THE *Advent*
Calendar

'If there was ever a book you would want to read yourself or share with your children at Christmas, then this is the one. Thoroughly enjoyable – well written and totally thrilling – every page is a complete gem. To find the adventure of Christmas you must first find *The Advent Calendar*.'

G. P. Taylor, author of *Shadowmancer*

THE *Advent* Calendar

STEVEN CROFT

with illustrations by Sarah John

DARTON · LONGMAN + TODD

First published in 2006 by
Darton, Longman and Todd Ltd
1 Spencer Court
140–142 Wandsworth High Street
London SW18 4JJ

ISBN-10: 0-232-52680-X
ISBN-13: 978-0-232-52680-6

A catalogue record for this book is available from the British Library.

Designed and produced by Sandie Boccacci
Phototypeset in 11/13.75pt Apollo
Printed and bound in Great Britain by
Page Bros, Norwich, Norfolk

To Paul, Andrew, Amy and Sarah
with much love.

30 November

On the day it began, Sam dragged himself out of bed (late as usual) and savaged his face in three places while shaving. 'Memo to self,' he mumbled to his imaginary PA. 'Try to wake up before scraping blunt razor over spotty chin. Change blade at least once a year.' The mirror revealed traces of red on his new white shirt collar but, of course, there was no time to change now.

There was a sharp knock on the bathroom door. Sam's niece, Alice, in a tearing hurry as usual.

'Sam! Hurry up!'

Alice was standing on the landing in her dressing gown, looking cross. 'You're making me late. Again!' The bathroom door was slammed and bolted.

Sam winced at the noise. He never spoke in the mornings unless he could help it. He finished dressing, grabbed his bag and made for the door.

Megs, his big sister, caught up with him just as he was leaving.

'Sam. You promised to call into Hamleys today to pick up that Advent Calendar for Alice. Here's the letter. Don't forget.'

Something stirred dimly in the back of Sam's mind. He took the line of least resistance and put the envelope in his coat pocket fully intending to leave it there.

Sam was staying with Megs and Alice for a while, having moved in three weeks ago. They were still getting used to each other. The house was a small terrace in a sloping street on the edge of Enfield. It was handy for the station. Sam worked in central London just near Farringdon tube. But it wasn't really big enough. Sam had the second biggest bedroom but it was piled high with boxes of his stuff, which overflowed sometimes into the small front room, much to Alice's annoyance.

There were no seats on the train (normal). The tube measured 17 on the Sardine Scale (where 10 is the maximum and 15 is get on board only by using both shoulders and looking straight down for the entire journey). Work was just a boring blur. After work Sam normally went for a drink with friends but first there was the note in the inbox from Megs.

> Sam. Don't you dare forget to pick up that calendar. Alice has come home from school and is screaming for daily chocolate. All her friends have had theirs for months, apparently. I'm a useless mother (as usual) and there's no way I can get in this evening. She was so excited to get that special offer. I've no idea where it came from.

Sam wavered for the first time. Megs was his only sister. And she'd had a mouldy time since that used teabag of a husband traded her in. *And* Sam was staying with her rent-free at the moment while certain things were sorted out (or not). 'Memo to self – let's not go there just at the moment, shall we?' But Advent Calendar? What kind of a thing was that for a stroppy teenager?

Dim memories from childhood stirred in the very shallow pond of Sam's soul. According to Tizzy at the next desk (long legs, short skirt, hot lipstick, big boyfriend) it was a countdown to Christmas with chocolates in. Germaine in Accounts (sackful of kids and no money) just smiled: 'What do *you* want with an Advent Calendar?' Maureen at reception (103 if a day and *massive* cardigans) said it was a shame really. 'You just can't buy religious ones any more. My vicar writes to the local paper about it every year.'

'What on earth has an Advent Calendar got to do with religion?' thought Sam, on the way to the pub. 'Pints of Jellyfish – it's the last thing I need!' It was the time of day when he began to slow down and get ready for the evening, the time when his mind began to catch up with his body, looking forward to the first drink of the day. The thought of a crowded toy shop was deeply unattractive. 'Beats me. *Sad*vent more like.'

Despite his best intentions, he fished the envelope out of his inside jacket pocket and took out the small white card edged in gold leaf. There were no pictures, just an old-fashioned copperplate script.

> Dear Miss Carroll
>
> I am delighted to inform you that you have been selected to receive our special Advent Calendar this year. Please present this card in Hamleys toyshop in Regent Street on 30 November.
>
> Yours sincerely,
>
> A. Gabriel Esquire

He dimly remembered Megs saying that Alice had cheered up a bit when the card had arrived a couple of days ago. She'd never won anything before – and she'd had a bad few months with the divorce and moving house and schools. But it was probably just some bad sales gimmick. Why couldn't Megs come and get it tomorrow?

It took real effort to wrench his guidance system out of autopilot and jump on a bus to Oxford Circus. Once he was on the bus, Sam remembered that the Christmas lights were switched on the day before by some kind of footballer's wife: Regent Street looked like a shimmering river of light peppered with winking Santas and frolicking penguins. Hideous. Traffic was nose to tail with much honking. There was a bigger jam still on the pavement which somehow wasn't wide enough. But the real battle began once you passed through the heat curtain and into the shops.

Hamleys was a mass of tiny gawping infants gripped firmly by exhausted parents. Novelty helicopters clattered overhead. Father Christmas had arrived yesterday: 'Try the Second Floor!' shouted an elf with a blocked nose when Sam showed his card.

'Note to elves: bring Tunes to work. Note to self: say no to big sister more often.' Sam thought longingly of the normal booth in the pub and the first pint of the weekend. Progress up the escalators was blocked by a humungous stuffed camel clutched by an embarrassed thirty-something. He was complaining to his wife over and over in shrill tones like a parrot on steroids.

'Fifty quid this cost me. She's wanted it for months. Fifty quid! Still, it's only once a year, isn't it?'

'Once too often if you ask me,' muttered Sam, staring up the camel's backside three inches from his nose. 'Note to self: no kids. Ever. And if kids, then leave home for Christmas. Suffering centipedes – look at that crowd.'

Elbows to the ready, Sam squeezed and shuffled through the Department of Cuddly Toys and the Ministry of Mechanical Models. There were still no signs of Advent Calendars. He looked again at the card, then looked around for some kind of information desk. There was a jolly green goblin at the top of the escalator. 'Try the information desk,' she said. 'Over by the Bear Factory.'

There was a bit of a queue. Sam listened impatiently to elaborate requests about Mechano, spare parts for radio-controlled aeroplanes and DIY chess kits. He checked his watch, cleared his throat and tapped his foot. 'Come on! Come on!' At last an assistant was free.

'Advent Calendar department, please. Chocolate ones,' he said, smiling and waving his card at the assistant.

'I'm sorry, sir,' the assistant began. 'Hamleys doesn't sell Countdown Calendars.'

'Countdown Calendars?' said Sam. 'I wanted an Advent Calendar.'

'We're not allowed to call them Advent Calendars any more,' said the girl, in a low voice, glancing right and left. 'It's not inclusive or something. They're called Countdown Calendars now. But we don't sell them anyway.'

Sam thrust the card under her nose. She read it, then shrugged her shoulders.

'Never seen one like that before. Must be some kind of joke.'

There was a low cough from behind Sam's left shoulder.

'I think I can be of assistance, sir. This way, please.'

A superior-looking man in a dark suit and tie and a bowler hat led him away from the information desk across the crowded, noisy shop floor to a small doorway set into the far wall.

Sam stepped through a curtain of tinsel and bells and then suddenly burst through to a place of calm and stillness.

'Take a seat, sir, I won't be a moment. We are expecting you.' The man's voice was deep and cultured with a lilting Welsh accent.

'Lolloping lobsters,' Sam gasped, sinking into the first chair he'd seen since leaving work. 'Stuff Christmas down a big hole. I'm sick of it already. Never understood it. A great madness that comes on all the world.'

The sense of silence in the little room was complete. The babble outside was cut off as if someone had flicked a switch. No chatter. No cash registers. No piped music. Sam felt as though he'd suddenly gone deaf. The light was dim, like some kind of stockroom (but without the stock) and it was pleasantly cool. The smell was clean sawdust.

Bowler-hat man came back and stood behind a low counter. Between them was a large brown parcel, tied with string.

'Here it is, sir, all ready for you. The Advent Calendar. I hope you like it.'

'Thank you,' said Sam, not quite knowing what else to say. It was larger than he expected. It was square and about the size of a very large picture. 'There must be lots of chocolate in there!'

'Oh, I doubt it, sir, I doubt it, although you can never be quite sure.' Sam didn't quite get that – but the man was so solemn he didn't like to ask questions – and time was getting on. 'Is there anything to pay?'

'Not just at this moment, sir, no, nothing to pay. You will be careful, won't you, to open the doors on the right day, otherwise things can get a bit, well, complicated, and we wouldn't want that, sir, would we?'

'I suppose not,' said Sam, humouring the man. What could go

wrong with a chocolate calendar?

'We'll need a mobile phone number, sir, if that's alright, for the texts. It's really very important to open them at the right time.' Sam scribbled his number down without thinking. Alice had one but it was broken. She was hoping for a new one for Christmas. 'And there's a help line this year for the first time,' said the man, proudly, as he held back the curtain for Sam to leave. 'Just dial 266 433 555 in case of complications. It works from any phone and it's free. Here's my card.'

'Thanks, Mr – er – Gabriel,' said Sam, puzzled, looking at the small business card. 'I don't expect we'll be needing it but good to know you're there. Must be off.'

'Goodbye, sir. See you again.'

'Oh, I doubt it,' Sam muttered, as he pushed through the curtain of tinsel out into the main store again, blinking in the light. The large brown parcel was secure under his arm. It was surprisingly light – like a large sheet of cardboard – but very awkward to carry. He looked at his watch. 'Bother and bananas.' Should he join his friends or get this back to Alice and Megs? Just one, for the road? It was Friday, after all. Christmas cheer and all that. Sam smiled in triumph as he saw the camel man still in the queue for stuffed bears as he rode the escalator to freedom and the weekend ahead.

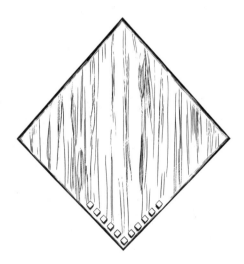

1 December

Alice yawned and shook herself awake around nine – her normal time on a Saturday. Almost her first thought was chocolate and the special calendar.

She hoped against hope that Sam had actually been to Hamleys and hadn't lost the card. Last night Megs had feared the worst.

'Never mind, love,' she sighed. 'We can go in and get it tomorrow if we have to.'

As she pulled on her jeans, jumper and trainers, Alice thought, not for the last time, that the word 'uncle' was much too adult to describe Sam.

'The English language needs a new word,' Megs would say on a good day. 'For someone who is your mum's brother but has no sense of responsibility.'

She heard Sam come in, of course, around two in the morning: his regular time on a Friday night. There was the normal accompaniment of friends throwing him out of the taxi; of Sam looking for his keys; the odd 'Barrels of barnacles' and other less savoury expressions.

He would be fast asleep on the couch in the front room. One of his many annoying habits was crashing out on the sofa when he came in from a late night.

Alice rattled down the stairs. Sure enough there he was, looking as if he'd done battle in the night with giant mushrooms. Normally, if she was feeling merciful, Alice would leave him to sleep for a bit. Today she wanted only revenge and chocolate and so she drew back the curtains and turned on the lights.

'Hand over the calendar, Sam. It's wake-up time. Did you get it?'

Sam made cow-like noises and pulled the quilt over his head. His boots stuck out at the bottom. A hairy hand pointed to the large brown parcel, tied with string.

'Leave me alone, monster. S'there.'

Alice threw a cushion at the lump that was his head and fetched the scissors. Sam had one eye pushed over the duvet watching like a hermit crab. She peeled away the cardboard wrapping.

'Sam, this isn't funny! I thought you were collecting me an Advent Calendar. I wanted a big one with Maltesers or Terry's Chocolate Orange segments or Galaxy. What's this exactly?'

Sam farted and looked pleased with himself. He was waking up now, reaching back into yesterday for the memories. He spoke slowly.

'That's the one the man gave me. I handed over the card like you said. Strangest blinking calendar I've ever come across.'

Alice took off the last of the wrapping paper and held the object up to the light. It was like nothing she'd ever seen.

The Advent Calendar was very light and made of wood a couple of centimetres thick in the shape of a large diamond. They found out later that the wood came from an olive tree. It had a lovely sweet smell and a polished surface. The centre was light brown with a darker strip around the border which tapered to a thin, smooth edge. Alice turned it over. There was no label or marking on the back to say where the calendar had come from but there was a small gold-coloured chain so it could be hung on the wall.

Alice stood on a chair and threaded the chain over the spare picture hook where a mirror used to be. The calendar somehow fitted the room and made itself at home immediately, blending in with the surroundings and looking as though it belonged. Alice stayed on the chair and looked more carefully at the front. On the bottom edges of the frame were eleven square wooden buttons.

The one in the middle, at the very bottom of the diamond, had two dots, one above the other. On the left were the numbers 0, 1, 2, 3 and 4 carved into the buttons. On the right were the numbers 5, 6, 7, 8 and 9. Alice felt them with her fingertips and traced their shape.

Sam was standing behind her now with the duvet wrapped round him from neck to ankles looking like a vast, vertical blue caterpillar. 'There's just one problem,' he mumbled.

'Where's the chocolate?' she snapped, intrigued but still cross.

'No. Where are the doors? Shouldn't there be little doors? One for each day?'

Right in the centre of the frame there was just a single square double door. You had to look a second time to see it as the colour was just slightly darker than the main surface of the calendar. Alice and Sam peered more closely. It was made of rougher wood and stood out a little. The number 24 was printed on it in tiny letters. But there was no sign at all of 1 to 23.

'Coffee,' moaned Sam, and began to shuffle off towards the kitchen still wrapped in the duvet.

'Just one moment, Sam, you great lump,' said Alice, blocking his path. 'This arty nonsense is all very well but where is my … ?'

Sam's phone farted. Sam looked pleased with himself again. It was set to do that when a text message arrived. Sam began his normal game of hunt-the-phone.

Alice gave up in disgust and turned back towards the calendar without knowing why. Something was different. She looked carefully and ran her fingers across the smooth surface. That was it. Another door had appeared in the centre of the space at the top: black and very distinct against the light wood. How had she missed it the first time?

'Sam! Look at the calendar!'

Sam crawled out from under the sofa, grinning in triumph, phone in hand. He came over. 'Found it. Lummy, look at that. Trick of the light?'

Alice peered a bit closer. There was a small number 1 painted in dark grey on the surface of the door. She had to look sideways to see it.

Sam was trying to read his text: 'Nine, colon, two?' he said, puzzled. 'Strange.' Alice ignored him and tried to open the new door with her fingernail, part of her still hoping for chocolate. It wouldn't budge.

An unusual, thoughtful look came over Sam's face. He rummaged in his coat pocket (always dangerous) and fished out a small white card (along with an assortment of bus tickets, small change, paper clips, biro tops and gum). Alice looked over and pulled a face.

'What are you doing?'

'Mr Gabriel!' said Sam in triumph. 'The man in the shop who gave me the calendar. He said they would text through the code for each day. I gave them my number because your mobile is broken. It's obviously some kind of gadgetry. The door appears at a set time and they send out the codes. Clever stuff. There's more to this than meets the eye. Try those little buttons.'

'At last,' said Alice, brightening up. 'Now maybe we get the chocolate. This could be fun.'

She grabbed the phone, read the message herself, then punched the buttons one at a time. Each one stayed down with a satisfying click as it was pushed home. 'Nine.' Click. 'Colon – that's the two dots.' Click. 'Two.' Click. Sam caught hold of Alice's arm, reaching for his phone.

With the last click, something was happening. The door at the top of the calendar slowly began to swing open. There was just blackness on the other side – a richer, deeper blackness than a painted square on the surface of the calendar. For Sam and Alice it was like looking down a tiny, dark hole or through a window into nothingness.

They both took a step backwards in shock. A split second later, the tiny door was as big as a large window and it came rushing toward them. A moment after that, before they could move or think or do anything at all, they were completely swallowed up by the great and utter darkness and, at first, complete silence.

Without having experienced it, it is impossible to understand how vile it is to be swallowed by darkness. Perhaps a blind person would have some idea or someone who lives in a place without electric lights. Alice had never been in a completely dark room before or out in the countryside at night. Nothing had prepared her for the sheer blackness of everything. For the first time in her life she gripped Sam's hand and was glad he was there.

'What's going on?' he whispered, shivering. The duvet had disappeared and Sam was left in his T-shirt and boxers. 'Who turned the lights out? Power cut?'

'I've no idea,' said Alice. 'It feels as though we're outside.'

'We can't be,' said Sam.

Together, still holding hands, they bent down and felt damp earth between their fingers. The air was clammy and still.

'So what happened?' said Sam, fully awake now.

'I punched in the numbers. The door opened. It got bigger. The darkness kind of swallowed us.'

They turned around slowly, hoping to see something behind them. There was nothing.

'Sam, this is scary. What can we do?'

There was a dank, rotting smell and the air was completely still. For ages, as it seemed, they stood rooted to the spot, looking around but seeing nothing, ears straining into the silence.

Then very gradually their eyes began to adjust to the dark and began to sift blackness from blackness and make out shapes. Their ears began to catch soft, muffled sounds in the distance. Sam took a step forward, very carefully, and discovered they were standing next to a kind of rough cobbled track. Stooping down, they discovered that to each side was soft, boggy ground where hardly anything grew. Ahead was the silhouette of some kind of great city surrounded by a high wall. The track they were on led up to an open gate.

Still holding hands and trembling as much from fear as from the cold, Alice and Sam moved slowly forward, up the gentle path to the gate, still not daring to speak. They inched their way slowly along, keeping to the edge of the path. The soft, low sounds were coming from the city itself. The gates were open and unguarded. They passed through.

Once inside they began to make out the shapes of people shuffling to and fro, great crowds of them going about their daily business. Most were very thin and stooped. They moved very slowly and carefully in the darkness, keeping as close to the walls and making themselves as inconspicuous as they could. Sam and Alice stayed well back from them and the strange people avoided contact even with each other. They were still frightened but Alice's curiosity was beginning to get the better of her fear.

Occasionally, someone would brush past them and Alice and Sam noticed that their skin felt clammy. They walked deeper and further into the city for longer than Alice cared to remember. It was like a long, grey dream. She couldn't ever remember being without light for so long. The same stooped, sad figures wandered aimlessly to and fro. The darkness began to eat into them after a time, sapping hope and life. Sam had hardly said a word since the journey began.

Then, gradually, very gradually, there began to be a change. As they came nearer to what felt like the centre of the place, there seemed to be more and more people moving in the same direction, slowly at first, then the movement picked up momentum and even some speed. Sam and Alice were caught up and walked swiftly with the crowd.

In the end Alice had to do something. She was bursting with questions. She looked around at the crowds rushing past and then spoke to a girl her own age as softly as she could: 'What is this place? Where are we going?'

The girl came close and looked at them in amazement and in dread. 'You must know, surely?' she whispered, looking over her shoulder. 'This is the City of Choshek.'

'How long has it been dark here?' asked Alice. 'Does it never get light?'

'How long? It has always been dark here, miss, always and always. We have always lived like this. There is a longing in our hearts for something else, something different, and we believe it was different once, but the memory is so far in our past. It eats at us when we wake and beckons us in our dreams but we have no name for it. In the meantime we have learned to live in this darkness.'

Something stirred in Sam now Alice had made a beginning: 'Where are all these people going?'

The girl turned to him and, again, spoke with respect but softly, as if not wanting to be overheard.

'To the great assembly, sir, in the centre of Choshek. There has been a rumour that the oracle will speak and name the thing we all seek. You must come. We have not seen a moment like this for many generations.'

She moved away, her eyes full of fear and hope. Sam and Alice followed as best they could but lost her quickly in the crowds. They kept on walking until they came to the place where all the people in the city were gathered: a spacious cobbled market square which Alice guessed was in the very centre. There was a stillness, an expectancy over the gathering. For as far as they could see on every side, the crowds waited in silence.

On a raised mound of earth in the middle stood an old, crooked man with a long staff, silhouetted against the perpetual night sky. He raised his staff high. Sensing the time was near, a rippled whisper passed through the crowd: 'The oracle speaks.' Then all fell silent, straining to hear. The oracle too spoke softly but his words cut through the night and carried across the vast square and out into the streets of the city.

'People of Choshek, hear this. There will be light again in this dark place. One day, the dawn will come. The time is near. People of Choshek, take heart and hope again.'

His voice was thin and weak but his words carried strength and life and hope. The crowd around Alice and Sam became a little more alive, some angry, some excited.

They watched together as the oracle raised his staff high above his head and then plunged it into the ground where it seemed to take root and grow taller. There was silence again. Then, the very tip of the staff burst into a tiny flame. Alice gasped. She felt as if she had been starved of light for so long. From where she stood, at first it was like a candle in a football field; then, as the people watched and waited, it grew in intensity until somehow its brightness began to light up the entire city.

For hours, it seemed to Sam, he had been longing for light and warmth. His senses leapt towards the strengthening flame. He began to look around and see the city for the first time. But the people around them had never seen light at all, it seemed. Some reached forward straining towards the burning torch, fascinated by its glare. Others shrank back, shielding their eyes and looking for the familiar shadows. There was a buzzing and commotion all around.

'Childwoman! Childman! Come quickly!' There was a soft, gentle voice behind them. 'The oracle would speak with you.'

One of the people of the city carrying a smaller staff was beckoning them to follow. He took Alice by the hand and led her through the crowds, with Sam following. They moved away from the flame, to a building with a high balcony where the oracle was waiting. Alice looked out across the mass of people drawn to the light which still burned brightly.

Sam saw that the oracle stood taller than the other inhabitants of the city because he refused to stoop. He looked around him as if he could see even without the light.

'Childwoman, childman, do you know where you are?'

Sam chose that moment to come to his senses and start to protest. To Alice's alarm, he was being protective but Sam's voice sounded hollow after all that she had seen and was seeing.

'Now look here. We want to go home. Straightaway. This minute. I need coffee and this young lady needs chocolate.'

'You are right, childman,' said the oracle (very patiently, Alice thought). 'It is indeed time for you to return home. But remember. Remember the City of Choshek and the promise of the light. Carry the hope within you.'

The oracle stretched out his hand and touched first Sam then Alice lightly on the shoulder. They fell backwards together just as though they were tumbling back into a deep, dark sleep.

Minutes later, as it seemed, Alice opened her eyes. They were back in the front room. There was the duvet. There was the phone. There was Sam, screwing up his eyes against the light. There was the winter sun streaming through the windows. There were the normal household noises: the traffic outside, the radio in the kitchen, Megs getting ready for the day.

And there was the Advent Calendar on the wall, making itself at home. The small dark door at the top was now wide open. Alice looked more closely. There was no chocolate to be seen. Inside was something even better. Inside all was darkness, except for a tiny, living candle flame.

2 December

Waking up, for Sam, was always difficult. As he and Alice tumbled back he rubbed his eyes and blinked. There was a moment's quiet. Their gaze met just for an instant. What had happened, exactly? Was Sam simply waking up after a particularly hard night out? It was nearly the Christmas party season after all. Thoughts swirled round inside his head looking for words to capture them but finding none.

'Suffering swordfish,' he mumbled, falling back into well-known territory.

That was enough to rouse Alice from gazing up at the calendar and light the blue touchpaper. All the fears and anxieties which had been stirred up by the strange experience of Choshek came to the surface. She turned on Sam ready to give him both barrels.

Then several things happened all at once to take him out of range. Megs stumbled into the room, looking rather dishevelled but cheerful. 'Morning, darling. Morning, idiot brother. Time to get ready to go. Hairdresser's in ten minutes.'

At that very moment, the doorbell rang very loudly several times. Alice opened it on her way upstairs. Four of Sam's mates stumbled in dressed in Chelsea colours. It was Saturday and a lunchtime kick-off. They swept through the house like a tornado and when they left, moments later, Sam was with them, washed, scrubbed (well, almost) and dressed in football shirt, scarf and woolly hat. Alice saw him from the bathroom window wedged into the back seat of his friend's car clutching a large mug of coffee and blinking his way into the day. Just as they pulled away, the house phone rang. Alice could tell from the way Megs spoke that it was Josie, Sam's ex. Megs liked Josie. So did Alice – though they both thought she was much too nice for Sam.

'You've missed him by a whisker, my love, sorry. Football. Early game, I think. I would have given him your message but I didn't see him last night, you see. I'll write him a note. Yeah, you too. Have a good weekend. Bye.'

Megs had a good look at the calendar when she put the phone down. 'Strange-looking thing. What does it do? No chocolate? Never mind, Alice. Want me to buy you another? Not to worry then.'

That was it for the rest of the day really. Hairdresser's. Visit to grandparents over in Luton. Saturday night telly. Alice had left all her friends behind when she moved house, so there wasn't much to do at weekends. The calendar was, well, just a bit too strange to talk to your mother about, wasn't it? Or your friends for that matter. Or anyone really. From time to time, in the advert breaks or in the middle of *Who Wants to Be a Millionaire?* she glanced over at the wall. Once, when Megs was out of the room, she turned out the lights and the little candle in the open door gave out light as if it was real, which of course it couldn't be. Her mum hardly noticed it after the initial fuss. Alice saw this was a Two Bars of Dairy Milk Saturday. She wasn't sure, but she thought Saturdays were probably the very worst days for Megs. Whenever Alice asked how she was, Megs would just smile and pretend.

Sunday mornings were always lazy, do-nothing, please-yourself times. For Megs and Sam, that normally meant sleeping in (if Sam was around at all). But Alice couldn't sleep past eight o'clock today. Her dreams were full of strange events in different worlds. She could hear Sam's snoring through the living-room door. He was here then and taking over the front room again. Softly she pushed open the door and tiptoed into the room. She went first to the calendar and her heart skipped a beat. She could just see it by the light of the tiny candle in the first window. A second door had appeared in the bottom half of the calendar. She touched it with her fingertips: it was icy cold and seemed to be made out of tiny strips of steel welded together. She picked at the edges with her fingers but again there was no way of opening it.

Half in excitement, half in fear Alice punched in the code: nine, colon, two. She closed her eyes and braced herself for the journey back to the strange city. Nothing happened. She opened one eye. Everything in the room was still the same. She opened both eyes, looked around and saw Sam's phone spilling out of the pocket of his jeans.

Like a hobbit stealing treasure from a sleeping dragon, Alice crept over to Sam without making a sound. She stretched out her hand, grabbed the phone and flipped open the lid. Message waiting. That sound she thought was snoring – well, never mind. Yeucch. She pressed the buttons and brought up the message: two, colon, four – just the same as yesterday. Different number.

Alice held the phone close to the bottom of the calendar to see better and pressed the first two buttons. Again, they felt large and important, like the combination of a safe. She hesitated just for a moment with her finger above the figure 4, remembering what had happened yesterday. Should she or shouldn't she – especially without Sleeping Sam? Then the next instant she remembered how useless he'd been in the dark and pressed the number.

There was a distant, echoing, grating sound, as if huge hangar doors were being cranked open. Alice kept her eyes on the new door. Sure enough it was opening very slowly from the bottom, rolling up like the garage at her old house. Out of the gap at the bottom of the door came wisps of something like very thick fog. As the door opened wider, it poured out faster, filling the room in a matter of seconds. It was clammy and cold. Alice held up her hand in front of her face and began to feel afraid. She could see about a metre – that was all. She turned around. The light was changing somehow to an outdoor kind of light on a damp winter morning. She bent down to touch the ground: instead of living-room carpet there was moist earth. What had she done?

Just to her right Alice glimpsed a familiar shape, hunched up on the ground, shivering and rubbing his eyes. Sam! What was he doing here? Waking up – that was clear but only very slowly.

'Sam! Sam!' She shook his shoulder. 'Sam! Wake up. It's happened again. The calendar. The second door.'

In an instant, Sam was wide awake, staring round, mouth open. The fog cleared, carried away on the morning wind. They were standing on a broad, flat plain just in front of an enormous building stretching away as far as the eye could see in every direction. Think of the biggest aircraft hangar you have ever seen, then try and imagine it's the size of four football pitches, then eight, then double it again.

Alice and Sam were still standing in front of the door from the Advent Calendar only now it was as high as a three-storey building. Inside the door, from within the hangar, came a deep roaring and choking sound like a thousand tractors. The ground began to shake. The smell of the engine fumes reached them a second or so after the sound and then, coming through the mist, they saw the barrel of an enormous tank.

Sam drew Alice back a little away from the door. The tank was at the head of an enormous procession of vehicles, six or seven abreast. Sam said later it reminded him of the great parades of armaments from the old newsreels – except that the weaponry was from every different age and empire. There were ancient canons and armoured cars, huge missiles towed by tractors, jet fighters and massive futuristic bombers, chariots and submarines. Among the larger fighting vehicles were huge wagons filled with guns and knives, armour, shields and helmets, bows and arrows, decorated shields, muskets, landmines and hand grenades. Other vehicles carried spy satellites and robots and weapons which seemed to have come straight out of *Doctor Who*.

Every single weapon invented by humankind was there: the whole inventory of destruction and despair: widow-makers; limb-renders; city-slayers, all in one procession, a river of death. Alice looked closely: there were no people in the vehicles – they drove themselves, all in perfect timing, all in the same direction.

'Come and see what happens next,' said a voice in her ear, shouting above the noise. 'It's really rather good.'

Turning around Alice and Sam saw the oldest people they had ever set eyes on: a man and a woman standing a little way back. The man's fine grey hair and beard reached his waist. He wore a brown robe with a hood, tied with a rope girdle, and carried only a staff. He was about as tall as Sam and not at all stooped. His skin was old, dark brown and leathery as if he had spent hundreds of years in the hot sun. He wore a pair of ancient sandals: no socks, thought Alice, for some reason. He smelled just like a fusty old library, Sam thought: full of wisdom from the years.

His companion was shorter and stooped a little. She was dressed in grey. Although very old, she was still somehow very beautiful. Once they saw them, neither Sam nor Alice was the least bit afraid.

The old man and woman led them back away from the grim parade to a place where a grove of ancient trees gave shelter from the morning sun, now just beginning to warm the earth. The noise of the engines became a distant roar. They sat down together in a comfortable semi-circle of rocks and gestured for Sam and Alice to join them.

For a few moments the four of them sat and watched the procession. The elderly couple offered Alice and Sam their binoculars so they could pick out the details. Alice noticed for the first time that the weapons were not new. They had all seen many years of wear and killing. She shuddered. Then she watched as a single white dove flew out of the great hangar, soared and swooped over the military procession and finally flew towards them and settled in the branch of the tree.

'Who are you?' said Alice. 'Where are we? What does all this mean?'

The man smiled at the woman and looked tenderly at her, as if he was enjoying the moment hugely. Then he touched Alice's face gently and spoke softly.

'My name,' he said, 'is Folkfather. In your tongue, I am known as Abraham. My wife's name is Laughter: in your language she is Sarah.'

The old woman smiled and squeezed his arm. Somehow she brimmed over with gladness.

'We are to be your guides in this place and in the other places you will see as each door opens for four more days.'

'What is this place?' said Alice. 'Is it the same as Choshek, the place we saw yesterday?'

'No, child,' said Abraham, eyes twinkling. 'They are all different worlds and different places, yet all in some strange way part of the world in which you live. The calendar draws back the curtain for just a moment. It gives a different view, you might say.'

Sarah looked excited: 'The vision here on the second day is one that many in every age have longed to see. In your world it is yet to be fulfilled.'

'What do you mean?' said Sam. His tone of voice was different from any that Alice had heard him use before. Younger, somehow. Less sure of himself. 'What do you mean? It just looks like a procession getting ready for war.'

Sarah smiled. 'You've not yet seen where this road leads,' she said. 'If you are ready, you must come and see.'

Abraham offered Sam and Alice some water in stone cups and some olives taken, he said, from this very grove. Then they began to walk slowly, at the pace of the old people, following the broad river of war at a distance and leaving the hangar far behind. The dove followed them, a sprig in its beak from one of the trees. They walked, Alice thought later, for about an hour. All the time more weaponry passed them.

'How long will it last?' she asked Sarah.

'It will last for a thousand years,' she said with a sudden sadness in her voice. 'Every hour of daylight for every day for four times three thousand months. In every part of history, in every place, men have given their best efforts to destruction and the arts of war. But look, we reach the turning point.'

Sarah pointed to where a small wooden shed stood in the midst of the vast flow of weaponry. Alice watched, expecting it to be crushed in a moment by a tank or tractor towing guns but the stream parted just a little and flowed around the hut exactly like a river round an island in midstream. Then as soon as she passed what she realised was a stable, Alice could begin to see a line a long way ahead where the column of vehicles simply seemed to disappear.

She pulled forward but Abraham caught her hand. 'Careful now, child. Not quite so fast.'

They walked on together. It took another hour of walking to begin to see what happened.

Sam realised a moment ahead of Alice that, in actually fact, they were coming to the edge of a massive cliff: a sheer drop of 2,000 metres or more. The four of them edged slowly nearer until they could see exactly what was happening. In some ways, it was exactly like the top of a waterfall. The great flow of destruction came to the edge of the cliff and drove straight over. Swords and guns, bombers and armoured tanks were smashed to pieces on the rocks below. The debris spread for miles and miles.

Sam was afraid of heights and stood well back from the edge. Alice lay down and put her head over the cliff, staring through the binoculars at the destruction below. 'There are people down there,' she said. 'Around the edge. As small as ants. They are carrying pieces away and making things – look, there are buildings and roadways and farms stretching into the distance.'

Sam came nearer at last and looked carefully over the cliff. He held the binoculars to his eyes and saw the people like ants below, hovering around the edge of the enormous scrap yard, hauling away the hunks of steel and metal. He saw the fires set up for the forges and then focused on the blacksmiths transforming the weaponry again into objects of purpose and of beauty. He saw the markets around the forges and men and women coming to trade and exchange and reuse all that had been created for destruction.

Alice stood up again and looked back at Abraham and Sarah who were watching as the deadly river of weaponry flowed to its end.

Abraham raised his staff and pointed it over the river. 'Behold,' he said, stretching out his hand. 'See what every generation of humanity has longed to see since Cain walked the earth,' he cried. 'Behold the end of war.'

A moment later – a blinking of an eye – and the river and the cliff and the valley were gone. Sam and Alice were rubbing their eyes and back in the front room. Sam looked at Alice. Alice looked at Sam. Then both turned to look at the calendar. The second door was open now. A tiny ribbon of steel stretched across the top. In the open doorway was a tiny carving of a white dove, its eyes glistening blue like sapphire. In its beak it held an olive branch. In the Sunday morning silence, Alice put her ear to the doorway. She could still hear the distant roar.

3 December

Monday morning: the very worst day of the week. Double biology first lesson. As a matter of principle, Alice always switched off her alarm clock on Sunday nights. She cherished the secret hope that Megs and Sam would both go off to work and forget all about her. Sam, of course, never took the slightest notice of anyone or anything in the mornings. He managed to get himself dressed (sort of) and out of the house by half past seven without waking up at all as far as Alice could tell. Megs likewise was utterly predictable. She hadn't even twigged that this was a regular protest yet. Alice was shaken back to life every Monday morning at 8.15, curtains jerked back, light on.

'Come on, darling, come on.' Megs was trying to squeeze cheerfulness out through her teeth but not quite succeeding. 'Monday morning. Rise and shine. School awaits. That awful alarm clock has failed again.' Megs was not a morning person.

For Alice, conversation wasn't really for mornings either. She went into autopilot. Bathroom. Disgusting school uniform. Rabbit food for breakfast. Also disgusting. Megs was on the healthy-eating trip again. Her school bag weighed half a ton.

'Come on, darling, come on.' Megs' voice was rising in volume and in tone, like a kettle coming to the boil. She held the car door open. Alice slammed it behind her. They were halfway to school before she even thought about the calendar.

Just for one fleeting moment the word 'chocolate' came into her mind and her mouth watered. Then a split second later she realised that Sam had gone off to work with his mobile phone. How would she get the code? Would it be a different time during the week? What if Sam wasn't coming home tonight? Should she contact him at work? She could text him from a friend's phone if only she could remember the number. And if one of her two friends had broken school rules and smuggled a phone in. Would the calendar still work if they missed a day?

'Here we are, my precious,' said Megs, leaning across to give her a kiss. Alice made a strangled 'Gollum' sound and leapt out of the car. 'Bye,' she called, but the car had already pulled away.

Her heart and her shoulders sank a little every day as she walked through the school gates. Everything about the place seemed ten times worse than her last school. The buildings were falling apart. Most of the classes were out of control. The Year 9 bullies were particularly vicious.

Something strange was happening. As Alice turned the corner into the main entrance a dark shadow moved across the edge of her vision. As she walked down the long spinal corridor to her form-room she turned round in mid-stride. There it was again (she thought) following her but she was not quite sure.

Since the beginning of term, Alice had teamed up with Suzie and Alex. They were both new as well. She knew that, like her, both of them had moved to the area because of problems at home. The three had become unlikely allies without ever declaring friendship. Suzie was much better spoken than the other kids in their year but Alice thought she was really nice. Before her parents' divorce she used to go to a private school. She found it difficult to take in everything at class and often rang Alice in the evenings to talk about homework. Alex was a geek, pure and simple, the brains in the outfit. He'd moved into the area from somewhere in the north because of his dad's job.

There were three clauses to the three friends' unspoken treaty: always stick up for each other, be there at break and lunchtime (the worst moments), and never, ever ask questions about home. Because they all lived a long way apart, the three of them hardly ever met up outside of school hours. Their archenemy (apart from the bullies) was Miss Newton, the biology teacher, who was at least seventy. Suzie reckoned she was the Trunchbull reborn to torment her.

'Hi, Alice! Good weekend?' Alex was there first. Suzie arrived a moment later.

'S'alright. Nothing special. You?'

'Same old thing. Ready for biology?'

Alice, of course, was still thinking about the Advent Calendar. Her mind kept going back in spare moments to the doors and the new worlds. But she was much too sensible to mention it to Alex, especially as it was so new. It felt fragile, somehow. As if it could disappear if she talked about it. Not to mention the weirdness of it all.

Biology always, always, always started with a test. They got through as best they could. Then Miss Newton announced one of her special educational films. Most of them were ancient and crackly but this one was actually rather good, Alex thought. Miss Newton kept talking about nature 'red in tooth and claw'. The film traced the food chain in an African game reserve. Alice was seriously thinking of becoming a vegetarian by the end.

She daydreamed whenever she could. There was no way of knowing whether Sam had a new code or if they would go somewhere new this evening. Once or twice during the day she had the weird feeling that she was being watched or followed and caught the shadow in the corner of her eye but the moment passed. At long last it was time to go home.

Normally, she caught the bus. Megs was still at work on the other side of town. She was just turning out of the gate when there was a fierce beeping on the horn. 'Over here, Alice.' It was Sam. He was calling to her from his rusty blue sports car parked over the road. 'Over here, quick, jump in!'

Alice crossed the road and hopped in beside Sam. 'What are you doing here? Why aren't you at work? Is it something to do with the calendar?'

Sam grinned, shifted into gear, revved the engine and pulled away. 'What happened? Tell me.'

'The trains weren't running this morning. Something to do with a bomb scare in London. It turned out to be a hoax but there was no way of getting to work. As soon as I got to the station, I had to turn round and go back for the car. I must have just missed you. I was walking home when the text message arrived. Here it is.'

Alice grabbed the phone. The message was just like the others but a different number: 'Eleven, colon, six.'

'Great. And thanks for coming to get me. Let's go home and punch in the number.'

Sam went a bit sheepish. 'Erm. Well … ,' he said, choosing his words very carefully. 'I already did that.'

Curiosity and temper both flared up at once. Curiosity won, but only just.

'What happened? If you went anywhere without me I'll get Mum to chuck you out.'

'Calm down, dear,' said Sam, in his most annoying TV voice. He caught the look in her eye and stopped halfway through the quotation. 'I was at home anyway so I thought why not just punch in the number? So I did. Another door had appeared.'

'What did it look like?'

'Strange really,' said Sam. 'Like a five-bar wooden gate. I couldn't resist it and punched in the numbers and, well, nothing. There was just nothing. No different world, no smoke, nothing. I was just about to turn round and go back to work when there was a whirring sound and out of the door came this tiny strip of tape.'

He handed Alice the ribbon of paper with tiny letters neatly printed in a single line:

> Alice and Sam are warmly invited to take tea at 4 p.m. at
> St Saviour's Church, Eden Road on Monday 3 December.
> A and S.

'A and S?' said Alice. 'Alice and Sam?'

'Abraham and Sarah, I think,' said Sam, pleased that for once he'd got there first (but he did have all day to think about it).

'The old couple from the world with the weapons.'

'Exactly,' said Sam. 'And here we are.'

He turned sharp left into Eden Road and pulled into St Saviour's. It was a tall, dark church, set back from the street, surrounded by gravestones. The noticeboards had been spray-painted, the grounds were overgrown and several windows were smashed through. It was dark now and forbidding. There was a single electric light over a small side door.

Sam knocked three times. Alice stood there shivering. There was just a hint of a shadow in the street outside.

An instant later, the door opened. Warmth and light flooded out into the cold night. Abraham and Sarah were both there, both smiling, both kind of excited.

'Come in, come in the pair of you.'

'How wonderful to see you.'

'It's a cold night but warm as toast inside.'

'Let's take your coat and bag.'

'My, this is heavy.'

'We've been so looking forward to you coming.'

'The kettle has just boiled this very minute.'

'Perfect timing.'

It was like visiting the nicest grandparents you can imagine – except for the house or church or whatever it was. Alice never quite worked out which. Abraham and Sarah bustled them through a small, ordinary-looking hallway into a huge space which was like some glorious indoor jungle. Alice thought of the greenhouses at Kew Gardens. Sam thought of the rainforest in Brazil. There was every kind of tropical plant imaginable: palm trees and ferns and exotic flowers of every colour: blue and yellow, orange and pink. It was buzzing with birds and insects. The whole place teemed with luxuriant growth and life. There was a strong smell of rich earth mingled with the perfume of orchids. On either side of them, Alice saw enormous bananas, coconuts and oranges ripening on the bushes.

Abraham led Alice and Sam slowly down a raised pathway made of logs towards a large clearing where there was a table and some chairs laid out with afternoon tea. They were just about to sit down when a great black bear came walking out of the trees to the left on all fours and ambled towards the table, sniffing the cake. Alice jumped behind Sarah for protection.

'Not for you,' Abraham said to the bear, which ambled straight on again back into the trees. 'Don't be frightened, dear,' said Sarah. 'None of the animals will hurt you. But they might want to come and say hello.'

Sam and Alice looked around a bit more carefully when Sarah said this. Sitting at the table while Abraham poured the tea, they peered into the bushes. Wherever they looked, eyes and ears and snouts stared back at them. On the ground were hedgehogs and mice and voles. From where he was sitting, Sam could see an enormous buffalo, a leopard and what looked like an old grey wolf. Alice saw the stripes of a great Bengal tiger not ten feet away. Playing round its feet were a pair of young monkeys and a goat. In the distance the long neck of a giraffe was visible above the fruit trees. Alice loved snakes whilst Sam was frightened of them. To Alice's lasting delight (something she remembered for days afterwards), an enormous python slithered from the long grass at the edge of the path, underneath the table and into the bushes on the other side. Sam lifted up his feet and gripped the sides of his chair in terror.

'So is this another world?' asked Alice.

'It's more like another window on our world,' said Sarah. 'How are you enjoying the calendar?'

'I like it a lot,' said Alice, with her mouth full of the most delicious scone and strawberry jam. She helped herself to more cream and Sarah passed her a napkin. 'Much better than cartoons and chocolate. Will it be like this every day?'

'Wait and see,' said Abraham. 'We don't want to spoil the surprises. But we will say that nothing that happens when you open the doors will hurt you or cause you any harm.'

'Do we always need to be there together?' asked Sam. 'What about school and work and stuff?'

'The codes will arrive at exactly the right time every day,' said Sarah. 'But it might be a different time on different days. Don't try to plan it all out – just let it happen. If only one of you is there, punch in the code anyway. The calendar will find a way to draw you both in together.'

'How long will it last?' wondered Alice.

'There are twenty-four days on the calendar,' said Sam.

Abraham took Sarah's hand and gazed at her, his eyes full of love and tenderness. Sarah smiled back at him. He turned back to Alice, eyes twinkling.

'If you want it to, it lasts for ever.'

There was a moment's pause, then Sarah took their cups.

'Come on, dears, you've finished your tea. Let's show you round.'

Slowly they walked around the garden. Abraham walked ahead with Sam, pointing out the species and varieties of birds and flowers and the different types of fruit. It was a very long time since Sam had taken a walk in a garden. It was also a very long time since he had had a proper conversation with someone older than himself. Alice thought he seemed to relax a little and he began to breathe more deeply. He was strangely quiet as he looked around. At Abraham's invitation he picked an apple and began to eat it. Alice walked quietly by Sarah's side. Conversation was unnecessary: it was just good to be here. She tried to see beyond the trees and the bright light to the roof of the building but found she couldn't. For all she knew, they could have been in the middle of a real garden with an open sky above. At every turn in the path there was a different scent of blossom or fruit or rich earth smell. For some time they walked beside a stream with the most enormous peaceful carp just below the surface. Sarah had brought the remains of a scone and showed Alice how to hand-feed the great fish.

They came at last to what Abraham said was the very centre of the garden, and to an enormous tree. Its canopy made a roof over the central glades. Its branches reached up as high as Sam could see, alive with birds and a tribe of monkeys playing and swinging through the upper branches.

But at the base of the tree, Alice saw, in among the roots, something was moving. She looked more closely. There were snakes. Snakes of every kind, coming and going, in and out of the ancient roots of the tree. Some of the roots themselves stood proud of the ground and the creatures wrapped themselves around the fibres or else lay still across the top. She recognised a cobra and a rattle-snake and an adder. On the far side was an enormous boa constrictor. Sam had turned pale and gone into hiding behind Abraham.

Then, as they watched together in silence, Alice caught her breath. A tiny child, no more than two or three years old, came to the tree from a different direction. He was carrying a large open bowl of what looked like milk or cottage cheese. He smiled at Abraham and Sarah, and Alice and Sam and walked straight past them in amongst the roots of the tree. The snakes took no notice of him but glided past his ankles and over his bare feet. He set down the bowl on the floor and, as he turned round to walk back into the garden, he laughed as the snakes began to drink. It was a strange and beautiful moment.

Abraham and Sarah then led them back by a different pathway to the front door of the house. Alice hadn't said much in the garden: she was too busy soaking in the smells and the colour and the life. As they reached the end of that day, she did just have one question.

'Sarah,' she said quietly, out of Sam's hearing, 'I had a sense something was following me today. A kind of shadow. Is that something to do with the calendar?'

'You've begun to see it, then,' Sarah replied. 'Don't be afraid. It's not from the calendar itself – in fact it's always been there. The calendar is helping you to see it, that's all. I'll tell you some more tomorrow.'

They were outside now, in the cold December evening, saying goodbye. Alice waved as Sam drove off. They both wanted the drive home to be in silence.

They arrived home and the house was in darkness – Megs had an evening class on Mondays. Together they opened the door of the house. Alice ran ahead into the front room.

There, just as Sam had described it, was the third door: a garden gate made from wood. Only now the gate was open. The picture inside was a beautiful garden, a riot of colour and life and tiny detail. When Alice looked closely, tiny eyes looked out at her from the bushes and the long grass. When she stood close by the calendar, she thought she could even smell the scent of apples and the dew on the wet grass.

4 December

Sam sat on the tube wedged between two large ladies, each with an empty carpet bag on her knee. They were heading for a serious day's shopping in the city. Like tennis professionals, they passed backwards and forwards their complaints about December: too much to do; too little money; no one to help out; the crowds in the shops. Sam resisted the temptation to turn his head from side to side and imitate the Wimbledon crowd. After two stations, he tuned out and checked his mobile phone. Five texts from Josie all asking him to get in touch. All sounded urgent. As each message came up, he pressed delete. Still no code.

After the excitement of last night, today felt kind of flat. Sam was enjoying the calendar so far – sort of. Weird but nice. He knew that Alice had been into it from the very first moment and the shock of the darkness. But Sam lived his life in so much of a dream world it had taken a few days to sink in. There was so much coming at him – so much he wasn't thinking about – that it took a while for anything to get beneath the daily grind. After yesterday in the garden, something had begun to stir.

He emerged from the underground blinking in the half-light. The Christmas decorations and the streetlights shone through the early morning fog: they somehow looked indecent in the mornings. Each shop window tried to draw him in.

The man from Accounts shared the lift, swaddled in a bright green scarf and bobble hat. 'Christmas. I ask you, what's the

39

point?' he mumbled to no one in particular, bemoaning his week-end of shuffling round the shops. He got out at the second floor before Sam could reply. There was always a funny sense of gloom and pointlessness in the first weeks of December. Later on in the month the pace picked up. Parties and gossip and the prospect of a few days off lifted the spirits but this first week or so there was still work to be done. The Christmas decorations were enough to put you off your turkey sandwich.

Sam was working on what he felt was a particularly pointless project at the moment. The firm worked in public relations. Sam's job title was junior account manager. He was a member of a team charged with persuading corporate clients to part with large amounts of cash for websites, advertising campaigns and the like. His boss, Richard, was the same age as Sam but a rising star in the firm, promoted six months ago. He had one smile for those above him in the pecking order and another for those below him.

Richard's present project was a review of new markets for the firm's partners. Most of the donkey-work was being done by Sam and Tizzy – his colleague. Their report was due in weeks ago. Every day Richard asked how it was going. Every day, Sam or Tizzy made up a different excuse: leaves on the line; no replies from suppliers; problems with the IT system. They dared each other to think of an ever-more outrageous reason. Before Josie, Sam and Tizzy were an item for three and a half days after the last Christmas party. That fling was in the background now – her present partner was a black belt in some obscure martial art – but every so often there was the odd spark between them.

Normally Sam had a thousand different ways to pass the time at work. He could get through a whole week effortlessly without producing anything. There were games to play on the computer, new websites to explore in the name of research, flirty emails sent backwards and forwards from the marketing department, gossip round the kettle (the nearest the firm got to a water cooler), urgent meetings at the coffee shop on the corner, office gossip with Tizzy disguised as a project meeting. Today he couldn't be bothered even to look as if he was employed.

He switched on his computer and opened his inbox. 'You have

fifty-seven new varieties of spam,' he groaned, clicking down the list pressing the delete button. Josie's message was halfway down. It was gone before he realised – but he knew what it said anyway. There were two sharp reminders from Richard about that wretched report and five circulars. Nothing remotely interesting. The post tray came round: nothing. Coffee break. A bit of banter about the match on Saturday. A task-group meeting. Sam sat quietly, stayed awake, kept his head down. Tizzy kicked him under the table when his turn came to speak. He managed to make up something. A long walk at lunchtime on his own, not with the normal group today.

Tizzy ambushed him when he came back into work. 'You OK, Sam? You don't seem yourself today.'

'S'pose,' said Sam. 'Nothing wrong really – but then nothing much right either. Something to do with the time of year I think. I can never work out what it's about.'

'Christmas? Season of goodwill and peace to all – that kind of thing. Speaking of which, Richard was really on the warpath this morning. You should have heard him sounding off after the meeting. He wants that report and wants it now! He almost turned purple.'

Sam managed half a grin. 'You done anything yet then?'

'As if!' said Tizzy. 'But I think we might have taken this one as far as it can go. I promised close of play tomorrow, absolute scouts' honour. We've got to get moving. OK?' She squeezed his arm fondly. 'Let's surprise the little toerag.'

'S'pose,' sighed Sam. 'I'll get to it. It's not rocket science.'

Tizzy moved back to her desk. Sam tried to engage. He stared at the screen but it was all a blur. He swore that the hands on the office clock moved more slowly in the afternoon. There was a kind of stupor over the large open-plan office. The worker bees dozed gently in their cubicles.

The sharp ring of the telephone interrupted the nothingness of his day.

'Hullo.'

'Sam, Sam, it's me, Alice. How's it going?'

'S'boring,' Sam whispered. 'How about you?'

'Pants,' said Alice. 'Pants as anything. Have you got the code?'

'Don't think so,' said Sam. 'Hang on.' He scrambled for his phone. Richard had just come into the other end of the room. He was looking in Sam's direction. Sam looked serious, concentrating on his work.

'There's a new door, Sam. There was nothing when I went to school. When I came home this new shape had appeared. It's tall and thin and made of brown wood. There's a number 4 in the very centre.'

He took out his mobile. Richard was coming nearer. There was no doubt he was heading for Sam.

'Hold on – I think something has arrived. There's a new text.'

'Tell me, quick.'

Time was short. Sam read the code to Alice. 'Two, seven, colon, six. Got it?'

'Got it.'

Sam put down the phone. He smiled what he thought was his most winning smile at the advancing figure of the boss, now just feet away, and fled down the corridor.

'Sam,' called Richard. 'Sam, wait.'

'Back in a minute,' Sam called. 'Left something in the stock-room.'

He knew it would be beneath Richard's dignity to chase him through the office. Through the corner of his eye, Sam saw him stop to talk to Tizzy. He did not look a happy bunny.

'Suffering shellfish, now what shall I do? No alternative,' he thought. He would have to get something important from the stockroom, take his time, go to the loo on the way back and hope against hope that Tizzy had bought them more time.

Sam opened the stockroom door and gasped. A wave of heat caught him full in the face. It felt like opening an oven door. He shielded his eyes from the bright sunshine. Instead of the familiar shelves and boxes of paper and dim light of the stockroom, he was looking out onto what looked like … like a desert? In the middle of a London office? There was blue sky above. The barren landscape stretched away into the distance as far as he could see: sand and scrub. Hardly anything grew there at all, just clumps of dry grass and low brown shrubs. The landscape was still. Nothing moved.

His mind struggled to take in the change. Alice was waiting inside. She grabbed him firmly by the hand and pulled him through the door, closing it behind him. 'Quick, you dummy. Someone might see.'

'What happened?' said Sam, brightening up. 'I was at work. I was having the most awful day. Did you punch in the numbers without me?'

'I had to,' said Alice, defensively. 'You did the same yesterday, remember. They said not to worry if we weren't together. The calendar would find a way – and, look, it did.' She peered back down the corridor. 'Your office looks just like my school.'

'What happened to you?' said Sam, turning round and round. His eyes drank in the desert landscape. Even though hardly anything grew there it was much more interesting than his office. The stockroom door had melted in moments, as if it was made from ice.

'Well,' said Alice, enjoying the moment, 'I got home from school as normal and saw the new door so I rang you at work. I punched in the code you gave me. It was a bit scary like it was two days ago but the weird feeling is beginning to go. I felt a slight tingling feeling as if something was starting but just at that moment, Mum came into the front room. I mumbled something and ran upstairs to my bedroom. I opened the door, saw this and stepped through and shut it behind me. Two minutes later another door appeared in exactly the same place and you arrived. My door melted as well. It's so cool.'

Sam loosened his tie and slung his jacket over his shoulder. 'S'warm not cool,' he said. 'What do we do next?'

'The only thing I can see is that tower in the distance,' said Alice. 'Look, over there in the east.'

Sam screwed up his eyes. 'How do you know that way is east?'

'Because of the sun, you dimbo. Don't you know anything?'

Sure enough, the horizon was unbroken all the way around: just scrub and desert as far as the eye could see. In just one point, Sam saw a tower, tiny in the distance but clearly man-made.

'That must be it then. Shall we go?'

Although it was hot and dry it was not unpleasant for walking. Both of them knew that the strange world was much more interesting than the office or biology homework. They set off towards the tower.

The landscape around them was absolutely barren. No trees, no flowers, no weeds even – just dry grass and hardy shrubs. No water that they could see. Nothing lived there at all. For the first half-hour of walking, the tower looked just the same. After an hour it was much bigger on the horizon. They could see that it was about six metres tall, made of wood. It seemed to be enclosed by a high stone wall. It was a long, dry walk. As they came nearer, the shape of the wall was clearer. It enclosed an area about the size of a football pitch but in a great oval: there were no corners. In the very centre of the wall as they approached was a large brown door, arched at the top and set into the wall.

'It's the door from the calendar,' Alice said.

There was no handle on the door. Sam walked up to it and pushed. Nothing. He knocked loudly three times and stepped back. The sound echoed in the still air. The door opened silently and swung towards them.

'Aaaaaaaah,' sighed Alice.

'Whistling wombats,' cried Sam.

The enclosure was a vineyard. There was row upon row upon row of vines in orderly formation beginning just inside the wall and filling the entire space, except for an area around the base of the tower. They were well staked and cultivated. The ground inside was well watered. In between the vines the grass was green; there were wild flowers and brambles against the walls. To the left of the door was an enormous barrel of the coolest, clearest water Sam had ever seen.

Side by side they stooped over the barrel, cupped the water in their hands and drank in silence. Sam felt his strength and life flowing back. He said later, looking back, that it was a turning point. The water was deeply refreshing not just after the long walk in the desert sun: it began to refresh other parts kind of worn out by daily life. It gave him an inner strength he couldn't name. When they had drunk from the barrel, both of them splashed the clear water over their arms and faces, both more alive somehow than when they came through the doors.

While Sam was still washing, Alice turned to look properly at the vineyard. The vines were pegged out in neat rows leading away towards the tower in the centre. It was clearly a very ancient place. The stock of each vine was gnarled and old: innumerable branches had grown from each stem. It seemed they had arrived at exactly the right moment. The branches now were laden with bunches and bunches of rich, red, juicy grapes, ripe and ready for harvest.

'Do you think it's allowed?' said Sam as Alice reached out her hand.

'I don't think I can stop myself,' said Alice, softly. She picked a grape from the nearest vine and bit into it. It was sweet and full of flavour: the richest, most refreshing taste she'd ever known.

'Sam, Sam, you must try one.'

Sam followed her and tasted his first grape. His face burst into the most wonderful smile Alice had ever seen. 'They're amazing, so sweet, so – so good, if you see what I mean.'

Sam and Alice walked now towards the centre of the vineyard, eating as they went. Each row of vines led inwards to the tower, like spokes of a wheel. It looked as though they were the only ones here but there was clear evidence of activity at the centre. At the base of the tower, surrounding it, was a group of olive trees which gave shade and cover. In the centre of the olive trees, beside the foot of the watchtower, was a small stone house. In front of the house was a table made of olive wood. Four goblets stood at the centre of the table. Four olive-wood stools were round the edge. Two of the stools were occupied already. On this day, Alice glimpsed a little more of what she called the sheer majesty of the two old people: their age sat lightly upon them.

'Welcome, Alice. Welcome, Sam. How do you like the vineyard?' asked Sarah.

'It's amazing,' said Sam.

'Beautiful,' said Alice. 'The taste, the smells, the life. Your garden yesterday was so full of life and colour and surprises all mixed up just growing everywhere. But this is different. The life is still here but it's ordered. It has a kind of purpose to it, don't you think?'

'We do,' said Abraham. 'And here it is.' He pointed to the goblets. 'Come and taste the wine.'

'How old is it?' said Sam, taking the cup and holding it to his nose.

'The vineyard has been here for twenty-five times five-score years,' said Sarah, almost singing with the joy in her voice. 'For the first five hundred years, there were hardly any grapes. Despite all the care you see around you, the owner failed to produce a harvest. But for the last two thousand years, the wine each season has been the same: rich and deep, bringing joy.'

Silently, Sam again raised the cup to his lips and breathed in the fragrance of the vineyard. His mind was filled with images of light and summer. He sipped and let the wine slip over his tongue. His whole body was for a moment perfectly still, focused on the joy and sheer life poured into the cup of wine. Never again, he knew, would he taste such a vintage, however long he searched. Never again in his life, he knew, would he drink wine and not remember this moment.

Alice also tasted the wine – just the tiniest sip. She too recognised the moment as special though she had nothing to compare it with. A curious kind of warm, tingling happiness spread out from her tongue over her whole body, reaching in moments to the top of her head and to the tips of her fingers and toes. Somehow, she was more alive than when she awoke this morning. There was joy bubbling up within.

Abraham and Sarah drank also – the four of them in silence, savouring the moment.

Eventually, Sam broke the silence.

'What happened two thousand years ago?' he said. 'What did the owner do to produce this kind of wine?'

Abraham and Sarah looked at each other, long and silently. There was a strange mix of sadness and of wonder in their eyes and in Abraham's voice as he gave the answer.

'He sent his son.'

When they talked later on, those were the last words either of them remembered from the table in the vineyard. The taste of the wine lingered for the rest of the day. Sam woke up a few minutes later, to his great surprise in the corner of the stockroom. Tizzy had come to look for him. The coast was clear, at least for today. Alice woke on her bed after the deepest sleep she could ever remember and tiptoed downstairs to the front room.

The fourth door on the calendar was open now. It was tall and brown and made of wood, arched at the top. Inside the door, carved in wood relief and painted the deepest red, was a miniature bunch of grapes still attached to the branch of the vine.

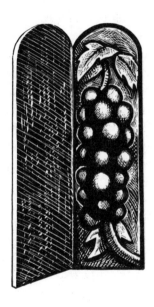

5 December

The next day, Alice sat at the back of the biology class in between Alex and Suzie, yawning every three minutes. No matter how hard she tried, her eyelids kept closing. Neither of her friends could understand it. Alice had been dozing off in corners all day long with a gentle smile on her face. At first they thought she'd stayed up until the early hours reading or chatting on-line. According to Alice, she had been in bed well before seven. Whatever the explanation, she was in no shape to face Miss Newton, so Suzie sat on one side with Alex on the other. Whenever her eyelids drooped even a little, one or the other of them would poke her with a pencil or kick her under the table. Alice already had a row of purple bruises down her left shin.

'*Ouch*!' she cried, when Miss Newton's back was turned. 'Watch it, Suzie. That really hurt.'

'Just keep your eyes open then, dopey,' Suzie hissed in a very upper-class way as the teacher looked in their direction, leering at them over the top of her spectacles. 'You're on the brink of triple detention as it is.'

'And the answer to the second question down on page 42 is …?' Miss Newton's shrill voice hung in the air. This was her favourite gambit. There would be five seconds' silence and then she would select the name of her least favourite pupil that afternoon, demanding an answer. If the chosen one stammered out a reply, all well and good. If he or she failed the test, Miss Newton would fix them with one of her beady eyes just like a bird of prey. Then, in a fraction of a second, she would swoop down from the other side of the classroom, push her face within inches of yours and screech the answer in loud, mocking tones.

Suzie and Alex both knew that this time it would be Alice. There had been tell-tale signs all through the lesson. In a last brave attempt to rescue his friend, under the eye of the teacher, Alex flicked the ear of the student on the row in front. As he expected, it was enough:

'Alexander Buchanan.'

'Yes, Miss Newton?'

Alex winced as the teacher's malodorous breath descended on the back row. Alice gagged and came fully awake.

'The answer to the second question on page 42 is?'

Just in time, Alex caught sight of Mandy Braithwaite mouthing the answer behind the Newtron's back.

'Carbon dioxide?' he muttered, weakly.

Miss Newton stalked away, looking disappointed, the vulture deprived of her prey. She turned away and spoke crisply to the class, clipping her words. 'Carbon dioxide – correct this time,' she said. 'Now, pay attention – all of you. That includes you, Miss Carroll.'

'We start a new topic tomorrow. Homework is advanced reading of Chapter Five: "Origins of the Universe". End of lesson.'

The bell sounded for the final time that day. Alex, Suzie and Alice bolted from the classroom. 'Thanks, you two,' yawned Alice. 'Sorry to be so dopey today.'

'Maybe you're catching something,' said Suzie, hope rising. 'You might get the day off school tomorrow!'

'No fear,' said Alice. 'You have to be really sick before you get a day off in our house. I think it was something I ate – or maybe drank – last night.' She seemed suspiciously cheerful about it all.

Alice was on the point of saying something about the calendar when the two friends had to go. She made her way to the bus stop, biology text in hand. 'It's not that the subject is so bad really,' she thought later, pressing her face against the bus window and looking out into the winter sunshine. 'It's just that Miss

Newton has a special gift for making interesting things dull.' As the line of traffic crept past the park gates, she looked and wondered and thought that the world really was very beautiful – even the ordinary things – at least the parts that she could see.

Megs was home. Wednesday was her half-day. No sign of any message from Sam. In the hall, Alice saw a bright red brolly and some red Wellington boots. 'Josie,' she thought, instantly. 'What's she doing here?'

'I have to see him, Megs, I just have to,' Josie was saying as Alice walked down the passage to the kitchen. 'I've left him messages; I've been emailing him for the last week. Nothing.'

'Are you sure about the test?'

Alice slowed down a bit. Josie was crying and Megs was giving her a cuddle, back to the door.

'Sure as I can be,' Josie said, then her tone changed to cheerful and she wiped her eyes. 'Oh. Hi, er, Alice! Good to see you.' She rubbed her eyes with the back of her hand as she disentangled herself from Megs.

'Hi, darling,' said Megs. 'Had a good day?'

Megs was making all kinds of weird facial gestures to Alice from behind Josie, trying to make her go away. Alice was having none of it. She hadn't seen Josie for ages and she liked her a lot. Sam was a total nerd to give her up.

'Whassup, Josie? Here to see Sam?'

'You bet,' said Josie, rubbing her eyes. 'We need to talk. Grown-up stuff.'

Alice knew when she wasn't wanted. By this time she had milk and biscuits sorted and she was making herself really comfortable at the kitchen table. Megs and Josie exchanged looks.

'I was just going to put the kettle on,' said Megs, eyes again flashing daggers behind Josie's back.

Just then the phone rang.

'Could that be Sam?' asked Josie, voice trembling.

'Doubt it,' said Meg. 'Never rings here during the day. Never rings here at all really. Just comes and goes when he feels like it. Probably double-glazing again.'

Just as Megs reached out to pick up the phone, it stopped

ringing. They heard Alice on the cordless extension in the hall, moving into the lounge. 'Oh, hi Suzie, just a minute' – she came back and closed the kitchen door. 'Private!' she mouthed to Megs, tapping her nose, phone pressed to her ear.

'Sam – you'll never guess who's here,' she whispered. 'It's Josie. She's sitting in the kitchen with Megs.'

'Walloping warthogs,' said Sam. 'What's she doing there?'

'She looks upset – kept going on about some kind of test.'

'Weird,' said Sam. 'I'll hang around out here for a bit then.'

'Where are you?'

'Just parking the car in the back lane. How's the calendar?'

Alice went to look.

'New door. Right-hand side near the bottom. Looks like a folding leather blind of some kind. Have you got the code?'

'It just came through as I was driving home. Punch it in, then meet me in the back garden. I'm almost there.'

'What is it, dummy? Quick, Mum's coming.' Alice heard the kitchen door open again. 'Are you sure that's Suzie on the phone, my love?' Surely she hadn't listened in on the extension? Alice didn't *think* Megs was that sneaky but you never knew. Lots of things happened at once in the next ten seconds.

Sam gave her the code: four, zero, colon, two, two. Alice cut off the call as her mum came into the room and peered deliberately at the calendar. As soon as Megs' back was turned, she punched in the numbers. Megs brought Josie back into the room. 'Alice, you go and do your homework in your room, will you? Josie and I need to sit in here for a while.'

Out of the corner of her eye, Alice saw the leather blind beginning to move to one side. A tiny strip of blue began to appear in the doorway. She flew past Megs and Josie, through the kitchen and out into the long back garden, hoping to meet Sam coming in at the back gate. Down the garden, past the swing and the great yew hedge and ...

There was Sam, all right, by the back gate, mouth open like a bulldozer. Alice stopped in her tracks.

Standing in front of Sam, as still as statues, facing each other were two magnificent golden eagles. Each was as tall as the back door. The top of their heads was the same height as the shrubs which surrounded the garden. The rich golden brown of their feathers stood out against the greys and greens of the winter landscape. They carried, as eagles do, an enormous sense of dignity, even on the ground. The great birds were plainly aware of Alice and Sam: neither afraid of them nor looking down on them – just kind of there.

Alice and Sam took a long look at each other, then at the eagles, then back at each other. Sam shrugged his shoulders and raised his eyebrows: 'What do we do now?' Alice took a step towards him. As she moved her foot forward, the eagle on her left bowed towards her. The eagle on the right did the same to Sam. Alice and Sam, together, instinctively bowed back, each to a different eagle. Alice's bird then lowered her body gracefully to ground level. Alice followed her cue and moved two paces nearer. The eagle on the other side of the path mirrored his companion. As Alice moved a step closer still, her eagle fixed her with one eye, lowered her right wing and, with her beak, motioned to Alice to climb onto her back.

With the utmost care, Alice stepped forward and around to the back of the bird. She tried not to think about the sharp beak and the powerful talons buried under the feathered body. Half closing her eyes, she climbed onto the bird's golden back, face buried in its neck, legs extended on each side. There was a powerful, warm smell unlike anything she had experienced before. The bird reached behind with its bill, gently coaxed Alice into the best position, and then began to stand. On the other side of the garden, Alice could see Sam finding a similar position. His hands gripped tight to the eagle's neck feathers and his eyes were screwed shut. Sam hated heights.

With one graceful unfurling movement, both eagles stood tall, spread their wings and in a moment were in the air. Alice's stomach leapt into her mouth on take-off, then quickly settled again. The eagles flew together, immense wings beating for a matter of minutes, gaining height, searching for something. Sam's eagle found the up-draught of warm air first. Alice saw the great bird simply spread his wings and begin to glide on the thermal current up and around in huge circles. A moment later, the second eagle did the same.

Sam, she noticed, had opened his eyes but still gripped his eagle tightly with both hands and knees. Alice tried to relax both and found that she felt just as safe. The eagle's feathers were soft and warm. She found she could sit up and see in all directions. There was a gentle breeze on her face, blowing back her hair. The air smelt clean and fresh. Down below her was the garden and the house with the wide curve of the main road. The eagles were taking a broad sweep over their part of town. Alice saw the detached house where Suzie lived and the school in the distance. At this height she could still hear the traffic noise.

On the second circuit they went higher still. There was hardly any sound now. She could see the shape of the roads, like looking down on an oversize living map. She saw the market-place with the parish church just behind it; the high street; the new shopping centre. Even at this height, the green spaces stood out most clearly: the school playing fields and the parks around the town. Round again and higher. Now, only the sound of an ambulance reached them. Alice followed its white roof as far as the hospital on the hill. The people were just dots moving on the streets, the cars simply coloured shapes, queuing at the roundabouts, moving freely on the major roads.

Still the eagles climbed, occasionally coming close enough for Alice and Sam to exchange a few words, to shout and point. 'There's the station. See the train coming in?' The two train lines led away from the stations at each end of the town and away towards London. 'Over there,' Alice called, 'you can see the city.' The centre of London was now clearly in view. She could pick out the Gherkin and St Paul's. The thin blue ribbon of the Thames sparkled in the winter sunshine. A familiar skyline – the strangest of angles.

Looking beyond the city centre Sam smiled as he saw the entire ring of the M25. Two-thirds of it was solid traffic – thousands of cars in a pointless procession. This, he thought, was what it must be like to fly in a hot-air balloon: silent, gliding, still. But no balloon could match the beauty and symmetry of the eagles' wings spread out on each side, tips extended to the furthest horizon, steering upwards with the gentlest of movements.

Neither Sam nor Alice could remember later feeling cold during the flight. It was as though the eagles each radiated warmth and life. There was no need on this journey for blankets or even for oxygen. Higher and higher they went, carried by the thermals. The gentle breeze had now become a steady wind. Alice had to lean into it as her eagle turned to stay balanced. Sam said later that this part was like riding pillion on a motorbike, riding into the bends. He pointed now to his left to where the line of the river met the sea. As they climbed still higher, they could see the shape of the coastline beginning to emerge. It was then that Alice noticed for the first time that if she concentrated hard on any part of the scene below her, she saw it with the eagle's own power of sight. She looked straight down and still she could see her own part of the city, her own street, her own back garden, her own bedroom window. She looked harder and could see the school playground – even the caretaker locking the gates as the last of the teachers left. A tiny Miss Newton walked to her car after the staff meeting. Sam had picked out the office where he worked and was pointing, but the wind was so loud in her ears now she could no longer hear what he said.

Still the eagles climbed. The south of England was spread out below them now like a quilt: dark patches were cities and towns separated by square fields connected by tiny roads and railway lines. Higher still and the view was more like a weather map – the clouds were below them. Planes criss-crossed the skies, circling in huge patterns around Gatwick and Heathrow. A couple of helicopters buzzed across London. There was a weather front coming in from the north-west. The eagles rode through a cloud, and Alice's clothes and face were suddenly soaked. Sam waved and pointed to the east. In the distance, Alice could see the place where day met night out across the ocean, moving towards them as the earth turned. From this height the horizon was a circle now extending all around them for hundreds and hundreds and hundreds of miles.

The great birds reached the top of the thermal. Both Alice and

Sam held on a little tighter as they beat their wings again, carrying them forward on the very borders between earth and space. The familiar shapes of the British Isles and Europe were spread out like a carpet below them. Endless blackness stretched above them. To the east again, away from the setting sun, the stars came into view clearer than Alice had ever seen. For a few moments at the very highest point of the flight, the winds dropped and there was complete silence. For the first part of the journey, Alice had been caught up in the detail: seeing everything from a new perspective. Now both she and Sam simply sat back and wondered at the earth and the skies spread out before them, drinking in the sense of space and size and order. Alice wanted to cry out but she had no words for what she felt.

Then the eagles turned, reaching the edge of the atmosphere, gliding but now down again in gentle, wide circles as the journey was reversed. The broad features of the land came into view first: the coasts and hills and forests and rivers; then the cities and towns; then the individual streets and houses; then the cars. Alice was surprised at how close to the earth's surface she had to come before she caught again the first sound of the traffic moving in the rush hour, the trains from the main-line station heading for the North, the helicopters on traffic patrol over the M25.

Now with each vast, gentle circle, the familiar sights came nearer, rushing to meet her like old friends. The roof of her own house was there, her bedroom window, one of the neighbours in his garden. No one looked up. The eagles swooped in low for the final time, clipping the tops of the trees and landing neatly exactly where they had begun, on either side of the garden gate. Alice and Sam slipped down from the back of the birds trembling with excitement. Both looked up into the sky, searching for the hidden pathways they had just explored. Then, together, they looked back at the creatures which had carried them so high. Both eagles bowed low to the ground. Sam and Alice bowed their heads in return in silent thanks and wonder. With a single, graceful movement, the birds stretched their wings and flew, this time away in the direction of the west and the setting sun.

Sam and Alice stood in silence until the birds had disappeared, then walked together into the house. Alice took his hand. Neither wanted to be the first to speak.

'Sam, what about Josie?' asked Alice as she put her hand on the back-door handle.

'It'll be OK,' said Sam. 'Don't worry!' Alice noticed for a moment how different he looked after the long flight. She wondered if she looked different too.

Josie and Megs were back in the kitchen, fixing something to eat. Both looked up as Alice and Sam came in.

'Hi!' said Sam. 'Back in just a sec.'

Together he and Alice went into the front room. Megs and Josie followed. There, on the wall, was the calendar. The fifth door was open now. The black leather blind was rolled back, secured with the neatest of tiny straps. The view through the door was one of wide-open winter skies. There, in the distance was the outline of an eagle in full flight, heading into the sun.

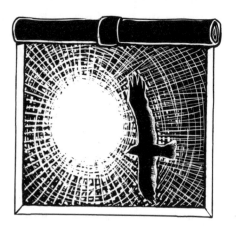

6 December

Sam's alarm went off the next day at half past six. A hand shot out from under the duvet and silenced it. An instant later the second clock went off – this one positioned just out of reach. This time a hairy arm and shoulder emerged, stretched, groped about on the chest of drawers and found its prey. Sam snorted, turned over and tried to get back to sleep. He'd been up late with Josie talking into the night and had not slept well. Two minutes later, though, alarm number three got him. This one was on the other side of the room. Sam stumbled out of bed and turned it off along with alarms four, five and six.

'Not bad,' he smiled to himself as he reached for his dressing gown and headed for the loo. 'Whassat?' The familiar sound of flatulence came from his mobile phone. A text message had arrived. 'Can't be this early, can it?'

Sure enough, the code had arrived. 'Galloping giraffes, that's a blow. I just can't be late for work today.' What Sam hadn't told Megs and Josie yesterday was that Richard had caught up with him on Wednesday and had given him a formal warning. He needed to get into the office early to do some extra work on the wretched report which was due in by noon Friday – no mercy and no last chances. He simply had to progress it this morning. They would just have to open the door tonight. Tizzy's job was on the line as well.

Sam's brain only worked very slowly in the mornings. By the

time he'd puzzled all this through he was showered, shaved, dressed and tiptoeing down the stairs. Normally, of course, Sam leaving the house sounded like a herd of gnu but today he particularly did not want to wake Alice.

She, however, was waiting for him in the hall at the bottom of the stairs in jeans, jumper and trainers.

'Aaaaah,' he jumped. 'What are you doing here?'

'Ready to go, stupid,' she said. 'The code's arrived, hasn't it?'

'How did you know that?' Sam asked suspiciously.

'My bedroom door was open,' Alice said, innocently. She didn't add that she had propped it open last night to see if she could catch some of the grown-up conversation going on in hushed whispers. 'I heard your stupid text-message signal. While you were in the shower, I checked. Today's code is three, zero, colon, two, one. You must have heard it. Why are you dressed as if you're going to work?'

'Is there a door?' Sam asked, despite himself.

'It's in the bottom left corner. It took me a while to see it. Simply a rectangle shape made of logs. Come and look – we can punch the code in together before Mum wakes up.'

'I just can't today, Alice. It's a work thing. I'm behind on something. I just can't be late. And what about school?' Sam was not convincing when he tried to sound like an adult.

'What about it?' said Alice. 'I couldn't care less about school. It's only assembly first thing. It's so boring. The calendar is much more fun. Come *on*.'

She tugged at his sleeve. Sam wavered, then began to back away.

'Alice – look, sorry. I really like the calendar. It's been fantastic. Normally I wouldn't mind missing work but I've run out of excuses, I really have. It's serious. Bye.'

He ran out through the kitchen door before Alice could stop him. She was not to be beaten and headed straight for the calendar. 'OK, Mr Keeno. Let's see what this does to your work plans.' For the sixth time she punched in the code one number at a time, pausing only slightly before the final number: 'Three. Zero. Two dots. Two. One.'

At first, nothing. Then a soft cranking sound as the rows of tiny logs began to part in the centre like a stage curtain. In the middle of the small doorway was something that looked like a tiny spinning tornado. 'Uh oh!' thought Alice, just feeling the wind moving her hair. By the time the door was half open, she was holding onto the back of the sofa to stay upright. The instant it was fully open, Alice felt her feet lifting off the carpet as she was pulled into the air and towards the calendar. Instinctively, she closed her eyes, thinking she was going to hit the wall of the living room. She never saw whether the door got bigger or she got smaller. An instant later she felt something like wet branches brush her face and she was sitting on cold soft earth. The smell of pine trees was all around. It was raining very gently. There was a soft mist just lifting with the dawn.

Alice opened her eyes. It was early morning. She was in the middle of a great forest of Christmas trees as tall as lampposts. A single path led away between the trees. And to her great delight, as she had hoped, she was not alone. Sam was about two metres away, his clothing crumpled and torn. He was grumpy and pleased at the same time.

'Suffering centipedes! You punched in the code.'

'What happened?'

'I was just putting my bag in the back seat of the car when I was caught up by an enormous blast of wind, spun through the air and set down here. You?'

'Same, only in the living room. Where do you think we are?'

'Dunno,' said Sam, getting to his feet and brushing pine needles off his trousers. 'In a wood? Lost? Late for work?'

'Sorry, Sam,' said Alice, grinning meekly.

'Bit late for that,' Sam said with a wink, pulling her up. 'The timings have all worked out so far. I was wondering how we might manage it today anyway. You've got your parents' evening tonight, haven't you?'

'Don't remind me,' said Alice. 'Mum and Miss Newton meet at seven. I've been trying not to think about it. What about your work and stuff?'

'Something,' said Sam, 'will just have to turn up. Let's go – there's only one path. Come on.'

They moved forward together down into the forest away from the clearing. The path was straight at first but then began to meander gently through the trees. It was a couple of metres wide and clear of the ivy and undergrowth that covered the forest floor. The canopy of branches sheltered them from the rain apart from one or two drips which made it through. The early morning sunlight cut shafts through the pine trees and made endlessly shifting patterns on the forest floor. The air was sharp on their cheeks. Both of them breathed in deeply. Wherever they were, it was good to be here.

'So what happened with Josie?' Alice asked once they were into their stride. 'I heard her talking to Mum about a test or something. Did she fail an exam? She's so nice.'

'It was a pregnancy test, nosey. I suppose you had to find out sooner or later. Josie's going to have a baby.'

'But she was crying.'

'I know,' Sam said. 'Having a baby's not exactly in the plan. A few months ago we were really close and we did talk about, well, you know, the future and stuff and being together. Then we had this big bust-up. Around the same time, I had to move out of my flat and I came to live with you. Since then we've seen each other every so often – but I never expected anything like this.'

'So what's going to happen? Are you going to get back together?'

'Dunno. It's kind of a lot to think about just now. If we stay together, then there's the baby to take care of. Not sure I'm ready for all that. It's just not a good time. Then there's all this stuff at work.'

'Have you thought about, you know?'

'Getting rid of it? Yeah. That might happen too. But it's not something to take lightly, is it? And if we go that way, then it really is over between Josie and me. Have you seen what's happening to the path?'

Alice looked back. The pathway was getting narrower, the bends were sharper now, and a few smaller tracks led off to the right and to the left. One or two were clearly dead-ends but some looked as if they would lead somewhere else completely.

Out of the corner of her eye, Alice caught a glimpse of something else.

'Something's following us again. It's the shadow I saw the day we went for tea to that church or garden or whatever it was. I've not seen it since. There was no sign of it at all in the vineyard and with the eagles. But it's there now.'

'Best keep moving then,' Sam said. 'What about these side-paths? Do you think we should explore them?'

'I'm not really sure,' said Alice, 'I think we're meant to stay on this one.'

But as they moved forward, the path they had been following became smaller and smaller until it began to look like the other pathways which criss-crossed the forest floor. There was no sign of civilisation of any kind. Each time they could tell which the main pathway was but only just. They couldn't see much beyond the trees but occasionally they caught sight of mountains on each side of them. They were clearly in some kind of great valley.

After an hour's steady walking they came upon a large rock by the side of the road. A very tiny spring bubbled up through a crack in the centre of the rock and ran across the pathway only to disappear into the ground on the other side. Sam tasted the water first. It was clear and fresh. They both drank deeply, cupping their hands to gather the ice-cold refreshment. Sam looked curiously at the rock and the way the water just appeared. Alice was looking at where they went next.

'We need to go more carefully here. We could take a wrong turn.'

Up ahead of them, the path divided into two. This time, the two ways looked exactly the same but each went off in a different direction, twisting and turning away from the other.

'Eeny, meeny, miny mo,' said Sam. 'Come on, it's this way.'

'Sam, wait!' cried Alice. 'Stop and think.'

Sam stopped, three paces down the left-hand track.

'This is the first time we've had to make a choice since we began the calendar,' Alice went on, glancing over her shoulder. 'None of the other roads have divided. I think it means something.'

61

'The shadows are still there,' said Sam, looking back. 'I can see them too now. There seem to be more of them. We can't just wait here. There's no way of telling which of the pathways we are meant to take. This one is exactly the same as that one. They are the same width; they head off in approximately the same direction. They look identical. So the only way is to just choose. Do you want to flip a coin or something?'

'But suppose it's important?' said Alice. 'Suppose there is another way to decide? Suppose we just wait and listen.'

To Sam's amazement, Alice squatted down by the side of the road and just looked at the two paths. 'But Alice, the shadows – we can't wait here.'

Alice had a deep, irresistible and strange sense that she needed to stop and think. It came from deep within her.

'Just do it, Sam,' said Alice. 'Just trust me on this one. It's a feeling.'

Sam did as he was told. Nothing happened for about a minute. Every ten seconds or so, Sam looked back over his shoulder. The shadows were slowly coming nearer. He was no wiser at all and about to give up when Alice stood up and pointed down the right-hand path.

'This is the way,' she said, setting off at once.

'How do you know that?' said Sam, amazed.

'I just know,' said Alice. 'I listened. Come on – no time to lose. We might throw them off the trail.'

Glancing behind him again, Sam set off after Alice, keeping his eye on the pathway. Fifteen minutes later they came to another rock by the side of the road. Again, there was a tiny spring bubbling up and running across the path. Beside the spring this time were two tiny flat loaves.

'Look, Sam. This must be the way.' Alice took a drink of water and broke off a piece of bread. It tasted of honey and herbs. 'I'm starving.'

'S'good,' said Sam, a bit reluctantly. 'I'm impressed, Alice. How did you know the way?'

'It was just as I said. I just kind of concentrated and listened.'

They set off again refreshed, nibbling the bread as they went. Sam looked at his watch to see how late he was for work already. The hands had stopped at ten to seven. A bit further on the trail divided again, this time into three almost identical paths. The central path was a little wider.

'Straight on?' wondered Sam.

'OK,' said Alice, and followed him slowly. Then she stopped. 'Hold up, Sam. I'm not sure this is the pathway. Just wait a moment.'

Sam turned back. As he did, he thought he caught a glimpse of three shadows lurking in the trees ahead but said nothing. Alice squatted down beside the road again in the place the paths divided, lines of concentration on her face. This time Sam heard the little whisper too. 'Left,' it said, soft as a kiss on the cheek.

Alice pointed left. 'This way,' she said. 'Quick.'

'I know,' said Sam. 'I heard it too. There are shadows down that middle pathway and at least five behind us now.'

On they went through the forest trail, twisting now this way, now that, climbing steeply. The path had become so narrow that they had to walk in single file, Alice first with Sam bringing up the rear. Despite the bread, they were becoming tired because of the pace. The third junction was different again. One pathway began to climb very steeply up to the left. The other was broad and wide and led down into the valley.

'It must be this way,' said Sam, pointing down to the right. 'It looks like the original path we followed at the beginning.'

'Just wait, Sam. We have to wait and listen again. I know we do.'

Both of them knew the shadows were gathering in the trees behind them and much closer now. Every time they looked round at least three or four flitted across the paths, keeping to the darkness of the trees when they could. Despite that, Alice squatted bravely in the road and tried to concentrate. Sam did the best he could to listen for the soft voice in his head but this time could only shuffle and look round. He caught nothing.

'This is the way, I think,' said Alice, pointing to the left.

They set off. The climb was steep. Sam had to help Alice now over the rougher parts. Twice they slipped: the sharp rocks cut a hole in Sam's suit trousers and bruised Alice's knees. The left-hand path led them up and out of the forest onto the side of a great mountain. As the trees thinned out they were able to look out onto the vast expanse of trees ringed by hills. As far as the eye could see there were no clearings or pathways. They could not see where their trail had started. From where they were, it looked as though this mountain was at the very centre of everything they could see.

'Faster,' said Alice, out of breath. 'I think we need to go faster.'

Sam looked round. The shadows were still with them and gaining ground. Alice and Sam were growing tired and the air was thinner. Then the path turned a sharp corner and, fifty metres ahead, it entered a kind of tunnel in the side of the hill. Across the entrance to the tunnel was what looked like a thin wall of water. As they drew nearer to it Sam looked up. Right above the entrance to the tunnel was a pool fed by a rushing mountain stream. The pool's overflow formed a waterfall which fell across the tunnel's entrance and away down a steep gorge. The path stopped just before the gorge and a tiny bridge led through the curtain of water and into the tunnel beyond.

'Quick,' said Sam. 'We have to reach the mouth of the tunnel.'

The shadows were close behind them, within ten metres and gaining. Sam and Alice both began to run. The drop on their right was steep now. The pathway was cut into the side of the hill. The shadows also gained speed. Alice began to feel a curious heat from the pursuit on her neck and the back of her calves. She sensed them reaching out to catch her hair or the heel of her shoe. Then moments later they reached the bridge. Without stopping, they plunged into the curtain of water. It was wider and stronger than they thought. They held tight to the handrails, breath taken away. Alice and Sam were completely drenched in an instant. They paused panting on the other side. The fiery shadows gathered on the other side of the bridge: black shapes with a flicker of red running through them. There were at least ten or more. They dare not or could not enter the water but reached out their arms, clawing at the air in frustration.

'Come on,' said Sam, taking Alice's arm. 'Let's move further in. They might find a way across.'

Alice knew, somehow, that they could not pass. But they moved forward in any case. The path led on through the tunnel in the side of the hill. They could see a patch of light ahead where it came out into the open. The sound of the water falling filled the space. Alice squeezed the moisture out of her hair and her clothes as they emerged blinking into the light.

'Alice, Sam, welcome! You made it through. We're so glad. We thought you would but we never know, you know. Well done. Come in. Everything's ready. Here's a towel for your face. Take these clothes. There's space to change behind those rocks. This side for you, Sam. That's the way. Over here, Alice.'

The greeting from Abraham and Sarah was as warm as ever. As they came out of the changing areas, Sarah brought Alice new shoes for her feet and a clear crystal ring for her finger. Abraham did the same for Sam. Together they led them to a table under a spreading oak tree in the centre of the glade and served them with fresh bread, water from the spring and fruit from the trees which grew in that place. There was kiwi fruit, melon, pomegranates and cucumber. Everything smelt and tasted so fresh.

'You have passed the calendar's first test,' said Abraham as they began to eat. 'We were hopeful that you would. We can now tell you more and send you on your way. This is the last day we will meet with you. There will be other guides as your journey continues.'

'The calendar has twenty-four doors in all, one for each day of the last month until the greatest of nights comes round again. A new door appears each day. This much you know already.'

Sarah took up the lesson. 'The days are in four groups of six,' she said. 'For each group there will be different guides. On the sixth day of each group comes the test. To move on to the next part of the calendar, you must complete the challenge and pass the test.'

'The pathways,' said Alice. 'The choices.'

'What would have happened if we had taken the wrong pathway?' asked Sam.

'The other roads simply lead back to your own world,' said Abraham, with sadness. 'As we promised, no harm can come to you in these different journeys and worlds. But there would have been no code tomorrow, no more doors appearing. The adventure of the calendar would have ended here for you. There would be no harm done – but nor would you have seen the blessing that the calendar holds.'

'What about the shadows?' Alice asked. 'Would they have followed us back to our world?'

'They are there already,' Sarah replied. 'You brought them to this place but see them more clearly here, that's all. The closer you came to the waterfall, the more clearly you could see. All that you learn through the doors of the calendar will enable you to over-come them in your own world and in your own life.'

Sam and Alice rested for a while with Abraham and Sarah, enjoying their last moments with the couple who were so full of years and full of wisdom. Then Sam looked at his watch and noticed the second hand had started to move again.

'Come, children,' said Abraham. 'It is time for goodbyes.'

Abraham and Sarah enfolded Sam and Alice each in an embrace. Held in Abraham's arms, Alice felt his great strength and courage and faith flowing into her. 'Well done, child,' he said. 'Well done.' Alice kept the words in her mind for a very long time: it was the first time she could remember hearing anyone saying that to her. Held by Sarah, Alice felt as though she was breathing in deep wisdom and laughter and joy, despite all the difficulties and dangers of her life. After the embrace, Sarah held both her hands and looked deep into Alice's eyes, her whole face alight: 'Enjoy the gift of life,' she said. 'Enjoy the gift.'

Abraham led them both to the entrance of a small cave in the side of the mountain, no more than a crack in the rock. 'This is the way back,' he said, standing back so first Sam and then Alice could walk through. 'This time, only seconds have passed in your worlds. Go well.'

His voice faded. Sam and Alice were standing again in front of the calendar in the living room. The sixth door was open. As Alice expected, when she looked closely she could see a forest of tall pines. Winding its way through the forest, showing the way, was a single, golden thread.

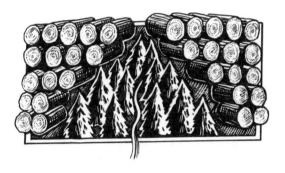

7 December

Friday was a very bad day for Alice and for Sam but for different reasons. For Alice, the rot set in on Thursday evening. Suzie and Alex dropped their guard in biology. Alice was tired again in the lesson after her long walk through the forest. They were getting very fed up with protecting her. The Newtron pounced again. This time she caught her prey and Alice was given a detention the night of her first parents' evening.

Megs was very embarrassed and very, very angry. It was the kind of parents' evening where pupils came too, so Alice had to listen again and again to reports of how she was always yawning in class; of late homework; of sloppy work. Again and again, she listened to Megs defending her with the same excuses. 'It's been a hard few months ... lots of changes ... her father left us ... moved into the area ... I've had so much to do ... sure she'll do better next term ... won't you, Alice?' Once or twice, she even had to wipe away the tears.

Alice knew that behind the smile for the teachers, the pressure in Megs was mounting. In turn, she glowered back, grunted out her replies, slouched in her chair and shuffled reluctantly from room to room. The only light moment in the evening came when Alice joined the long line for Mr Watkins, the fit PE teacher. He didn't even teach Alice but everyone said that he didn't have a clue who anybody was at parents' evenings and so he always said exactly the same thing to everyone. They were right, so at least

Megs left assured but puzzled that Alice always behaved herself and tried hard in PE. Alice could tell by the way Megs smiled in that meeting that she thought Mr Watkins was pretty fit as well. 'Yeucch,' she thought. 'He's much too young for her. Yeeuurrgh.'

The interview with Miss Newton was, of course, the blackest moment of the evening. It was the last appointment. Alice had been kind of hoping that they might run out of time. Instead, she could tell, Miss Newton's patience was running very low at the end of a long day.

'Alice has a lot of work to do, Mrs Carroll, a lot of work to do. She's got the brains, haven't you, Alice?'

Alice had been practising swearing in front of the mirror and she really wanted to tell Miss Newton to 'F off' right then and there just for the hell of it. 'S'pose,' she mumbled.

'But she won't apply herself. The homework is sloppy and late. She never contributes in class. Yesterday and today she looked as if she was asleep in the lessons. It simply has to stop.'

Megs looked as though she was about to burst into tears. 'What have you got to say, Alice?'

The head teacher was hovering nearby, clearly wanting to encourage everyone to go home. Miss Newton, by a superhuman effort, pulled her features into a mask of concern and said, rather loudly: 'Is everything alright at home? Are there any problems we should know about?'

Megs pulled herself back together and began to gather her things. Whatever else was happening she wasn't playing that game.

'Yes, thanks. We're fine. I'll be coming back for a longer conversation about what the school's strategy is for all the problems I've been hearing about this evening. You seem very good at pointing out people's faults here but not very good at constructive solutions – except for that nice Mr Watkins. Goodnight.'

Set and match to Megs, thought Alice, as she was dragged by the hand through the main school door. There was much nose blowing and wiping of eyes before Megs could start the car.

'Alright, Mum?' said Alice.

'Shut up, madam. Just shut up, OK. I'll deal with you when

you get home. I have never been so humiliated in my entire life.'

Megs turned the ignition key and pressed the accelerator to the floor. The engine turned over but the car would not start. She did the same a second and a third time. Nothing. Megs swore as Alice had never heard her swear before and thumped the dashboard. There was a tap on the driver's window, which had steamed up. Megs wound it down.

'Hi! Andrew Watkins – we met inside a few minutes ago. Mrs Carroll, isn't it? Anything I can do to help?'

'Car won't start,' said Megs, wiping her eyes.

'Hop out – let me give it a try. Evening – er – Lucy.'

'It's Alice,' said Alice.

'Course it is,' said fit Mr Watkins, winking at her. 'I think I can see what's happened.' He pushed in the choke and gave the slightest of touches on the key. The engine sputtered into life.

'There we go, Mrs Carroll,' he said, leaping out of the car and standing, Alice thought, rather too close to her mum. Megs didn't seem to mind and made no move to get into the driver's seat.

'It's Megs,' she said, holding out her hand.

'Andrew – pleased to meet you. I don't think I've seen you here before.'

'We've just moved into the area. Gordon Hill.'

'I know that part well – just round the corner from my flat.'

'Oh,' said Megs. 'That's nice. Perhaps see you around then. Thanks for your help – and for what you said about Alice tonight.'

'Cool,' said Mr Watkins. Alice cringed. Megs got back into the car. 'Oh – and don't be embarrassed or anything – but I don't actually teach your daughter. It's a bit of a school joke, I think – quite a few of them queue up to see me on these evenings. I try not to show them up. Teenage girls – you know.'

'Quite,' said Megs, blushing and crashing the gears in the rush to get away and winding up the window. 'Wait till I get you home, young lady. Do not say a word. Not a word.'

So Alice had the ten-minute drive home to think of all the things that were wrong with her mum. When they got home Megs was angry and tired and upset and let fly at Alice. Alice let fly back. She told Megs it was her fault Dad had left; that she was impossible to live with; that she always felt sorry for herself; that she had no time for Alice; that Alice didn't care what she thought. Quite a few of the new swear words she had been practising came rushing out. Alice stormed off to her room, slammed the door and lay face down on the bed.

A few minutes later she opened the bedroom door so she could hear her mum talking on the phone – to her dad.

'Nick – look sorry to ring so late. I'm in a bit of a state about Alice. It was parents' evening tonight. Absolute disaster. She's clearly been much more affected by all the changes than I thought. I just don't know what to do. I think we need to talk ...'

Alice got up and slammed the door again – just for effect really – and sobbed herself to sleep.

The next morning, you could cut the atmosphere in the house with a blunt butter knife. Sam clearly had a lot on his mind. Megs had let him know that she needed some support but it was just one more thing to cope with: 'Sis, I've got problems of my own right now. Back off, OK?'

Alice and Megs were not speaking at all. Breakfast and the journey to school were in complete silence. Alice was like a bear with a sore head with Alex and Suzie. She called Loren Graham a stuck-up cow after break for no reason and very nearly got into a fight with Elaine Webster, the toughest girl in the year. Fit Mr Watkins smiled at her a couple of times in the corridor, making her want to run to the toilets and throw up. Miss Newton looked daggers at her when she arrived at the labs for chemistry – no biology today, thank goodness. When she got home there was no message from Sam and, for the first time, she couldn't be bothered to ring him. What was the point of passing a test in the world of the calendar if all this stuff was happening to her now?

Meanwhile, Sam had been wrestling with his own problems. Outwardly, at least, things were OK. The wretched report was finished and handed in though Sam had no real enthusiasm for it. At least Richard was off his back now for a little while. He and

Josie had agreed to spend some time together at the weekend to think about what to do. Sam knew he was going to have to make some choices: he knew his life was simply drifting. But he was also very frightened. The adventures in the calendar were helping in some ways. But they also made certain things much clearer which was very uncomfortable.

All of this meant Sam had too much to deal with that Friday. Like Alice, he had snapped at Megs, growled at Richard, been too sharp with Josie and even told Tizzy to back off. A week ago, he thought, he would have simply drowned out all the noise and gone off to the pub after work. Three different people rang to ask him but he made excuses. If there were any answers, he knew by now he would find them somehow through the journeys through the calendar.

At home, Alice just sat quietly in the living room, hugging a cushion, staring across at the calendar wall. Six doors open. The candle. The dove. The garden. The grapes. The eagle in flight. The golden thread. Despite herself, she came closer and looked at each in turn, thinking, wondering, wanting things to be different. The memories of each experience came back as she looked into the doorways. What was it all about? She knew it had to have some kind of meaning. She caught a glimpse of her face reflected in the windows: tear stained, moody. Why did she have to be like that? Why was she everything she didn't want to be inside? Somehow the calendar was helping her to see at least that more clearly.

The back door opened – Sam called through, softly in case Megs was back. 'Home. You there, Alice?'

'In here,' she called back, turning to look at the calendar again. She felt a tingle of excitement. A seventh door was there: two miniature stone columns on either side of a door overlaid with what looked like tarnished gold. 'Sam – the door has appeared. Do you have the code?'

'Arrived two minutes ago – I was just parking the car. Suffering centipedes, you look awful.'

'You don't look that good yourself. Have you eaten today?'

'Come to think of it, no. Too much going on, I think. Here's the code. Very simple today: six, colon, six. Wonder what these numbers mean anyway?'

'I thought they were just random codes,' said Alice. 'Do you think there is something more? Six, colon, six. There.'

Sam peered closely at the calendar. The tiny golden doors began to open – but inwards. How could that happen? A narrow line appeared down the centre and grew bigger. This time, the first thing they noticed was the music.

The deep sound of what sounded like a football stadium of top-class male voice choirs filled the room in slow rhythmic chant on a bass line:

> 'Q'a ... dosh ... q'a ... dosh ... q'a ... dosh.'

The power of the sound grew as the doors opened. The whole house began to shake, not able to contain the song. A choir of women's voices came in with sharp, clear harmonies to the same words, leaping and tripping across the bass lines:

> 'Q'a ... dosh ... q'a ... dosh ... q'a ... dosh.'

The power of the harmonies seemed to cause the living room, the house and their entire world to shake and then simply to melt away. Drumming began underneath the bass sound: a steady, syncopated rhythm reminding Sam of African dance music. Alice looked round. She and Sam were in the centre of a vast, open space surrounded by a colonnade. All around them were pilgrims, pouring in through the many gates in the colonnade, summoned, it seemed, by the choir and musicians. The crowd took up the simple songs, swaying, rocking and dancing in time to the music's gentle rhythms.

> 'Q'a ... dosh ... q'a ... dosh ... q'a ... dosh.
> Adonai ... seva'oth ... q'a ... dosh.'

At the top of the steps, the entrance to an inner courtyard, trumpeters sounded a rippling fanfare.

The male choir continued its rhythmic chant while the women changed their song, singing the words over and over until Alice knew them by heart and could join in:

> 'Adonai ... seva'oth ... mil'o ... col ha'retz ... c'vodo.
> Q'a ... dosh ... q'a ... dosh ... q'a ... dosh.'

As the pilgrims poured into the vast space, all bound together in the music and the rhythm of the dance, so Alice and Sam were gradually pressed forward towards the steps. On each side of the stairway the crowds parted. Men and women and children were there from every race and in every kind of national dress. All joined in the song and moved together. Every face was alive with joy and hope. On either side the people turned back towards Alice and Sam holding out their hands in welcome, smiling and beckoning them forward.

Sam and Alice held back. Without a word being spoken both of them became aware of what they had been feeling all of that day and the day before but couldn't name: a deep sense of not being worthy, a discontent with the person they had become.

A thin young man stepped out of the darkened doorway at the top of the stairs and came down to welcome them. He too held out his arms and motioned for them to climb the stairs and enter. With each step Alice took, her sense of unworthiness grew. She remembered how she had looked in the mirror, the way she had treated her friends at school, most of all the stuff she'd said to Megs. Sam's mind was on the shallowness of his life, the way he always ran away from problems and couldn't help it, his responsibilities to Josie.

The trumpets stopped. The drum beats were hushed. The singing dropped to a deep, soft whisper all across the courtyard, filling the space:

> 'Q'a ... dosh ... q'a ... dosh ... q'a ... dosh.
> Adonai ... seva'oth ... mil'o ... col ha'retz ... c'vodo.
> Q'a ... dosh ... q'a ... dosh ... q'a ... dosh.'

Sam and Alice reached the entrance to the building. The young man took them through the immense doorway. Once inside there was a sense of vast empty space and a great, deep stillness: all the silence in the world gathered into one place. Somehow the inside was bigger than the outside – the building stretched away above and in front of them. The only light came from a brazier of hot coals just a few metres away.

Without knowing why, both Alice and Sam fell to their knees just a few steps inside the entrance. The sense of unworthiness was still growing inside each of them. This was such a special place.

Without a word, when he saw that they were kneeling, the slender young man walked towards the brazier of hot coals. He took some tongs from the floor beside the brazier and, with great care, picked up one of the coals. Carefully and slowly, in the silence, he carried the glowing coal towards Alice and Sam as they knelt side by side. When he stood before them, he held out the coal first towards Sam, stopping a few inches from his face. Instinctively, Sam moved his head backwards. The young man motioned to him not to be afraid. Sam took Alice's hand as the man moved the tongs nearer until the red-hot coal just touched Sam's lips. Alice felt Sam squeeze her hand tight in a moment of pain and then relax. A moment later and the coal was offered to Alice. Bravely she did not flinch. The stab of pain on her lips was sharp and clean. After that, Alice felt a warm, cleansing fire move slowly from her lips to her head, to her heart and then to her hands and feet. Suddenly, the sense of unworthiness was gone.

Sam and Alice remained on their knees, heads bowed.

The young man raised them to their feet. 'Welcome to this new part of the adventure.'

Alice and Sam could not reply. For both of them, the moment was too special for words. There was a fire playing on their lips and in their minds and on their hearts, burning, cleansing, making new.

'I am Col,' said the young man, solemnly. 'Your guide for this day and five more. We will speak again in a different place.'

Col signalled to them to move back now to the building's entrance. Alice and Sam did as they were asked, still not able to speak. They came out of the great silence of the hall and towards the courtyard. The soft singing and music still filled the air, more gentle now:

'Q'a ... dosh ... q'a ... dosh ... q'a ... dosh.'

Slowly, as they crossed the threshold, the courtyard faded from view and they stood side by side in the living room. The chanting continued for a few moments more, then it too faded into the distance.

For a few seconds Alice stood looking at her reflection in the front windows, holding her own gaze. The fire was still there, playing inside her. There was so much that had to be put right.

Then, with Sam, she turned towards the calendar. Right in the centre in the top half of the calendar stood an open door: a slip of gold on each side flanked by a delicate stone column. In the centre of the doorway was a tiny brazier of coals. Whenever she looked through the doorway in the coming days, Alice felt the pain and the wonder of fire on her lips.

8 December

Alice woke with the burning sensation still on her lips and knowing what she had to do. Saturday. Normally a good, lazy day. Yesterday had been so *very* strange. Cold and frosty in the house. A foggy atmosphere at school as she struggled through the day. Then sunny intervals without warning. She turned the calendar journey over and over in her mind's eye: the rhythmic singing and music; the crowds; their new guide. What had she seen in the temple? Looking back, she wasn't sure. There was just this sense, this feeling, that she was in the presence of something deep, terrible and strange, yet not at all frightening. Slowly Alice unravelled the knotted ball of string in her head and began to understand what she was feeling. The closer they had come to the presence – and they only went a few steps into the temple – the more the atmosphere kind of thickened; the more solemn and serious things became; the more the feeling of her own, well, unworthiness grew until it became overwhelming. Sam had said similar things in the short conversation they had had last night. Then there was an instant of fear and the searing heat of the coal and, just as suddenly, a deep sense of cleansing and of stillness.

Alice hadn't wanted to say anything to anybody on Friday evening. Sam went out for a walk and a think. Megs was still very angry. The worry of her dad coming round today made that much worse. They hadn't seen or heard from him for weeks. Megs had said to be ready at eleven. The house sounded very quiet. Alice looked at the clock: ten already. She had to do it now.

She pulled on her new jeans and T-shirt, brushed her hair and went downstairs. Megs was vacuuming the front room, getting the house ready for the visitor. Everything looked a bit cleaner than normal. The calendar looked exactly the same. Megs looked nice, kind of polished. She turned off the vacuum as Alice came in.

'Mum, I'm – er – it's just – I'm really sorry I was so horrible – I'm sorry I said all that stuff. You're a great mum. I feel really bad about the way I've been. I'm just really sorry.'

By the time she got this far, Alice was in tears and Megs was holding her tight and crying as well, squeezing the breath from her lungs.

'It's OK,' she said. 'It's OK. I think I needed to hear some of it. I've been too caught up in myself lately. Not coping well with ..., you know.'

'I know,' said Alice, brushing the tears away. 'What time is he coming?'

'He said 11.00. It is time the two of us talked – and at least your parents' evening gives us a reason. There are things that need to be sorted.'

They sat down together on the sofa and cuddled together. Megs stroked Alice's hair. 'So what is happening at that school? Is it really that bad?'

'It's pants. Alex and Suzie are nice but they live so far away. I think I upset them yesterday. Some of the teachers are OK but some of them are really, well, unkind, even though I don't like to say so.'

Alice was about to go on to say some horrible things about Miss Newton and biology but she found the words got stuck somewhere between her mind and her throat.

'That biology teacher was a bit of a dragon, I thought,' said Megs. 'Still, the PE teacher was nice – even if he doesn't actually teach you.'

Alice went very red indeed at this point but to her great relief Megs still had loads to do. 'Will you be OK in here while I get things ready? I told Sam to get lost for the day. He and your dad are not getting on at the moment. I don't want little brother starting fights to make things any worse.'

'Sure.' Alice smiled gratefully and switched on the TV. She flicked over the channels. Normal Saturday morning kids stuff. Zillions of adverts for toys and Christmas presents: talking dolls and plastic soldiers; racing cars and board games made of bright plastic; DVDs and the latest gadgets. Even on the channels with sport and old cookery programmes there were adverts for more gifts; supermarket adverts for food and drink; adverts for credit cards and loans.

As she watched from her favourite chair, Alice kept on looking from the TV to the calendar and back again. Was this all it was about? Plastic presents and plastic food with plastic cards to pay for it all. She looked again at the door at the very centre. What would be there? What was at the centre of it all? For the first time, something inside woke up and started asking questions. Just what did it all mean?

Megs came and sat with her on the sofa just before eleven. 'It's a funny old thing, your calendar,' she said. 'Shame about the chocolate – but it's nice having something different on the wall. I've got used to it now. The code thing is good. Wonder what all those little pictures mean?'

'Dunno,' said Alice, suddenly realising her tongue had started to tingle.

Just at that very moment, that very moment, the doorbell rang.

Sam's Saturday was strange and empty. There was no football – the match was away from home and he couldn't afford to go. All his mates were busy. Megs had asked him to be out of the house by ten just in case Mr Toerag arrived early. He and Josie had agreed to meet for lunch but that gave him a couple of hours to kill. Against his better judgement, Sam found himself pulled, like everyone else, to the shopping mall.

The lights here were nowhere near as good as the ones in London. Reindeer alternated with Father Christmases all down the high street but lots of the bulbs were missing. In the mall itself, there were green Christmas trees and pink fairies. Another colour-blind designer! The queues at the cash points were six deep already. Christmas shoppers were out in force. Mainly women, Sam thought. What men there were lagged three steps behind looking as though they would rather be somewhere else – anywhere else. Lots of little children, either rushing ahead and pointing to the shop windows, eyes growing bigger all the time or else dragging behind, tired and sulky. Some people on their own, dashing about, little headphones in place, living in two worlds at the same time.

Sam drifted for a while, wondered about a lottery ticket, then thought better of it. Eventually he found a Starbucks and sat down in the window, just watching. For once he switched off the iPod and just stared. He, too, had a strange, burning sensation on his lips where the hot coal had seared and burned something – though not his flesh. He remembered the sense of unworthiness, poverty, emptiness which came as they stepped inside the temple building. Some of the intensity inside him had gone with the burning coal: he felt able, as it were, to go on with the journey. But the emptiness was deeper, if anything. Sitting in the coffee-shop window, watching the crowds, with no music playing made it worse. So many people, thought Sam. So much activity. So little point and so little purpose. Nobody looked as though they were enjoying themselves. Everyone was in a hurry. Christmas seemed more about survival than anything else. Getting ready for this great and terrible event that nobody really enjoyed.

He pressed a number on his mobile. 'Alice. Hi, how's it going? Has Mr Meatball arrived?'

'Late as usual,' said Alice. 'The doorbell has gone three times. First some woman with a card from the church. Then a window cleaner. Then a man delivering telephone directories – but no big bad Nick.'

'How's Megs?'

'Nervous, I think. But I said sorry and we made up. Kind of had to after yesterday. Any codes?'

'Nothing.'

'You feeling OK?'

'Kind of,' said Sam. 'But different. Got to go. Meeting Josie. Love to Megs.'

⧗

As Alice put the phone down, the doorbell rang again, twice, very loud. This time it had to be Dad.

'Nick, hi, come in. Bit later than you said,' she heard Megs saying.

And so it starts, thought Alice with a sigh.

'Sorry, Megs. Had to drop Janie at the hairdresser's. You know how it is. Hi, Alice – how's things?'

Why did he have to mention his girlfriend in the first breath? And why was he wearing enormous combat trousers? And what was that thing in his ear? Wasn't the shaved head bad enough?

'Come through,' said Megs. 'Do you want a coffee or something?'

'Only if it's fresh. Never drink instant these days. But I've not got that long really. Kind of short notice, you know. This place is looking a bit better, but what kind of junk is this?'

'It's my Advent Calendar,' Alice said as Megs went out to the kitchen. 'Sam got it for me.'

'Did he indeed?' said Nick. 'Looks just like the kind of rubbish that Sam would pick up. I brought you this – thought you'd have one already but that you might like another.'

Alice was always amazed at how her dad kind of filled a room. He was big and broad physically but his personality kind of took up the whole space and squeezed everybody else into the corners. You had to fit in or just be ignored. She took the bag. It was a cheap, chocolate calendar with a big rabbit on the front.

'Thanks,' she said.

'No problem,' he said, smiling. 'Reduced at Woollies all this week.'

'Come and look at the kitchen,' Alice said, leading him out to where Megs was fussing over the coffees. They sat down at the table. There was an awkward pause.

'So,' Nick said after a while, 'what's all this about school, then, Alice my girl? Not too good?'

'S'alright,' said Alice, looking down at her glass of orange juice, thoughts buzzing round her head. Why can't I say all the stuff going round in my head? Why can't I ask you why you're not here, why you never call, why you went off with Janie, why you've had your head shaved like a billiard ball? Why you're such a stupid nerd of a dad? Why Mum is so upset?

'I think we can sort school, Nick,' said Megs. 'It's been a bit rough in the first term but Alice and I have had a good talk this morning. But you and I need to sort a few things out. Alice, can you get that, love, and give us a few minutes?'

Alice picked up the receiver in the hallway. 'Alice, it's Josie here. Do you know where Sam is? We met for lunch a quarter of an hour ago. He was really sweet and nice to me, back to his old self. Then all of a sudden he got a message on his phone and he dashed out of the restaurant and said he has to talk to you. What's going on?'

'That's funny,' said Alice. 'No sign of him here. It might be the code for the calendar.' The butterflies jumped in her stomach. There was a soft tap on the door.

'Josie – I think that's him,' Alice whispered. 'I'd better let him in quietly. He's not supposed to be here because Nick's arrived. Mum will go spare. Can I get him to call you? Will you be OK?'

'That's fine. Sam asked me for lunch tomorrow – see you then, pet.'

Alice put the phone down and crept over to the door. Sam was outside, hiding behind the holly in the front garden. 'Is he here?'

'They're in the kitchen. Got the code?'

Sam nodded. They crept quietly through the hall and into the front room. Alice tried not to listen to the sharp, rising voices from the kitchen. There was a new door – it must have appeared in the last few minutes: a round glass window a bit like a porthole on a ship.

Sam showed her the phone message. 'Two, five, colon, seven ASAP.'

'As soon as possible,' he whispered.

'I know that, dummy,' said Alice, punching in the code.

'Alice, you OK?' Megs called. 'Is someone with you?'

'Fine, Mum,' she called back, lips tingling again. The room began to fill with thick green smoke pouring out of the bottom of the calendar. 'Don't worry about me.'

Alice and Sam held hands as the smoke thickened and deepened, swirling round their knees. In a moment it was up to Sam's chest and over Alice's head. It smelt like mushy peas. Soon it was over their heads and for a few seconds they could hear and see nothing. Then, slowly, the smoke began to clear a little. Shapes appeared through the mist. Alice rubbed her eyes and looked around.

They were standing on what looked like a motorway construction site in the middle of what would be a six-lane motorway. It was very, very cold. There was half an inch of frost on the ground. Sam still had his jacket on but Alice was freezing in her T-shirt and jeans. Work on the roads was at an early stage. Alice could see the shape of the new road stretching away behind them marked out with stakes and with a foundation of gravel and concrete – but ahead of them it looked as though work had just begun carving a way through a low hillside. Coming towards them at great speed was an enormous, bright yellow bulldozer.

'Whistling walruses, it's cold,' said Sam, rubbing his arms furiously. 'Where do you think we are?'

'D-d-d-dunno,' shivered Alice through chattering teeth. 'Th-th-think we're about to f-find out.'

The bulldozer braked hard as it approached. Sam jumped back and pulled Alice out of the way as the great digger came within a couple of feet. Col was at the wheel.

'Hi, you guys,' he called. 'How d'you like the green smoke? Cool or what?'

He handed them down some bright-yellow workmen's jackets and safety helmets, just like the one he was wearing. Alice's was much too big. The jacket came down below her knees and the helmet covered half her face. 'This digger's amazing. Never driven one before. Come up and have a look. You look a bit blue.'

'We're freezing cold,' said Sam.

'Whoops,' said Col. 'Never thought about that. Climb up in the cab. It's warm up here.'

He helped them up the ladder. 'Isn't this fantastic?' Sam had to admit the view was amazing. 'We're in Scotland. This is a new bypass. Fantastic engineering. You can have a go in a minute. Seriously, how was the green smoke? Never tried it before – personal touch.'

'It smelled of mushy peas,' said Alice.

'My favourite,' said Col. 'Pea soup.'

'Mum nearly saw it as well.'

'Ah, not quite so good then.'

'What's all this "ASAP" about?' said Sam. 'Why so urgent?'

'To tell you the truth, I slept in,' said Col. 'I thought this would be a good place to come and the workmen all arrive for a new shift in an hour. I thought if you came quickly we could have more time on the digger.'

Alice rolled her eyes. To her amazement, Sam instantly understood. 'Great move. Always wanted to have a go at one of these. Can I drive?'

'Watch this,' shouted Col, shifting into gear. They lurched forward, much too fast for safety, Alice thought. Col steered the digger towards a huge mound of earth at the side of the road and lowered the shovel.

'I'm a bit new to all this,' he called as he moved the levers to fill the shovel with earth.

'I can tell,' said Alice, caustically.

'Not the bulldozer – the calendar. We have to take it in turns for week two. Normally, you would get one of the others. I'm the youngest. This is only my second time. I want to try a few new special effects.'

'Like the green smoke?' said Sam, warming to Col all the time.

'Exactly,' said Col, crashing the gears into reverse and then racing forwards again. Alice was beginning to feel sick. She wondered if her cheeks were green as well as blue.

Col dropped the earth down into a great dip which the road builders were trying to fill in, then went back for some more. After a couple of goes he handed the controls to Sam, much to his delight. Alice sat bored and cold in the corner, refusing even to have a go at driving. After the hole was filled in, Col seized the wheel again and turned the digger round. He lowered the blade at the front which looked something like a snowplough. 'You'll love this,' he said, crashing the gears and putting his foot down. The monster truck charged forward, ploughing into another huge mound of rubble. 'They were blasting here yesterday,' Col explained. Effortlessly, Col moved the earth to one side. Despite herself, Alice began to be impressed. At the very end, when Col asked if she wanted to help drive the digger back to base, she agreed, despite herself. It was quite a feeling driving the enormous yellow monster back along a new stretch of highway.

'Cup of tea?' said Col. 'I love tea. One of the great advances of modern times. Come on.'

The workmen's hut was open and warm. Sam boiled the kettle, Alice found the mugs. They sat together round the gas stove, hugging the steaming mugs of tea for extra heat.

'Nobody knows the meaning any more,' Col said, suddenly serious. 'Nobody knows the stories and the pictures.'

Sam thought back to the coffee shop that morning and all the people milling about. Alice remembered Nick and the chocolate calendar.

'To find the meaning again you have to find the stories. Put them together, a bit like a jigsaw, and it will make sense. But not till the end.'

Col smiled, as if it should all be perfectly clear. Alice looked at Sam and tapped the side of her head. Sam was kind of mouthing the words again, trying to remember them.

Col looked at the clock on the wall. 'Time to go,' he said. 'Bulldozer or green smoke?'

'Neither.' 'Bulldozer.' Alice and Sam spoke together.

'Alice won by a fraction,' said Col, eyes sparkling. 'Stand up and close your eyes.'

Sam and Alice did as they were told. Col came up behind them one after another and spun them round by the shoulders. Alice felt herself spinning. A second later she tumbled onto the sofa. By the time she had opened her eyes, Sam was there too. They looked at each other and grinned.

'Better go,' Sam whispered. 'Your dad might still be here.'

'You need to ring Josie,' Alice whispered back. 'She rang after you left her in the restaurant. She sounded happier though.'

'Will do,' said Sam.

Together they turned towards the calendar. The glass porthole was open now. Through it, Alice could see a brand new road, perfectly level, stretching away through hills and valleys, beckoning her on to new adventures.

9 December

Brrrrinnng. Alice's alarm went off at half-past eight on Sunday. It took a moment or two to remember why. The card. That was it.

She pulled on her best jeans and jumper, splashed her face with water and charged into Megs' room. 'Mum, Mum, wake up. It's Sunday. Can we go to church, please? Come on.'

Megs opened one eye and looked at Alice as if she was bonkers. 'Don't be silly, sweetie. You know it's Sunday. It's my lie-in day.'

Megs turned over. Alice jumped onto the bed and peered over Megs' back right into her face.

'Mah-um, come on. I want to go to church. I've never been. I just want to see what it's like.'

'You won't like it, darling. It's really boring.'

'But, Mum, I want to go. Please take me. Grandma is always saying we should go.' Alice grabbed the bottom of the duvet and started pulling it off the bed.

Megs held on tight and pulled back. 'I don't know where any of the churches are round here, darling, or what time the services are. Maybe next week or the week after.'

'But, Mum, that lady brought a card around yesterday, when we were waiting for Dad. St Philip's. It's just in the next street – five minutes' walk away. The service is at ten and there's a map and everything. Come *on*.'

'Alice Carroll!' Megs was now sitting up, using her 'last straw' voice. 'What has got into you? I am not, repeat *not*, getting out of my nice warm bed this morning for any reason on earth short of a hurricane heading down the street and certainly not to take you to a church service you won't enjoy. Just what part of "no" don't you understand? Go away and stop winding me up!'

Alice was in full nag mode but she knew when she was beaten. A couple of minutes later she knocked gently on Sam's door. To her great surprise he was up and dressed.

'Whassup, little niece?'

'What are you doing up so early?'

'Josie's coming round for lunch. Thought I might get up and cook. Megs wasn't too good after yesterday. What about you?'

Alice waved her card. 'This may sound really stupid – don't laugh or anything – but I really want to go to church. A lady brought this round yesterday and it made me think – with the calendar and everything – that I've never even been inside a church building. I kind of want to see what it's like. Mum won't get up. Can you come with me? I don't want to go on my own. Come on, Sam, it can't be that bad.'

Sam thought for a moment, then said slowly, slightly to his surprise: 'OK. Don't mind if that's what you want to do. We won't be more than half an hour, will we? I could leave a note for Megs and she could start lunch off. I'm no good at cooking anyway. Let's go.'

Alice was so grateful to Sam that she poured out his cocoa pops for him and made him a cup of tea at the same time as she made her muesli. Sam turned up his nose in disgust. 'Don't know why you can't eat a proper breakfast,' he said as he finished the short note to Megs.

It was a crisp morning. Sam wore a scarf with his light jacket and Alice wrapped herself up in her woolly hat and duffel coat. The air was cold and fresh on their cheeks and the leaves crunched under their feet. They hurried (Sam had taken ages to get ready) but even so they could hear the organ playing the first hymn as they walked down the church path.

'Looks a bit derelict,' said Alice, pointing at the long grass and the broken fencing. 'S'pect it's nice inside though. Come on, Sam.'

She pushed open the big door which was just like the one at school. It opened much faster though with a great crash and Alice almost fell through it. She giggled and looked back at Sam who was motioning her to be quiet. Alice turned back into the church. The floor was made of wood and made a noise when you walked across it. The church had rows of long benches all facing in the same direction. There were about twenty old people spread out all over the building, one or two to a row. At least six of them were turning round and looking at her with a range of expressions.

Alice smiled and waved at a couple of them, but they just looked a bit cross. A nice-looking man came over and smiled.

'Hello – have you come for the service?'

A woman near the back turned round and tut-tutted at the noise. The hymn still hadn't finished. Alice presented the red card like a ticket. 'We had an invitation.'

'Really?' the man whispered, sounding a bit surprised. 'That's very nice. You'd better come and have a seat. Here, have some books.'

Alice and Sam crept into the back pew just as the hymn was finishing. The vicar said some words to the congregation and they all said something back, reading from one of the books. Then everybody knelt down. Alice copied them and pulled Sam down with her.

'Just do what everyone else is doing, silly.'

'OK,' said Sam, obviously trying very hard.

Five minutes later and after much searching, Alice found the right place in the service book. It wasn't too difficult really. She nudged Sam in triumph. He was just sitting quietly, staring at the building.

They had some readings and then there was a talk. Alice hardly understood a word but, to her great delight, there were two references to Advent and one to Abraham. Each time she nudged Sam again.

'All this has got something to do with the calendar stuff, Sam, I knew it.'

'Sssshh!' said the cross lady in the seat in front.

The prayers came next. Alice thought that part was really nice: the whole building was still. She loved the list of names of those who were sick. They passed a bag round and Sam put some money in, there were more prayers said by the vicar and then everybody started to move to the front of the church.

The nice man came over to them again: 'Would you like to come and receive communion?'

'What's that?' said Alice.

'Bread and wine,' hissed Sam. 'No – we'll just sit here, thanks.'

'Perhaps a blessing?' said the man.

'I will,' said Alice.

'Just kneel at the rail,' the man said. 'Keep your hands by your sides.'

Alice joined the line and waited quietly, looking at the great warm space around her. She liked the pattern of the roof and the pictures in the windows. Alice knelt at the rail and the vicar put one hand on her head and said a prayer: she felt a warmth go right through her. She stayed kneeling at the rail for a moment or two and said a kind of prayer for her mum, then slowly found her way back to Sam. One or two people were lighting candles in the side chapel so Alice joined them and lit one of her own.

After the service, the nice friendly man took them to the very back of the church where people were having coffee and mince pies. He introduced them to the lady who had called at the door.

'This is Brenda,' he said. 'Brenda, this young lady brought the invitation you took round yesterday.'

'You did?' said Brenda. 'That's wonderful. I'm so pleased to see you. Did you like the service?'

'I liked some bits,' said Alice. 'Where are all the children?'

'I'm afraid we don't get many nowadays,' said the man. 'We had to close the Sunday School a couple of years ago. Not enough helpers. A few families come at Christmas and Harvest.'

'Time we were going, Alice,' said Sam.

Alice finished her squash and said goodbye, politely. The nice man introduced himself as Derek. They offered Sam a parish magazine but when he saw it cost a pound he said, 'No thanks.'

'How was church then?' said Megs, kissing them both as they

came in the door. 'Thanks for taking her, Sam, that was really sweet.'

'It was peaceful,' said Alice. 'And some of the people were really nice. But there was hardly anybody there.'

'Did you understand it?' asked Megs.

'Some of it, I think,' Alice said. 'But that didn't really seem to matter. I said a prayer for you.'

'Thanks, my love,' Megs said. 'That means a lot. Maybe I could come with you next time.'

Lunch with Josie was fun. She and Sam were obviously getting on really well. Having them all there cheered Megs up lots after yesterday. She had even set up the old table in the front room.

'Great food, Megs,' said Sam, helping himself to thirds. 'Haven't had Yorkshire puddings in ages. Well done, old girl.'

'It's nice to all be together,' said Megs. 'Family. Sorry I've been such a grump this week.'

Josie gave Megs a hug as they cleared the table for pudding. Megs popped the question which had been in her mind all day. 'Have you two decided what to – er – you know?'

'Not exactly,' said Josie. 'It's still sinking in. But Sam's taken it really well. I didn't know how he was going to react at all. He's kind of different – don't you think?'

'Kind of,' said Megs. 'I know what you mean. He even took Alice to St Philip's this morning.' A great fart came from Sam's mobile, left in the kitchen. 'There's still some way to go though.'

The two of them chuckled as they brought Sam's phone back into the front room with the tinned peaches and custard and put it on the table.

'Text message,' said Josie. 'Probably your calendar code, Alice. Let's see you open it.'

Alice and Sam exchanged looks. 'Shame to spoil lunch,' said Sam. 'Let's do it later.'

'Do you mind if I stay in this afternoon, Mum?' said Alice. 'I know you wanted to go for a walk but I've got lots of homework. Biology.'

Megs and Josie had their backs to the calendar. Alice and Sam could see very clearly that another door had appeared. It looked strangely like the door of St Philip's that Alice had pushed open that morning.

'Me too,' said Sam, starting to clear the table. 'I mean, I promised to do a bit of tidying up on a report. I'll keep Alice company. But you two go. I'll sort the washing up.'

Josie and Megs were quite content to stretch their legs and went to get their coats before Sam retracted his offer. Alice suspected their route would take them past at least one coffee shop.

'Quick,' she said, closing her biology textbook as the front door closed. 'What's the code?'

'Three numbers,' said Sam. 'Three, five, colon, five.'

'Three, five, colon, five,' Alice repeated as she pushed down the keys. 'I wonder what Col has got planned this time.'

In the distance they could hear the faint sound of an organ being played, growing steadily louder and stronger. Sam recognised the tune from a friend's wedding. This time the mist coming out from the door was bright purple. Alice giggled as it filled the room and she took Sam's hand. It was like being wrapped in cotton wool. 'Nice one, Col,' she said as it grew thicker. Sam felt the ground under his shoes change from the living-room floor to a something rougher. They were in the open air, again.

A light breeze cleared the purple mist and carried it away over the horizon. Alice watched it gradually disappear in the pale winter sunlight, then looked around.

Sam and Alice were standing in the middle of an immense valley, stretching as far as the eye could see. The air was perfectly still now. There was no sound: nothing moved. The landscape was bare earth and white rocks. Nothing grew there. On either side the hills were completely bare, except for three trees on the nearest western range, silhouetted against the sky.

But there was something else – and it was more disturbing. Alice was still gripping Sam's hand tightly, frozen in horror. All across the plain, scattered in every direction, were bones, bleached white in the sun. Alice recognised some of the shapes: femurs and hip bones; vertebrae, ribs – sometimes connected and sometimes separate – fragments of fingers and toes – knee joints, and, most horrible of all, skulls, staring up at them with sightless eyes.

Sam realised in horror that the branches he thought he was standing on were pieces of arm and moved his feet, searching for a place to stand. Alice turned slowly, taking in the sight: thousands and thousands of bones, scattered over the barren soil, stretching as far as the eye could see. Col was standing behind them, silent, sombre.

'It looks like the site of a great battle,' said Sam, 'but there are no weapons.'

'Where are we, Col?' said Alice, frightened. 'Why have you brought us here?'

'This way,' said Col. Alice and Sam followed him, picking their way across the ground as best they could without treading on the remains.

Col led them to the only structure visible in the entire valley: a wooden watchtower standing about three metres high. He motioned that they should climb the ladder. Alice went first, then Sam, then Col himself followed them. At the top was a small platform, about two metres square, surrounded by a wooden railing.

The view was exactly the same but not quite so creepy as close up: fragments of people scattered over the earth. 'There is no need to be afraid,' said Col. Sam spoke to himself but out loud: 'One day all of us will be like this. This is all that's left.'

Col looked at them. 'This is for the very brave,' he said. 'Be strong and you will both see something you will never forget. Do you want to go on?'

Sam and Alice looked at each other. 'Can it hurt us?' said Sam.

'Absolutely not,' said Col. 'That rule never changes. But that doesn't mean it can't change you – that's up to you.'

Alice nodded. 'I'd like to go on.' Sam said the same.

'Speak to the bones,' said Col. 'Tell them to come together.'

Alice and Sam felt stupid as they moved to the edge of the platform. Alice said it first, just a whisper: 'Come together.' There was the lightest rustle across the plain, then nothing.

'Louder,' said Col. 'Say it as though you mean it.'

'Come together!' said Sam in his normal speaking voice. The rustling and shaking was louder. There was a shimmer of movement right across the plain, easing away into a whisper.

'Much louder!' said Col. 'A word of command – north, south, east and west.'

Alice faced north and Sam south. 'Come together,' they shouted in unison. Sam faced east and Alice west. 'Come together.'

The rustling and rattling grew louder and this time could not subside. The whole valley floor seemed to be in motion. Alice looked down at the ground underneath the tower: every bone was moving – rattling, searching, finding its neighbours. It was slow at first. Skeletal feet formed and hands and heads were drawn together as if by some invisible thread. Sam could see that although the bones were mixed up, the different bodies were still in the same general area. The spread on the ground was thinner now, the rustling softer as the different bone groupings came together: feet found ankles, thighbones located knees and hips, skulls were drawn onto vertebrae. Piece by piece, every skeleton was brought back together. There was silence right across the plain.

'Now a new command,' said Col. 'Call for muscle and flesh.'

Sam took north and Alice south, excitement growing: 'Muscle and flesh,' they called. Alice faced west and Sam faced east: 'Muscle and flesh,' they cried together.

This time there was hardly any noise. Again they looked at the base of the tower where they could see most clearly. Then Alice gasped: a tiny red streak ran down the thigh of the nearest skeleton, spreading steadily all over the body, bone by bone. Sam looked out across the plain: the same thing was happening everywhere spreading out from the centre until the whole valley was turned from white to red against the dark earth. They looked back again to the base of the tower and saw muscle growing on the bones beneath them; saw the organs taking shape; saw eyes appearing in the sockets; then a covering of flesh grow back as the process of decay was set into reverse. Skin grew over the flesh, then fingernails and hair. Clothes grew as well, covering the naked forms.

It took, Alice thought later, about half an hour. During that time there was absolute silence in the valley. What had been a field of white bones was now a multicoloured field of human beings from many different lands. Men and women, children, old and young, rich and poor. Still, nothing moved.

'Go down,' said Col. 'Go and look at them.'

Carefully they climbed down the ladder and walked a little way through the immense valley full of bodies. There were no wounds or signs of death. The flesh was perfectly restored. Alice put out a hand to touch the cheek of a girl her own age. It was as cold and rigid as a stone.

'Speak to the Spirit,' called Col, his eyes bright with anticipation. 'Tell the Spirit to come and breathe on them and they will live.' So Alice and Sam climbed again into the tower and faced to each point of the compass, calling the words at the top of their voices as Col commanded: 'Come, Spirit. Breathe, Spirit. Come, Spirit. Breathe, Spirit.'

Instantly, Alice felt a sudden soft breath of wind on her cheek and the whole air felt as if it was alive. Next they heard a great roaring, rushing sound, a mighty wind coming from the four corners of the valley, skimming the floor, billowing this way and that, filling every place. Alice and Sam gripped the rails of the tower, holding on in what became a fierce gale, sweeping, rushing, tumbling through the valley floor. Col stood right in the centre of the tower, arms spread wide, bracing himself against the wind. Sam turned and saw that he was transfixed with joy, singing in his deep bass voice, pouring himself into the music. The words of the song were snatched away instantly by the wind.

Then, just as quickly as they had come, the great winds retreated, each leaving behind a breeze to play and tumble across the valley. In a single instant, as the wind drew back, each heart began to beat, each chest began to swell with air, limbs began to stretch and move, eyes opened. All across that wide plain, children, women and men climbed to their feet, embraced like old friends, flexed their muscles and looked with wonder at hands and feet and at each other. Families clung together; many laughed out loud, many wept with joy. As far as they could see, people were walking and running, leaping and dancing.

Alice and Sam moved around the platform together, pointing, waving, amazed at what they were witnessing. At Col's signal, they climbed down again onto the plain, moving from group to group, touching them, hugging them, feeling the warmth and life and catching the wonder of the moment.

A great bell rang out across the valley. With one movement, the vast crowd turned together and faced the west, bowing low. Alice gasped. Her eyes caught a glimpse of the trees on the horizon, silhouetted against the setting sun. Without a shadow of a doubt, the central tree had burst into leaf again and was covered in new life.

For a few seconds, Alice held the moment then closed her eyes. Instantly, as it seemed, she and Sam were standing together, hand in hand again, in front of the calendar.

'We're home,' Megs called as she and Josie came back from their walk.

The church door stood open. In the doorway, silhouetted against the setting sun, a man, a woman and a child leapt for joy, dancing into the sunset.

10 December

Sam stopped at the cash point on his way into work. There was a queue. 'No problem,' he thought to himself, full of goodwill. 'I can wait in line even on a cold December morning.' It had been an excellent weekend. Fortified by a good Sunday lunch, Sam felt kind of rekindled inside and, for once, wide awake on a Monday morning.

There were four people in the queue. Everyone had headphones on. Sam's iPod was tuned to his mellow Monday jazz mix. The first person in line was very quick: twenty pounds for the week at work. The second and third took longer. Each one checked their balance. Shoulders sagged and faces fell. Number three even looked right and left, questions on her face. Each then withdrew what looked like a lot of money, stuffed it in their wallet and went on their way.

Number four was an attractive young woman in her early twenties. Sam could see over her shoulder. She checked behind her before punching in the PIN and looked fiercely at Sam. He studied the back of her rather nice knee-length boots. Then she checked her balance: £250 overdrawn. 'Shit,' Sam heard her say, even through the iPod. 'It's only 10 December.' Instead of money, the machine spat out one of those annoying white slips.

'Maxed out?' said Sam. 'Know the feeling.' He removed one earphone as a friendly gesture.

'Bog off!' said the woman. 'Wotsit to you? Stupid prat!'

Chastened Sam turned round to the watching queue behind

him and smiled weakly as he replaced his earpiece. They were all suddenly looking in different directions. Two of them were checking their watches.

Without knowing exactly why, Sam took ten pounds less out of the machine than he intended and escaped. He switched off the iPod to give himself space to think. At first the silence was extraordinary. He tried to see the High Street for the first time, like one of the worlds in the calendar.

Most of the shops were not open yet but each window was already a blaze of light in the cold morning mist. There were a hundred special Christmas offers in as many yards. Many advertised low prices and free credit. 'Unmissable deal!' 'Buy now, pay later!' 'Give your family the Christmas they deserve!' 'The experience of a lifetime.' 'Pamper yourself this Christmas. You know you want to.'

The banks, Sam noticed, were the same as the shops: brightly lit and covered in trees and tinsel. 'Interest free credit, sir? No problem. New cards. Suits you, sir. A loan for the turkey? Let me gift-wrap it for you.' Sam's mind went back to the pile of junk mail by the front door. Every other day, it seemed, there was a letter inviting him to borrow more.

'Strange, really,' Sam thought, turning into the office. 'Never noticed it much before. Must be getting worse.'

He waved a cheery good morning to Richard through the open door of his office. He growled something back. Sam hung up his jacket and booted up his computer. The first email was a circular from Richard. Something about punctuality, working hard and no frivolous talk in the office. Apparently he intended to stroll round the floor between the cubicles at irregular intervals: 'Stamping out the culture of time wasting' was a phrase from the memo. 'He's been on another management course,' sighed Sam wearily. Tizzy came in looking stunning and breathless, as usual. She waved, very cautiously, through the partition. 'How was the weekend?' she mouthed.

Sam's eyes signalled that Richard was on patrol. He gave her the thumbs up. 'Good,' he mouthed back. 'Yours?' he pointed. Tizzy's thumb turned down and she pulled a face. 'Disaster!'

Sam made what he thought was a sympathetic face. Actually it looked more like he'd swallowed a hairball. 'Coffee at eleven?' he mouthed, pointing to an empty cup and holding up two fingers.

'You're on.' Tizzy looked a bit more cheerful as she hung up her coat and hat.

The routine was well rehearsed. Tizzy and Sam left the office separately at two-minute intervals, clutching a file of papers. Sam had already checked Richard's online diary and discovered he was upstairs in a meeting from half past ten until lunchtime. Perfect. The rendezvous was the Starbucks across the street. By the time Sam arrived, Tizzy had the coffees and had grabbed a table well away from the window.

'Oh, I needed this,' she said. 'What a weekend!'

Sam didn't need to ask. He knew she was spending it with her parents in the country and taking the latest in a long line of boyfriends.

'How did they like Sim – er Gary?' he asked.

'Absolutely loved him. That was the problem, darling. Mum dropped all kinds of hints – you know the kind of thing. Big sister's wedding photos left all over the house. Drove past the local church on the way to the pub for lunch. Lots of hints about not getting any younger.'

'Did he get the message?'

'Rather too well. He was absolutely silent all the way home. We had a furious row when we got back to my place. He dumped me without ceremony, collected his things and left. That's it.'

'How many is that this year?'

'Thirteen. Catching them is not a problem. Keeping them is a disaster. How about you? You were as grumpy as hell on Friday. What happened with Josie?'

'It was good, I think,' Sam said. 'Sorry about the bad mood. It was all getting a bit much last week. I hate December.'

'Me too,' said Tizzy, leaning across the table. 'But there's always the Christmas party to look forward to!'

Sam smiled weakly for the second time that morning. He was searching for the right reply when out of the corner of his eye he caught sight of Germaine from the office, looking for a seat.

'Germaine! Hi! Over here!'

For once, Tizzy didn't look too pleased but she moved over to make some space for a huge mocha with whipped cream, an enormous slice of chocolate cake and Germaine, who just managed to squeeze himself in between the table and the chair.

'Don't normally see you in here, mate,' said Sam. 'I thought you were working for that promotion.'

To Sam's utter and lasting discomfort, Germaine sniffed and looked as though he might burst into tears.

'S'not going to happen,' he said. 'They'll give it to someone whose face fits better.' He took a slurp of his mocha and left a long white moustache along his upper lip.

Tizzy offered him a tissue. Germaine blew his nose. Heads turned. The moustache was largely untouched. 'S'not the problem anyway.'

'What's up then, old man?' said Sam. 'Wife and kids OK?' He knew there were at least three little Germaines at home – maybe more.

Tizzy offered another tissue. Germaine blew again and this time he wiped his eyes. 'It's Christmas,' he said. 'We just can't afford it.'

'Can't afford it?' said Sam. 'What do you mean?'

'We're still paying for the last one,' Germaine said. 'Things were really hard last year. The kids all wanted such expensive stuff. We just bought it on credit – seemed really easy at the time. Then Lisa gave up work for number four. The washing machine broke down. They all want dear stuff again this year. They nag me every time we go shopping or watch TV. Weekends are hell. These letters come from the bank most days about the overdraft and repayments. What am I supposed to do? I'm not sure I can even go on.'

Sam absentmindedly took a bite of chocolate cake and wondered what to say. Tizzy put a hand on his shoulder. Just then Germaine's phone rang. He listened for a moment, protecting the chocolate cake with his enormous hand.

'It's Maureen in reception,' he said. 'Top-floor meeting has just finished. Richard's on his way downstairs. Scramble.'

Sam was back at his desk just as Richard came back into the office. Tizzy arrived a moment later, papers under her arm, looking as though she had just visited the photocopier. She flashed Richard her most winning smile. His eyes turned to follow her down the corridor. While he was distracted, Germaine crept behind him clutching the remains of the mocha and squeezed back into his cubicle.

'Thanks for listening, guys,' he emailed later.

Sam thought hard about Germaine's situation all the rest of the day and all the way back home. What was the point of Christmas if it was just a time for people like Germaine to get deeper into debt? Sam found it hard enough to balance the books just for himself. Germaine had to provide for six on a similar wage. The bright lights and the advertising for credit took on a more sinister tinge in the evening light.

The text message arrived just as Sam got home. Megs was on her way out. She'd agreed to meet Josie to go swimming once a week. Alice was waiting impatiently by the calendar.

'Just got it,' said Sam. 'Honest.'

'I know,' said Alice. 'The door has only just appeared.'

Sam looked hard in the top-right section of the calendar, following Alice's finger. The new door, like the others, was just a couple of centimetres square. He ran his finger over the surface, checking what he thought he saw.

'It's bars,' said Alice, 'like in a prison. Come on, what's the code?'

'Six, one, colon, one,' called Sam. Alice punched them in.

Instantly, a kind of drum roll filled the air followed by a fanfare of trumpets. Sam took Alice's hand and they faced the calendar. The bars swung open slowly from the centre. Thick grey smoke began to fill the room. But ten seconds later nothing else had happened.

'This is strange,' cried Alice. 'We're not going any ... aaaaaaaayeeeeee.'

At that very moment, the floor disappeared. Sam and Alice plummeted through the grey smoke, down, down, down, at first through what seemed to be a large, black plastic pipe. Then, suddenly, the angle began to change and the pipe 'caught' them on huge doormats as it changed from a vertical drop to 80 degrees, then 70, then 60. Holding hands was impossible – Sam was now somewhere ahead of Alice as they plunged downwards, riding the slippery surface of the inside of the pipe. Alice's hair streamed back in the warm wind. Both of them screamed at the top of their voices.

Alice saw a sign saying '50 degrees', as the descent slowed again slightly. She found she could grip the mat, sit up and look ahead. 'Sam,' she called, 'it's like a water chute at the pool.' Sam was going down feet first on his stomach. He looked up at Alice, stretched out his arms wide and stopped screaming. By the time they passed the sign which said '40 degrees', he'd managed to sit up.

The inside of the pipe was polished like a giant slide. Alice found she could swing from side to side. As they hit 40 degrees, there were some sharp bends to the right, then the left, slowing them down a little. Sam found that by gripping the mat and leaning into the bend, he could ride up the side of the pipe, then back down again. The next neon sign said '30 degrees'. Alice's hair still streamed back. There was no grey smoke now, just a warm breeze coming from the pipe. Then the pace began to slow until it was 20 degrees. More bends and sharper ones. Before long it was 10 degrees and a very gentle pace. Finally, at the end of the pipe, it was 0 degrees and out they shot onto a bed of sand. Both of them tumbled off the mats at Col's feet.

They were in a dank cave lit only by the burning torch in Col's right hand. He motioned to them to speak softly..

'How was it?' he whispered. 'You're the first to use it.'

'Brilliant,' said Alice, softly. 'Best yet.'

'Fantastic,' hissed Sam, 'once I'd got the hang of it. Can we have another go, Col?'

Col glowed with pride. 'I told them it would work,' he said, punching one hand in the air. 'Follow me. No time to lose.'

'Where are we?' said Alice, falling in behind Col as he made his way down a dark passage.

'The dungeons,' said Col. 'Keep up!'

They were in a narrow stone corridor about two metres wide.

The walls were running with water. The ceiling was low and Sam had to stoop in places. The floor sloped gently upwards.

'Whose dungeons, Col?' called Sam, trying to keep up. 'Ouch! Blistering barnacles.' Alice couldn't help grinning as Sam bashed his head for the third time.

Col turned round and signalled again for them to be absolutely silent. He stopped at a sharp bend in the passageway and put out the torch. 'We'll stay here for just a moment,' he said, very softly. 'Let your eyes adjust to the dark.'

Alice could see nothing at first but sure enough, after two or three minutes, she could make out the dark shapes of Col and Sam and the droplets of water running down the wall nearest her. She shivered, partly with cold and partly with excitement. There was a soft silver light coming from further up the passageway.

'Follow me now,' Col whispered. 'It's almost time. Stay close.'

They moved round the bend and down the passage. Alice could see now that just ahead of them the way was blocked by a grid of metal bars. The silver light was coming from the other side. Col put his hand into the depths of his robes and pulled out the most enormous bunch of keys. He held them close to his face and selected a small grey key, set it in the lock and turned it anticlockwise three times. He held the keys in his right hand and turned the iron handle with his left. The heavy door swung open without a sound and Col led them inside.

Alice and Sam gasped. The dungeon looked like the deepest foundation of a great stone castle. A maze of thick walls and pillars stretched away on three sides as far as they could see. The floor was just earth with pools of water here and there. Chained to the walls and pillars by their hands and feet were the prisoners, each out of reach of the others. Each one had a few scraps of dry bread and some stale water, a chamber pot and a rough grey blanket. All looked thin and sick in some way. Most had long hair, some down to their waist. The only way to tell the men from the women were the long beards and moustaches. They were all dressed in rags. Some were held by stocks around their feet. Others wore steel manacles. Still others were tethered to rings driven into the dungeon walls.

Some were sleeping. One or two pulled at their chains in a half-hearted way trying to get free. The majority just sat and stared into space. They looked at the three visitors and one or two stretched out their hands to beg but with no real hope in their eyes. Alice and Sam had nothing to say, nothing to offer them.

Col led them through the dungeon stepping carefully between the rows, twisting this way and that in the maze of the foundations. Alice lost count after the first hundred prisoners. They were heading towards the source of the silver light which spread thinly through the darkness. From time to time they glimpsed the source, a high window in the far wall.

'It's almost time,' said Col, at last, stopping underneath the window which was far above them. 'One minute to midnight. Here, take this.'

He took from his belt two small glass lanterns and gave one to each of them. Alice looked closely. Engraved in each of the six panes of glass was a small key. Two stood open giving access to the centre. 'But there's no wick,' she thought aloud. 'There's nothing inside the glass at all.'

'I know,' said Col, still whispering. 'Now stand on this precise spot and hold your lantern high. Keep it very still.'

Sam and Alice did exactly as they were told. They stood a couple of metres back from the window holding the lanterns stretched out towards it with the open panes towards the window. Somewhere in the castle above them, a clock struck midnight. At that very moment, Alice and Sam saw the source of the silver light. A brightly shining star came into view directly overhead, right in the centre of the window high above them.

Alice gasped and turned her head a little away from the light. 'Hold still,' said Col. 'Keep the lanterns absolutely still.'

Like Alice, Sam couldn't look directly at the star. Instead, he watched the lantern. Something strange was happening. Instead of spilling evenly into the room, the starlight was being bent and drawn towards the open glass. The star's rays were caught and began to swirl and spin inside. As each lantern caught more and more light, so it began to grow ever so slightly heavier.

'Hold it still,' said Col again. 'Steady now.'

He stretched out his own hand and held Alice's wrist, support-ing her as the lantern grew heavier. Sam was using both hands now and stood with his feet apart. All the starlight flowing into the dungeon was bending and streaming towards the lanterns. Within each glass, the mist of light was spinning, faster and faster like a tiny hurricane. At the very centre, Alice saw forming a tiny, bright speck of silver light: the concentrated fragment of the star's reflection. As more light streamed in, the brighter and larger the centre grew, and the more the weight of the lantern increased.

Col stood between them now, supporting Alice with his left arm and Sam with his right, gazing up at the window. 'Hold still just a little longer,' he said. Alice's arms hurt. She pulled her eyes away from the lantern and looked back at the tiny window. The star was passing now, disappearing on the other side of the frame. A few last strands of light were drawn into the lantern and then it was gone.

'Enough,' called Col. 'Lower the lanterns very carefully.'

As if she held a bowl of molten silver, Alice held her lantern at the top and bottom and lowered her arms to her waist. Col closed the open panes of glass and sealed them with a tiny catch. He did the same with Sam's lantern.

Over against the dungeon wall were two long metal poles. Giving one to each of them, Col showed them how to set the pole in the top of the lantern.

'Lift them high,' he said. 'Don't be afraid. Sam, you go that way, to the right. Alice, you walk to the left.'

Alice lifted the star-lantern high above her head. That part of the dungeon was bathed in a pool of bright, white light. There was the sharp sound of metal striking stone. Alice turned her head and gasped. The chains of the nearest prisoner had cracked apart and fallen off. He stood up, astounded and stretched his limbs, gazing at the light. It was the same on the other side of the passageway. A pair of manacles holding a woman to the wall were shattered. She hugged her arms to her body, rubbing her wrists.

'Move forward, Alice!' called Col, no longer whispering. 'You too, Sam!'

Both of them began a slow procession through the dungeon, taking the light into every nook and cranny. Wherever the light of the star touched chains or manacles, stocks or handcuffs, they were instantly smashed apart. The dungeon was filled with loud cracking, splitting and rending sounds.

The prisoners looked on in amazement as they stood and stretched, trying to get the circulation back into their bodies. Sam saw that many of them instantly looked a little stronger.

As the lanterns passed them, they began to follow in two slow processions. Some stayed behind.

Alice chose her own route through the cavernous dungeon, twisting and turning between the enormous stone pillars so every part was touched by the starlight from the lantern. As she doubled back she saw that, whilst all of the prisoners had been set free, not everyone was following the procession. Col was bringing up the rear. He bent to speak to each person who had stayed behind. Some he was able to persuade to get to their feet and join the procession. Some simply stayed where they were, for one reason or another unable to follow. Despite the joy and wonder of the moment, Alice felt a sharp pang of sadness for each one who chose to stay in that dismal place.

On the other side of the dungeon, Sam was also scouring every dark corner for those who were held captive. Col danced ahead, now and then pointing out one place or another which was still hidden. Then, as he beckoned to them, Alice and Sam joined their lights together in the centre of the great space. They followed Col as he led them forward, now in as straight a line as they could manage with the pillars and foundations in the way. Behind them, the two processions became one. The silence of the dungeon was broken by the sounds coming from the crowd: quiet sobbing, whispering, soft cries of wonder.

Col led them to what seemed to be the main gateway to the prison: an impenetrable wooden portcullis, covered in heavy chains and padlocks. The crowd behind them fell silent again. Alice could feel the hope beginning to flow away. Col turned round to face them. 'Point the lanterns at the gates,' he cried. 'Use the word of command: *Ephathah!*'

Sam and Alice caught the note of excitement in his voice and lowered their lanterns, pointing them like lances at the bars, chains and padlocks. '*Ephathah!*' they cried together. '*Ephathah!*' called the crowd. There was a loud crack. Something like lightning shot out from the end of each pole. Alice and Sam braced themselves as the poles jumped backwards in recoil. The gates and locks and bolts and chains were reduced to a pile of debris. From behind them came an enormous cheering which went on for at least five minutes. Hope was rising again.

Col led them forward again over the rubble of the gates and down a dark passageway. Fifty metres further there was another door, this one made of steel. '*Ephathah!*' cried Sam and Alice. '*Ephathah!*' thundered the crowd and it was destroyed. The cheer behind was even stronger.

'There are nine gates altogether,' cried Col above the noise as he led them onwards. It seemed to Alice that she was seeing every kind of prison door; every kind of chain; every lock; everything that had ever been used to hold a person captive. Every single one was shattered by the starlight and the word of command. Each shattered barrier brought them closer to the surface.

The ninth doorway was an immense stone boulder rolled against the mouth of the tunnel. Col stood well back. The lanterns were lowered for a final time. This time the whole crowd behind them cried in unison three times with Col and Alice and Sam in the lead: '*Ephathah! Ephathah! Ephathah*! The stone was shattered. The cold, fresh air rushed into the dungeon.

Sam and Alice led the great crowd of prisoners out into the fresh night air. Instead of armed guards or just emptiness, Alice saw immediately that there was an immense welcoming party in the open air. There were tables piled with food in one direction. There were baths and showers in another. There was a first-aid tent. Each prisoner was met with blankets and a warm embrace and taken wherever they wanted to go first: some chose food and drink, others a medical examination, the majority headed for a bath and new clothes. There was singing and feasting far into the night.

Alice and Sam followed Col round for a while as he supervised all that was happening and stopped for a word, now with a prisoner, now with one of the helpers. From time to time, one of the prisoners would come up to them, tears in his eyes, shake them by the hand and say thank you in a language neither Alice nor Sam could understand.

'Well done, both of you,' Col said at last, 'and thank you.'

'Wouldn't have missed it for the world,' grinned Alice. 'Fantastic.' Then she yawned.

'I've kept you out too long,' said Col. 'Hold hands and hold tight.' He reached out his hands and took the lanterns from each of them.

As they let go, the scene on the cold hillside quietly faded. Alice felt immediately the warmth of the gas fire in the front room, the carpet, the sofa. She felt suddenly very tired and very hungry. Sam was dozing in the armchair.

Megs and Josie came into the room together and switched on the light. 'Come on, you two. You must be shattered falling asleep in the front room.'

Sam and Alice both blinked. A tenth door was open in the calendar. Set right in the centre of the opened prison bars was a pair of manacles on a stone floor. The manacles were shattered and the prisoner had gone.

11 December

lice got soaked to the skin the minute she left school on Tuesday. Her umbrella blew inside out on the way to the bus stop. There was an icy north wind stinging her cheeks. It was the first really cold day of the winter. By the time the bus came she was soaked and shivering. She warmed up a bit on the bus ride but then had to walk into the wind and sheets of rain all the way home. Great puddles had formed in the road. She was caught twice by cars sending up a curtain of freezing cold water.

Megs and Sam were at work and there was no message. Josie had been there at breakfast time – a good sign, Alice thought – but she must have gone off to work as well. She was an optician's receptionist in the town. Alice peeled off her dripping clothes and had a hot bath, then changed into her jeans and T-shirt and made tea and toast.

'That's better,' she thought, clasping her hands round the mug. 'Feeling's coming back.'

There were some letters on the kitchen table. The postman must have arrived before Megs went out. Alice looked through them. Two Christmas cards already. One had a picture of a reindeer. The other had a large comical snowman. Both were from the great aunts. They always had time to get really organised for Christmas. Three bills and a credit card statement. Alice looked carefully at that one. Megs never said much about money. She knew things were tight but she'd no idea they owed this much. Ouch! There were a couple of pieces of what looked like junk mail for Sam. Right at the bottom there was a note personally addressed to Megs in writing she didn't recognise. The envelope had been opened but the note was back inside it.

Without a second thought, Alice took out the single piece of paper and read it through.

> Dear Megs,
> You might not remember but we met briefly on Friday when your car wouldn't start. I couldn't find your phone number in the directory so forgive this note. I wanted to ask you a favour and wondered if I could call in briefly on Tuesday evening around 7 p.m.? Please ring if it's not convenient. The number is 020 8625 3856.
> Yours truly,
> Andrew (Watkins)

Alice read the note through a couple of times and thought about what it could mean. Strange. What kind of favour did he want to ask? Her mind went back to the car park and that moment after the car had started.

Mr Watkins fancied her mum? Yuk. Emergency. Alice reached for the phone.

'Suzie? It's me. I just got home and found a note for my mum. It's from Mr Watkins.'

'Fit Mr Watkins? From school? You're kidding. My mum met him at the parents' evening and thinks he's really cool. She was ever so cross when I said he didn't teach me.'

'He's calling round tonight. He wants to ask Mum a favour.'

'Do you think he fancies her?'

'Dunno. What shall I do? I'm not sure she's ready to go out with anybody – still less a teacher.'

'Hide the note.'

'She's already seen it. It was open when I got home.'

'You'll have to disrupt the evening then. Send him away. Throw a fit or something. Misbehave and put him off. It could be fun. I'm always putting Dad's girlfriends off him.'

Alice heard the front door bang. 'Home,' called Megs.

'So we have to do all the questions on page 46,' Alice said deliberately and rather loudly.

'Has she come in?' said Suzie.

'That's right,' said Alice.

'Best go then,' said Suzie. 'Good luck. Give me a call and tell me how it goes.'

Megs sounded unusually cheerful. 'Had a good day, darling? Excellent. Listen – er – someone might be calling round toni ...'

'I know,' said Alice, casually, 'I read this by accident.' She waved the note.

'Oh, well,' said Megs. 'It's not quite polite to read people's mail, darling. But yes – er – that Mr Watkins is calling around seven. Wonder what he wants. He didn't say anything to you at school?'

'Nothing,' said Alice. 'But it's not me he wants to see, is it?'

Megs blushed ever so slightly. 'I need to tidy up, have a bath, change out of these wet things. You OK with your homework?'

'Think so,' said Alice, smiling. 'You carry on!' She needed time on her own to plan.

Sabotage was her scheme of choice, of course. Why be merely annoying when you can be disruptive? However, it might be better to save that one for the first 'date' if things went that far. Distraction was a possibility. For a moment, Alice reflected on the thought of hurling herself down the stairs just as the doorbell rang or cutting her finger on a kitchen knife, but then her mind filled with images of Mr Slimy Watkins calling the ambulance and even coming to the hospital. 'No,' she smiled to herself, 'let's not do anything to help him. On this occasion, it might just be enough to settle for Operation Gooseberry. Constant presence. No time alone.'

Alice smiled to herself as she rehearsed all the different reasons she had to stay in the kitchen. It was bound to be the kitchen. Megs seemed incredibly happy as they finished tea. 'You run along now, Alice. I'll clear up tonight.'

'It's OK, Mum,' she said, cheerfully. 'I'll help you clear up. I need the kitchen table for my homework this evening. I need to spread out.'

'Oh,' said Megs. 'I thought I might, well, you know, talk to Mr Watkins in the kitchen.'

'You carry on,' said Alice. 'I'll still be able to concentrate. Then I can ask you questions if I get stuck – and he's not going to be here very long, is he? He only wants to ask a favour.'

'OK then,' said Megs, with a weak smile. 'You stay in the kitchen.'

The kettle was just coming to the boil at seven o'clock exactly when the doorbell rang. 'I'll get it,' said Alice and shot out of the room. Sure enough, it was Mr Watkins.

'Hello, Alice,' he said. 'Is your mum in? I left a note. Ah – Mrs Carroll.'

'It's Megs,' said Megs, wrenching the door open and pulling Alice back by the shoulders. 'Come on in, Andrew. Very nice to see you. Close the door behind you and come through.'

Megs marched Alice through into the kitchen, gripping her by the shoulders, pushed her down into a chair and held her there. 'A bit too hard if you ask me,' thought Alice, grinning.

'You don't mind if Alice sits with us while we talk, Andrew?' said Megs with a grimace. 'She's got rather a lot of homework this evening and for some reason she needs to do it in the kitchen tonight. Tea or coffee?'

'Coffee – er – please. White. No sugar. Had a good day?'

'Not bad,' said Megs. 'Not bad. We're getting busier in the run-up to Christmas.'

'Mum, I don't understand question six,' said Alice. 'What does it mean?'

Megs leaned over Alice's shoulder and gripped her arm, very tightly indeed. 'Do you mind if I look at question six later, darling? Move onto question seven, why don't you?'

'But Maaaum. I don't understand question seven either,' Alice said sweetly.

'Why don't I have a look?' said Mr Watkins. 'What subject is it anyway?'

'Biology. Alice's least favourite subject,' said Megs. 'Here's your coffee.'

There was the sound of the front door opening and closing. 'Home,' called Sam. 'Where are you, Alice?'

'In here,' called Alice.

Sam stuck his head round the kitchen door. 'Sam, this is Andrew Watkins,' said Megs. 'He teaches at Alice's school. Andrew, this is my brother, Sam.'

'Hi,' said Sam. 'Alice, can I have a word? Front room. Now. OK?'

Alice looked panic stricken. 'Can't now,' she said, trying to look meaningfully at Megs and Mr Watkins and then back at Sam. 'Loads of homework.'

Just for a moment, Sam took in the scene. Both his niece and his sister were giving him meaningful looks. Both clearly wanted him to do something but he hadn't the faintest idea what it was.

'Suffering swordfish,' he muttered. 'It's a text message, Alice. It's just arrived. Very urgent. For immediate use. Come on.'

Alice knew she had to go. 'OK,' she said, flinging down her pencil. She looked hard at Mr Watkins. 'I expect I'll be back in a second or two' and retreated backwards out of the room.

'Sam, why did you do that?' she hissed as soon as they were in the front room. 'Did Mum put you up to it?'

'Put me up to what?' said Sam. 'There really is a text message and it really does say "4NOW". See for yourself. And the door is there, look!'

Alice looked, first at the phone and then at the calendar. There was a new door in the bottom left quadrant: a simple blue square made of wood. 'Col had better not be in on this as well,' she said. 'OK then, let's go. Read out the numbers.'

'Four, four, colon, three.'

To Alice's surprise the number six sprang back up again the first time she pressed it but stayed down the second time, like the other numbers. She held Sam's hand as she pressed the final number and both of them tensed and looked anxiously at the floor.

Nothing happened. No gap in the floor. No coloured smoke

coming out of the calendar. Just a tiny crack, Alice thought, at the top of the blue panel.

There was a sharp tap on the window. Sam went over and peered through. 'There's a rope ladder,' he said, puzzled. 'Just outside the window.'

'Those windows don't open,' said Alice. 'They are painted shu – oooh ... '

Just as she said this, the large sash window in the middle of the bay slid open by itself. Alice climbed out first, put one foot on the rope ladder and began to climb, with Sam following close behind. It stretched up as far as she could see.

'Hold tight,' came a familiar voice. 'Can't stay here long.'

As they climbed higher, the ladder itself began to move upwards. Alice stopped climbing and leaned back to see what was happening. The rope ladder extended above her for about twenty metres. It led to a large wicker basket. Above the basket was the faint outline against the stars of what looked like a huge balloon stretching into the night sky.

Sam could hear the roar of the balloon's furnace. It was gaining height already. He looked down and already the rooftops were growing smaller beneath them.

'Hold on,' called Col, over the side of the basket. 'Don't climb. I'll pull you up.'

There was a faint whirring sound. Alice gripped the sides of the ladder tightly as she was winched aboard through the trapdoor in the bottom of the basket. She stepped onto the basket floor and peered over the side. They were passing through a very thick layer of cloud. Sam joined her a second later as Col refastened the trapdoor.

'All aboard,' he said. 'That was close. Nearly spotted.'

'It's not that easy to hide an enormous balloon in an English town,' said Sam. 'Where are we going?'

'We're there,' said Col. 'Look!'

Alice and Sam blinked as the balloon emerged from the thick cloud – to their great surprise – into the bright light of a new day and a different world. Suddenly, it was early morning. The sun was peeping over the eastern horizon behind them and the light was spreading over the hills and plains below. Alice saw immediately that they were very high, but the balloon was losing height as they moved deeper into the countryside.

'What can you see?' asked Col.

'It's beautiful,' said Sam, as the dawn light raced over the land below them. Hills and valleys, deserts and dunes stretched in every direction.

'It's so dry,' said Alice. 'Nothing is growing. There's no sea, no river, no streams.'

'No trees,' said Sam. 'No crops or flowers.'

The landscape was desolate – a vast tract of barren desert stretching for hundreds of miles.

'It's amazing,' said Alice as they flew on in silence carried by the wind. She was looking back at their flight path. The warm east wind made her hair stream out behind her face. 'Like a silent planet. Nothing lives. Nothing grows. Has it always been like this?'

'For thousands of years,' said Col, pointing. 'Look, ahead of us. We're nearly there.'

The balloon was descending as they flew. Alice and Sam moved to the front of the basket. They followed Col's arm in the direction of their flight.

There, in the centre of the desert at the top of a hill were some stone foundations in a regular pattern. They were different from everything else in that strange and silent world. Clearly they were not part of the natural landscape. Long ago the building had fallen down. The stones left behind were half-covered by sand.

'Ancient ruins,' said Alice. 'There must have been people here long ago.'

'The great temple,' said Col, clearly moved by the sight. 'See the pattern,' he pointed. 'You can still make it out.'

'That looks like a massive wall,' said Sam, 'with gates in the centre of each side. We're coming in over the east gate.'

'That's the temple itself in the very centre,' said Alice, 'where the stones are thickest.'

The wind had been fading for some time. Suddenly it dropped completely and the air was still. 'Hold tight,' said Col. 'I'll bring us into land.'

Alice and Sam gripped the edge of the wicker basket as Col pulled some cables and released more air from the canopy of the balloon. They flew low over the centre of the ruined buildings. Col set them down, exactly as planned, on the west side.

'Come and see,' said Col, helping them out of the balloon. 'Take your shoes and socks off though and leave them here.'

Sand drifted over most of the ground but underneath the stones were sharp. Sam and Alice slowly picked their way bare-foot across the dry ground and up the hill into the ruins of the great temple. They were clearly following an ancient pathway. As they drew near to the very centre, Alice saw, to her amazement, a tiny plant growing by the side of the path.

'Col – look. Something does grow.'

Col knelt by the side of the pathway and examined the small plant. Carefully he broke off a few leaves and gave them to Sam and Alice. 'Taste them,' he said. Sam placed one on his tongue. He immediately screwed up his face. 'A bitter taste,' he said. 'Sharp and unpleasant.'

Col led them now to the very centre of the ruins. At the top of the hill was a stone altar, cracked with age. As they approached it, a single cloud for a moment shut out the sun and the hill was plunged into shadow. Alice saw as they came nearer that there was something white on the top of the huge stone.

Col stood back, his head bowed, and motioned for them to approach. 'Don't be afraid.'

The air was still, now. Sam and Alice drew near to the altar. At its very centre was a lamb, lying still on the stone. Its throat had been cut. The lamb's body was still warm. Its blood ran down over the altar and into the cracks.

'Col!' cried Alice, turning round with tears in her eyes. 'What has happened? Who has done this?'

'Turn around, child,' said Col. 'Look on the east side.'

Alice took Sam's hand and together they moved around the altar from the west side to the east, not knowing what they were looking for. Alice saw it first.

In the middle of the east side of the altar, flowing down like a tear from one of the stone cracks was a trickle of water. Where the water met the ground, as Alice watched, it became a tiny stream, finding its own pathway over the stony ground. Where the stream touched the dry ground, almost in an instant, the ground on each side began to turn green before their eyes as new things began to grow.

'Follow it,' said Col, excitement in his voice.

Sam and Alice set off down the hill, following the tiny thread of water, which deepened as it flowed. It was tumbling and bubbling, like a tiny brook, catching and reflecting the sunlight. The cloud which shut out the light was suddenly nowhere to be seen.

They moved as fast as they could but it was hard to walk on the stony ground, and the little stream of water outstripped them. Alice looked back and saw that plants were appearing behind her in a green ribbon on each side of the water, spreading outwards.

After walking on for ten or fifteen minutes, their feet became very sore and they began to hobble. Sam wondered again why they had left their shoes and socks back at the balloon. Bit by bit the stream grew larger and wider, gaining confidence and strength as it went on. Col pointed to a stone by the side of the river bed: it read '1,000 cubits'. The stream was now a metre wide.

'Come and paddle,' Col said, standing in the centre of the stream. Sam and Alice followed him. The water was cool and gentle on their sore feet. It came up to their ankles. They bent down, scooped up the water in their hands and drank.

'Forward,' said Col and led them on again. The green ribbon on each side of the stream had grown wider, stretching away on either side. There was grass to walk on and wild flowers. Walking was much easier. A second stone read '2,000 cubits'. Again Col led Alice and Sam into the water. This time it came up to their knees.

They set off again. Fields now stretched away on either side. Alice looked carefully. The greenery was spreading out into the desert, almost as far as she could see. The next sign said '3,000 cubits'. 'Time to get wet again,' said Col and led them into the water.

Now the stream was fast-flowing and deep. Sam and Col stood each side of Alice. The water was up to Sam's waist and Alice's chest. Unsupported, she would have been washed away. They came out again and picked their way along the bank. Oats and barley were ripening now in the fields. To Alice's surprise she could see men and women and children working there. Their songs reached them as they arrived at the final milestone: 4,000 cubits.

Col led them again into the water, roped together for safety, but this time, it was clear, the river was deeper and wider than anyone could cross. Sam and Alice could both swim but neither ventured very far into the current. The water was clear and cold: good for a dip but too cold to swim for long. Both of them dived down under the current. To their surprise, it was teeming with fish of every kind.

Sam led Alice back to the bank and they collapsed, out of breath, on the shore. Together with Col, they sat and looked with astonishment at the far bank and then to the right and to the left and back the way they had come. Already, trees were growing by the river bank. Col reached out and gathered ripe fruit to refresh them. Sam bit into a peach: it was sweet and ripe and the juice ran down his chin.

Alice gazed about her for a few minutes, drinking in the sight, contrasting it with the barren country over which they had flown in the balloon. She stood to get a better view. 'Ouch,' she said. 'These cuts on my feet really hurt.'

'Let me look,' said Col. Both Alice and Sam showed him the soles of their feet: cut and blistered from the long walk. 'Hold on a moment.'

Col went a little way into the orchard on their side of the river and came back moments later with a handful of leaves. 'Try these,' he said, lifting each foot in turn and laying a leaf across the cuts. To Alice it felt cool and soothing, like a dock leaf on nettle stings.

'Look now,' said Col. Sam and Alice looked, rubbed their eyes and rubbed again. The soles of their feet were like new. Even Alice's verruca scar had gone. 'The river renews the whole earth,' he said. 'Even the salt lakes turn fresh when it touches them. The leaves of the trees are for healing and for rest.'

'Healing and rest,' thought Alice, dreamily, stretching out in the warm sunlight and closing her eyes.

The next moment, as it seemed, Megs was shaking her by the shoulders. 'Alice, Sam, wake up. Andrew's just gone. He's asked me to go with him to his club dinner. And I've said yes.'

She kissed Alice. Sam rubbed his eyes. 'Thanks for giving us a bit of peace, love. But what have you done with your shoes? And why, oh why is the window wide open on a night like this?'

Sam and Alice looked at each other and their bare feet and smiled. 'Goodness knows where Col has left our shoes,' thought Alice. Sam was staring at the calendar up close.

The blue door stood open. Inside the tiny space was the grey side of a stone altar, standing on brown sand. Running down the side of the table, like a raindrop on a window, was the beginning of a mighty river.

12 December

There was a light tap on the bedroom door. Alice rubbed her eyes and looked at the clock. Six o'clock in the morning? The tap came again, more insistent.

Without turning on the light, she struggled into her dressing gown and opened the door.

'Col! What are you doing here?'

Col pressed his fingers to his lips. 'Special day,' he mouthed, barely whispering the words. 'Early start. Meant to warn you but forgot. Sorry!'

'I'll get dressed and meet you in the lounge,' Alice mouthed back. 'You wake Sam.'

Col held out his thumb sideways on and smiled. Alice raised her eyes to heaven. 'This way,' she said, indicating her own thumb which was pointing upwards. Col grinned, put up both thumbs and tiptoed across to Sam's door.

Muffled groans found their way across the landing. 'Festering flamingos' was all she caught before Sam's voice was choked off by Col's signal.

Alice drew back the curtains as she got dressed and gasped. There was a white covering on every surface. The snow glowed orange under the streetlamps. The light picked out the frosted cobwebs on the drainpipe outside her room. 'Christmas is beginning to arrive,' she thought, pulling on her warmest jumper and socks.

Sam and Col were already in the front room when she went

downstairs. Sam was in his warmest jumper and scarf but barely awake. He shone the light from his phone onto the calendar. A new door had appeared in the three o'clock position, a wooden one with an arched top.

'This is the second test,' said Col, in a soft, serious voice. 'There is one at the end of every section. It's also my last day with you. If you pass this test, you will go onto the next part of the calendar and a new guide. If you don't, there will be no more text messages and no more doors. I hope you make it. You need to take this.'

Col handed over his staff. Sam took it. Then he shook both of them by the hand, rather solemnly Alice thought. 'Read out the code, Sam,' she said.

'Four,' said Sam. Alice punched in the number. 'Three,' he called. Click. 'Colon.' Click. Each button stayed in place. 'Two.' Alice paused for a moment with her right index finger over the button. She took a final look at the room, at the calendar, at Col. She took Sam's right hand in her left and pressed the number two.

There was a sharp crack of thunder. Time seemed to slow for a moment. Something like a bolt of lightning shot from the calendar and landed at their feet. Instantly the front room and everything familiar disappeared.

Alice and Sam were on their own again. It was early morning. The sun was rising to the east. They were standing in the centre of a wide pathway. In one direction, to the west, was a wilderness of scrub and thorn bushes stretching for miles. In the other was what looked like a lake or even the sea. The road ran down to the edge of the water and disappeared.

There was a low, rumbling sound coming from the wilderness.

'Whatever it is, it must be this way,' said Sam, pointing into the wilderness and away from the sea with the staff. 'Let's get going!'

'Wait, Sam!' called Alice, who was much more awake. 'It's a test, remember. We need to think about this one.' She looked around her in the dawn light.

The rumbling sound was growing louder. A line of dust appeared on the western horizon. Sam remembered the Westerns he watched as a child. He bent down and put his ear to the ground. He was suddenly grim.

'Horses,' he said, standing back up again and pointing, 'lots of them, coming this way.' They both looked west. They could see now beneath the vast dust cloud. The sun picked out the shields and weapons of a great army. Alice and Sam were standing in its exact path.

Alice felt the panic rising. She stood as still as she could, watched and listened. Nothing but the rumbling across the plain growing louder. She shook herself, then began to take a closer look at the edges of the pathway.

'There!' she said. 'How could we miss them – one on each side?'

Just behind them, clearer now in the dawn light, were two low stone pillars, one on each side of the path. Alice went to one and Sam to the other. On each was a great stone arrow pointing to the east. The entire surface of the pillars was covered in carved writing. Alice ran her fingers over the letters.

'None of it makes sense,' she called.

'It's all different languages,' said Sam. 'The same thing, I think, over and over again. Come on, we need to get out of the open. They're coming straight towards us.'

'We need to know what it says,' Alice called back. 'It's important.'

She tried to shut out the sound of hoof beats and wheels in the distance and focused instead on the shapes carved in the stone. Sam did the same but kept one eye on the western horizon.

'Here,' she called. 'Words in English.' Sam was beside her in a moment. The words were near the bottom of the stone. 'Stretch the rod over the sea. Don't be afraid.'

Sam glanced back. He could pick out individual riders now. He estimated they had about three minutes. 'Don't be stupid, Alice. We have to run. Now!'

Sam tried to pull her away to the side out of the path of the army. Alice pulled back.

'Sam, it's a test. Remember what Col said. You've got the staff. Follow the words on the stone.'

Sam looked out over the sea, down at his niece and then back at the advancing army. He felt absolutely terrified.

'Please,' said Alice, taking his hand. 'Remember all that's happened. I want to see the end.' She pulled him gently towards the sea.

In a moment, Sam's mind was made up. 'Madness! Whispering wombats!' he said, then ran after Alice towards the sea as fast as he could.

The thunder of the hooves was louder now. Alice looked back and saw a line of cruel faces galloping towards her. 'Stretch out the staff, Sam.'

Sam arrived, breathless. He held Col's staff stretched out over the calm sea, pointing straight at the rising sun. A light breeze touched his cheek and ruffled his hair. He braced himself as, in a moment, the breeze turned into a mighty wind at his back, rushing out over the waters. As it passed over the sea, to Alice's amazement, the waters separated, towering on either side and a pathway appeared beneath the waves.

'Come on,' she called over the wind. 'Now or never.' Alice ran ahead into the gap left by the waves. A second later, Sam lowered the staff and followed. The path was about as wide as a country lane. The waters were piled up on each side like enormous hedges, each as high as a house. The wind rushed and swirled down the alleyway, keeping the two walls of water apart long enough for them to pass through. The passageway in the sea stretched ahead of them. The path at their feet was made of cobbles, slightly raised above the bed of the sea. Others had been this way before them, Alice thought.

The crossing took about ten minutes. Neither of them wanted to linger. As they got to the far shore, the waters closed behind them, surged and swirled for a few moments and then were still. Alice and Sam looked back over the great sea. The army had stayed on the far side, the horses pawing the ground in frustration, the riders waving their spears in anger.

Beneath their feet the cobbled path stretched away to the east. Alice took Sam's hand. 'Narrow escape,' she said.

'Is that it, do you think? said Sam.

'Dunno,' Alice replied, 'but I think we need to keep moving.' The ground rose steeply on this side of the sea. The path wound up the sides of a mountain. Alice led the way. On the right side of the pathway Alice found another stone pillar similar to the first one. They knelt to examine it, hoping for a sign. This one was engraved with large ancient writing with moss growing in the lines of the letters but, whatever it said, it was in a language neither of them could understand. Twenty minutes later, as they climbed higher up the mountain, there was a second pillar, this time to the left, then a third and a fourth.

Alice and Sam were growing weary by this time. At the sixth and seventh pillar again they stopped, hoping for some kind of sign. Alice longed for something to eat or drink. It was now the middle of the day and the sun was high in the sky. Both were carrying the jumpers they had needed in the dawn.

They reached the eighth pillar. Sam again ran his fingers over the surface of the rock. Each inscription was different. Alice's eyes fell on a large rock a few metres to the left. 'Sam! Look!' she called. 'There is writing on the rock.'

Amongst the lines of carved letters there were again languages she recognised if not understood. They searched together with their fingers for something they could understand.

'Here,' said Sam. 'Strike me!'

Alice picked up the staff and aimed it at Sam. He leapt back. 'Not me you great bullfrog. It must mean strike the rock.'

'Sorry, Sam,' said Alice through parched lips. 'Tired.'

She picked up the staff again in both hands and swung it down onto the rock. Instead of bouncing off the hard surface, to her surprise, the rock gave way and the staff sunk in, splitting the stone. Alice leapt back in surprise.

'What happened?' she croaked.

'Come and see,' said Sam, bending forward in amazement.

Bubbling up from the rock in the place where Col's staff had landed there was a spring of water. It quickly flowed into and filled a small hollow at the base of the great stone. Sam knelt down, cupped the water in his hands and bent to drink. Alice did the same.

'That's very good,' she said, 'very good indeed.' They both splashed the water on their faces and arms and then drank some more. They sat together on either side of the spring, resting in the midday heat and looking back over the vast plain. With her eyes Alice followed the cobbled path along which they had come back to the edge of the sea and to where it emerged at the other side. It stretched away in the distance as far as she could see across the barren plain.

'Ready to go on?' asked Sam, looking across at his niece.

'Guess so,' said Alice, her eyes brightening. 'There must be something at the top of the mountain.'

Again they set off with Sam carrying the staff. There were two more rocks on the way to the top – both very old, both with the writing that neither of them could understand. And then, almost at the very top of the mountain, the path ended not at the summit or with another stone pillar but at the mouth of a small cave, just a hollow carved from the rock with a small stone bench set back from the entrance. Near the entrance to the cave was a large bush, the only living thing they had seen on the entire mountain, somehow clinging to the rock, managing just to stay alive.

'Is this it?' said Alice.

Sam sensed the danger a moment before Alice, grabbed her arm and pulled her inside the cave. All around them the very ground itself started to shake and tremble. There was first a low roaring coming from the heart of the mountain and then sharp cracks in every direction. Cautiously, Sam peered out of the cave. The whole mountainside was moving. With each large crack a vent opened in the earth and a spurt of steam shot skywards. Back down the path, Sam could see the sides of the mountain were trembling as if half the mountainside was about to break away and tumble into the valley below.

Neither of them could remember how long the earthquake lasted. To Alice, it seemed as if the ground beneath her had been trembling for hours and hours. She closed her eyes, clung onto the stone bench and hoped it would end. It was all she could do not to run back down the mountain. She gripped Sam's hand tightly in one hand and Col's staff in the other. The cave shook and trembled like a boat on a choppy sea.

At last, gradually, the quake subsided and the earth was still.

The mountain was solid again beneath their feet. Sam first then Alice stepped out of the cave and onto the pathway. Both of them looked back down the cobbled path which was still intact despite the tremors. On either side there were new shapes and configurations from the ones they had passed. Suddenly Alice gripped Sam's arm and pointed to the west.

'Back in the cave, Alice, quickly!' They retreated as far inside the cave as they could go.

Rushing in from the west covering the sky like a blanket was a mass of dark clouds: an ominous, threatening storm was approaching. A moment later the rain lashed the ground outside their cave falling to earth like rods of steel and creating instant streams in the gaps between the cobbles. Sam pulled his jumper on. Alice huddled against him for warmth and comfort. The wind at the heart of the storm whistled and roared over their heads circling round and round the cave. There were crashes of thunder overhead every ten seconds or so. Sheet lightning floodlit the horizon. Hailstones the size of peanuts rattled on the roof of the cave, covering the ground with an instant white carpet.

Sam had been in storms before but nothing like this. Watching the horizon from a distance would have been spectacular: creation's firework display on a massive canvas. But this was an intense, terrifying exposure to the power at the heart of the natural world. All of his senses were assaulted at once: the chill of the rain and hail; the sound of wind, rain and thunder; the changing tapestry of dark clouds; the smell of his own terror caught in an unknown world with only a small cave as protection against the elements.

The storm's ferocity mounted minute by minute. To Alice it seemed as though it would never end and the whole of her life would be caught in its eye. Her teeth shook with the cold and with fear and then, suddenly, there was a massive explosion close to the mouth of the cave which rocked her back further against the wall. In the same instant the wind dropped, the rain ceased, the clouds began to part.

Again, with great care, Sam and Alice looked out from the cave only to shield their eyes and cower back again into their refuge.

Lightning had struck the solitary bush at the cave's mouth and it was ablaze all at once. At five metres the heat burned their faces. The whole bush was on fire. As they watched the flames grew in intensity. But the bush itself was not consumed. At the very heart of the blaze Sam thought he saw something move – perhaps the figure of a man – but his senses had been so assaulted by this point in the journey that he wasn't sure of anything.

The fire flamed and burned licking up the water which had fallen on the pathway, warming and drying their clothes after the storm and then, just as suddenly, it was gone leaving the bush itself just as it was before.

And after the fire there was a calm and a peace stronger and deeper than any that Alice or Sam had ever known. There was no sound at all on the mountain. There was no sound at all in their hearts or minds, just stillness and calm.

And in the absolute quietness of that moment, in the single instant when everything was at peace, after the earthquake, storm and fire had gone, each of them heard distinctly a still, small voice speaking within them and around them and through them and beyond them. 'Beloved,' said the voice. And in hearing what was said, both Alice and Sam knew it to be true.

They remained as they were, side by side in the cave on the mountainside in the stillness, caught up in the deepest silence. In those moments, time had no meaning. There was no urgency, no hurry; it was enough to be there.

And then first Alice then Sam stretched and yawned and stood. Sam took up Col's staff. They held each other's gaze just for a moment. Together they stepped away from the cave, towards the bush. In the space of three steps, the mountain, the cave, the open sky all melted away and they were back at breakfast time on Friday morning in the front room staring at the calendar.

Col was there, kneeling as they entered the room. He stood to greet them. 'Welcome, Alice. Welcome, Sam. Welcome and good-bye!'

Sam handed over the staff. 'Thank you, Col,' said Alice, hugging him. Sam gripped his wrist and shoulder and their eyes met.

'Go well,' said Col, stepping towards the calendar. 'You are halfway through the journey. The best is saved till last.' As Col said the words he seemed to shrink and disappear, drawn into the twelfth door of the calendar, now fully open. Sam and Alice went up close to look at what was there.

In the wooden doorframe, against a black background, there stood a bush which had burst into flame – a flame which gave warmth and life but which did not consume. Depending how it caught the light, you could sometimes see at the very centre of the flame the figure of a person walking as if through fire.

13 December

Seven Christmas cards arrived on Thursday. Alice opened them over her muesli. Two had pictures of Father Christmas and the reindeer. Three featured snowflakes of various sizes. One more showed old-fashioned scenes from Victorian England and one had an elf. Alice ticked off the different categories on a chart on the pin board.

'What's that?' said Megs, fishing one of the cards out of a blob of marmalade.

'School,' said Alice, chewing toast. 'Project. Mr Davison. Survey of cards for some reason. How many we get, when, what the pictures are. So boo...ring!'

'What's it for?' said Megs.

Alice shrugged. 'Der!' she said. 'Since when did homework have a point?'

Megs checked the clock. 'Let's go!'

Alice arrived at school to find Suzie and Alex plotting in the playground. Since the beginning of term Suzie had been trying to think of some way of getting their own back on the Newtron. Many a desperate hour had been spent dreaming up foul, impractical schemes.

So far, none of the traps had been sprung but things were getting worse with Miss Newton by the day. 'We just have to do it this time,' she said. 'She's setting more homework every night.

Everyone hates her guts. She really took it out on Lucas yesterday.' Suzie had come from a school where the parents paid for their children's education. She knew how to call the shots.

Alex nodded, convinced that now was the time. 'We stand much more chance of getting away with it just before Christmas even if we're caught.'

'What's the plan this time?' said Alice, amazed that Alex was coming out of his geeky shell.

'Fire Hose Plan G – slightly refined,' said Suzie. 'The one on the back wall of the lab. I've worked out a way to bung up the nozzle with blutac – like a timer. We have double biology all afternoon – right after lunch. So at lunchtime we block the hosepipe with gunge and turn on the tap so the pressure builds up. Halfway through the lesson, with any luck, the pressure builds and kerpow! End of lesson. No one knows who did it. Perfect plan.'

'Genius!' said Alex.

'Are you sure?' said Alice. 'I hate the Newtron just as much as you do but it sounds pretty serious. Don't they expel you for something like that?'

'Don't be daft, Alice, we've been looking for a chance like this for months.'

'Are you going soft or something?'

The bell went for morning school. Alice shrugged her shoulders and followed her two friends into English. 'Funny,' she thought. 'Two weeks ago I would have done anything to cause a riot in biology.'

Sam's day began badly. Richard was in a foul mood, throwing his weight around, cracking the whip. He stormed out of his office just as Sam was taking off his coat and hat.

'Good of you to turn up ... at last,' Richard said to the whole floor in his most sarcastic voice.

Behind Richard's back, Tizzy was signing to Sam to be careful. He missed the cue completely.

'No trouble really,' said Sam, breezily. 'Circle line a bit slow.' Soft giggles ran round the edge of the room. Richard's eyes flashed dangerously. He hissed at Sam, 'I need those new sales charts, Brown. Now, if you don't mind.'

'Okayyyyy,' said Sam, very slowly, turning round. At last he picked up Tizzy's cue. 'I'll pop them in later then.'

'Now, if it's not too much trouble,' snapped Richard. Sam thought he almost caught sight of a forked tongue and had to blink and rub his eyes.

'They – er – um – they're not quite ready,' he said. 'Sorry.'

'Not ready?' Richard said softly, with menace. 'Not ready?' he threatened, drawing every eye to him in the room. Everyone tensed themselves preparing for the explosion. 'Not ready?' thrusting his face into Sam's. 'NOT READY? You useless bloody toerag. I want those figures on my desk by lunchtime or it's a written warning.' He was now speaking through his teeth but even so he could be heard in every part of the room. 'I've had it up to here with you – and you, Barfield, you simpering, useless pile of...,' he said, spinning round on Tizzy but not finishing his sentence.

'It may come as a big surprise,' he shouted as he stormed back to his office, 'it may come as a very big surprise but this is called a place of work.' The office door slammed on exactly the right syllable. Bang.

Silence.

Sam grimaced at Tizzy and tried to catch her eye. She was bright red, lip quivering, hands shaking. Sam's own knees felt a bit wobbly. He turned and gave a wave to the room. Everyone was back in their cubicles – all eyes on their computer screens.

'Right, then,' he said, mainly to himself. 'Sales figures.'

The lunchtime talk in the pub was all about Richard and his temper. Sam and Tizzy sat on their own in a quiet corner. Several people came over to speak their mind. 'The blinding cheek of it,' said Tizzy, blowing her nose, 'showing us up like that. I've a good mind to complain. He gets away with it time after time.'

'No point,' said Sam, quietly, hands clasped round his glass. 'No point letting it get to you. No point complaining. Just got to take it.'

'Hate this place,' said Tizzy. 'I'm going to look for something else after Christmas. Had it up to here with him.' Her head was in her hands.

'Really?' said Sam. 'I'd miss you. Best thing about coming to work.'

'Really?' said Tizzy, eyes brightening just a bit.

'Yeah,' said Sam, smiling. 'Mates. Got your outfit sorted for the party?'

The office do was four days away. 'Surprise,' she said, smiling through the tears. 'Wait and see!'

Sam was just coming through the front door when the phone rang.

'Anything?' asked Alice with her eyebrows as he picked it up.

Sam shook his head. 'Hello? Nick. Who do you want? Meggsie. Naughty Nick.'

'Don't call him that,' called Megs. 'Not in front of Alice.'

'He is though,' said Sam, very loudly, as he handed over the receiver.

Sam put the kettle on and got out one of his infinite supply of pot noodles. Pot noodles were Sam's answer to a warm nutritious meal. Alice turned up her nose and hovered at the door eavesdropping on the conversation.

'Nick, I'm sorry, I just don't think that's going to work. You can't just drop this on us at short notice. Yes, I know she's your daughter as well and it's Christmas but Alice needs stability just now.'

Alice looked back at Sam. 'What are they on about?'

'You by the sound of it,' said Sam, as Megs slammed down the phone and stormed into the kitchen.

'Your father thinks he can just announce he's taking you on holiday for Christmas without any consultation, any planning, just like that. I ask you.'

'Where to?' said Sam, tactlessly.

Megs gave him one of her looks. 'Never mind where to. It's the principle.'

Alice stamped her foot. 'Just talk about me as if I'm not here, why don't you?' (to Sam). Then, to Megs, coldly: 'Where to?'

The doorbell rang and Sam's phone signalled a text message.

'Talk about it later,' Megs called over her shoulder. 'This will be Josie coming to do my hair and help me decide what to wear tomorrow, for the big night out. Sam, you'll have to entertain yourself.'

Sam gave Josie a hug and then followed Alice into the front room.

'New day, new guide,' Alice whispered. The new door was visible in the left-hand quadrant, made of tiny logs placed side by side. 'Come on, they'll be ages on all that stuff. She's really nervous. Code.'

'Funny,' said Sam. 'One, one, colon, one.' Alice punched in the numbers and tensed herself for smoke.

Nothing happened.

The door on the calendar remained closed.

'Check the numbers,' said Alice. Sam fished for his phone. 'One, one, colon, one,' he said. Alice tried to punch them in again, but the buttons remained in place.

The doorbell rang. Bother.

'Sam, can you get that?' Josie called. 'Megs is in the sink.'

Sam looked puzzled. 'Hair washing,' said Alice, eyes raised to the ceiling.

''Kay.' Sam and Alice ignored the doorbell and waited by the calendar.

It rang again, three times – sustained.

Josie stamped down the corridor. 'You deaf?'

'Delivery for Mr Brown,' said a very deep voice.

Alice pulled Sam out into the corridor. There in the open door-way was one of the biggest men she had ever seen.

'It's for you, Sam,' called Josie over her shoulder, then turned round to find Sam was just behind her. 'I need to see to Megs.'

'What is it?' said Sam. 'I'm rather busy at the moment.'

'I know,' said the man, and winked.

Sam looked annoyed and puzzled at the same time. 'Another time, then,' he said, closing the door. Alice stopped him just in time.

'Sam. Stop. Don't you understand? It's got something to do with the calendar, hasn't it?' she said to the man.

The man nodded and his face lit up with a great smile. 'There is a parcel here for you.' He pointed to something very large and wrapped in brown paper.

'Sorry!' said Sam. 'Better come in then. Front room, just to the right. We were expecting something else.'

He and Alice stood back as the man came in through the front door carrying his large rectangular parcel. He led them into the front room and stood facing the calendar.

'Who are you?' said Alice. Now the man was in the room he seemed even bigger. He had to stoop slightly to come through the doorway and the top of his head almost reached the ceiling. Sam's head came up to his shoulders. The stranger threw back the hood of his coat and Alice saw that his hair was so long it came down to his shoulders and went down his back in the most enormous ponytail. His beard was big and bushy and his skin was burned dark by the sun. Fire danced in his black eyes.

'Good to meet you both at last,' their guest said, still smiling. His voice was so deep and low that when he spoke everything seemed to shake.

'Are you the new guide?' said Alice. The man nodded slowly. 'Fantastic. Are you Father Christmas?'

He shook his head. 'Call me JB. But Nicholas sends his love. And I have brought a present.'

'Sorry about the – er – mix up,' said Sam with a nervous cough. 'Bit rude.'

JB smiled again and looked at Sam with a raised eyebrow and a question in his eyes. 'Here's the parcel,' he said in his deep voice.

Sam took one end of the package and Alice the other. It was about the size of a table top, wrapped in brown paper and tied up with string. There were three labels. Alice read them as Sam untied the knots. 'Fragile. Handle with Care,' said the first. 'To Alice Carroll and Sam Brown,' said the second, 'Express Delivery.' And the third read, 'In case of difficulty call 266 433 555. Mr Gabriel.'

'Sam – it's from the same place as the calendar. Look.'

Carefully, they peeled off the three layers of brown paper. Inside was a beautiful, full-length mirror in a carved wooden frame. Alice was right. It matched the calendar exactly in proportions and in the carvings around the edge. 'It's beautiful, Sam,' she said.

'We need to hang it up,' said Sam, looking at three leather loops at the top.

'Over here,' said Alice, pointing to the alcove opposite the door to the room. 'Let me move these things.'

Carefully she cleared some space. 'Let me hang it,' said JB. 'I've done this before.'

From the vast pockets of his coat came a hammer and three large iron nails. Sam and Alice held the mirror at the right height. JB drove in the nails with six blows. Together they stepped back to admire the result, with Sam and Alice on either side of JB.

Alice looked in the mirror expecting to see her own reflection along with Sam and their strange visitor. Instead, the surface of the mirror was dull and misty. It must have steamed up because the room was warm.

'Shall I get a cloth?' she asked.

'No need,' said JB, taking something else from his great coat. 'Follow me!'

To Alice's astonishment the huge man was holding an enormous axe. He took two strides forward, stepped into the glass, over the edge of the mirror as if it were a threshold and disappeared on the other side.

Alice's jaw dropped. She looked at Sam, who was equally astonished. A second later, JB's head came back through the misty mirror surface.

'Come on! What are you waiting for?'

Sam nodded to Alice to go first. It was the strangest feeling. Alice walked up to the mirror, took hold of Sam's hand, lifted her left foot and put it through. Her leg disappeared up to the knee. It was like climbing through a window frame. There was just a very slight resistance as you passed through the mirror itself –

like putting your hand into a thin film of syrup. Her foot touched the soft earth on the other side. She took a deep breath, closed her eyes and put in her head and left arm. JB took her hand on the other side and pulled her through. A moment later and Sam had followed.

They were outside in the middle of a forest in the early morning. It was very cold.

'Take these,' said JB, producing two brown coats from inside his own. Alice took one. It smelt terrible, as if it had just come from a stable. The rough hairs grazed her neck and legs but once she had it on she was as warm as toast.

'What's it made of?' Sam said, sniffing his arm.

'Camel skin,' smiled JB and strode off in front of them, swinging his great axe over his shoulder. 'Come on.'

Alice had to jog to keep up with his huge strides. 'Where are we going?'

'About a mile this way,' he called. 'Hungry?'

'Yes,' said Alice. 'We haven't eaten tea yet.'

'Not got much,' said JB, fishing inside his coat. 'You can try one of these if you like.'

'Yeeeuch,' said Alice. 'It's a dead insect.'

'Locust,' said JB. 'Full of protein. Bit crusty on the outside. You can keep going for days on those if you have to.'

'Got anything else in there?' said Sam, hopefully.

'This might be better.' JB handed them each a piece of honeycomb, running with goodness. 'Scrape off the wax and lick out the honey,' he said, crunching another locust.

It was a bit tricky till you got the hang of it but the honey was one of the best things Alice had ever tasted, even if it did run down your chin and inside your clothes.

The forest floor began to rise steeply now. They stopped at a stream to drink and washed their sticky hands and faces.

'Nearly there now,' said JB.

'Where are we going?'

'Just to the top of this rise.' He pointed ahead. 'See that large tree sticking through the top of the forest?'

'What about it?' asked Sam.

'It's got too big for itself. It's diseased. Needs to be cut down.'
He patted his axe.

They walked on, all the time keeping up with JB's enormous strides. A bit further on and the forest floor changed. The grass, shrubs and trees were becoming smaller and weaker – then they stopped all at once at the edge of a great dark clearing.

'See?' said JB pointing at the ground. 'Nothing can grow. The poison is spreading through the forest. It comes from the heart of the tree.'

He walked on through the clearing towards the tall tree rising above them, its canopy casting a shadow over the whole of the surrounding area. It was even colder here. No birds sang. The ground beneath them felt unclean somehow. It was less solid and gave way when Sam stepped on it. Foul-smelling steam rose up from cracks in the ground.

'Watch where you step now.'

They walked together to the centre of the clearing. The closer they came to the tree's heart, the more the sense of evil in the air thickened. As they drew near, Alice could see cracks in the side of the huge trunk. The branches twisted upwards as if in pain.

JB paused a metre from the trunk. 'See now,' he called to the great tree. 'The time has come. You are poisoning the forest with your arrogance and pride. No more.'

The leaves above swirled and rustled. The branches creaked dangerously.

'It's time,' said JB. 'Stand clear, Sam and Alice.'

He shook off his massive coat, bared his arms and took up the axe. First he walked to the other side of the tree. Alice saw that the trunk there was more solid. With five heavy blows he cut a V shape into the tree across its whole width.

'Hold steady now,' he said as he came round to their side of the tree again. 'Hold steady.'

He raised the axe again and this time aimed a mammoth blow at an angle down towards the tree's base at knee level. The canopy above them shook with the force of it. Alice tugged Sam's sleeve and pointed. The axe had sunk half a metre at least into the rotten bark of the tree. The second blow came hard after the first, then the third and fourth. In moments, as it seemed, the axe had torn through the wood. JB's enormous arms were beaded with sweat and the muscles stood out on his neck and forehead.

He wiped his brow, set down his axe and braced himself against the trunk of the tree, legs bent. With a deep breath he pushed, straightening both legs, putting all his strength into this final effort. There was a dreadful cracking and splintering sound. The trunk split and gave way. The whole rotten lot came crashing down away from Sam and Alice. As it fell and touched the earth, the tree crumbled to dust.

There was silence.

The sunlight streamed back into the glade. The cracks in the earth slowly began to be sealed.

Alice spoke softly, 'Was it always bad?'

'No, child,' said the deep, bass voice. Now JB was trimming the wide stump of the tree, chopping off every branch and twig. 'Look at the rings.

'Neither of you can read the story in the rings of the tree. If you could, you would see a long history, a tree of beauty and goodness which loved the light and gave life to the forest. But you might also see a seed of corruption sown in its heart: a seed of pride which took root and grew within the great tree, growing stronger and stronger until every last part was twisted and blind. There was no choice but to bring things to an end.'

'What will happen now?' said Sam.

'We have cut out the corruption,' JB said. 'Watch.'

He put his coat back on now and the axe was safely stowed away in its folds. He offered Alice and Sam another honeycomb but neither was hungry. They sat and waited together, watching the stump of the tree.

At first, nothing. As they sat and watched, time around them began to move faster and faster. Day gave way to night. Time accelerated. The seasons changed. The grass grew back around the glade. The forest changed around them. The stump became blackened with age. Still there was no life. Hundreds of years, it seemed, went by in a matter of minutes.

But then, as she grew stiff and tired of waiting and time slowed down again to something like its normal pace Alice saw what was happening. Right at the edge of the tree's stump, something new was growing: just a shoot, nothing more.

'Here it is,' said JB, excitement in his voice as the rapid flow of time ceased. 'Here it is. Look and see. There has been terrible judgement and destruction – but the life is still here, the promise of the future.'

They walked back along the path they had come. Alice looked back as they reached the edge of the glade. The shoot was still visible – a slender sapling growing from the root of the great tree it had replaced.

JB led them swiftly and surely back through the forest until they reached the rectangle of mist hanging the air. 'Through you go,' he said. 'See you tomorrow.'

First Alice, then Sam stepped through the mirror and back into the front room. There in the open door of the calendar was the stump of a tree, blackened with age. Growing from one side of the stump, now in its first leaf, was the new shoot, the promise of the future where all had been destroyed.

14 December

Alice woke early the next morning, her mind full of the image of the great tree, rotten to the core and falling to the ground. What was it, she thought, that caused people to go bad? Where did the badness come from? How did it grow so that it took over your whole life?

After washing and dressing, Alice went downstairs and straight into the front room to look again at the calendar and the new gift of the mirror. As she walked through the door, she had the most unpleasant surprise. The surface of the mirror was clear now, not misty, so she could see her own reflection. Smeared across her face and down her neck was a dirty brown streak.

'Where did that come from?' she said aloud. Carefully she pulled her shirt open at the top and looked at her reflection. Sure enough the streak ran down onto her shoulder. She licked her fingers and rubbed at the dirt on her cheek. It made no difference.

'Morning, darling,' said Megs. 'Hey! Nice mirror – where did that come from?'

'Same place as the calendar, Mum. We put it up last night.' Alice turned away from the mirror, expecting Megs to leap back in horror and reach for a flannel. Instead, Megs gave her a kiss on the forehead and went into the kitchen, humming.

'Very strange,' thought Alice. She checked back in the mirror. The dirt was still there. She ran upstairs to the bathroom and looked in the mirror there. Her face was as clean as when she washed it ten minutes ago. She filled the sink and went through the whole process again, scrubbing really hard. Then she came down again to the front room. The streak of dirt was back in place.

'Time to go,' Megs called, still humming.

'You know I'm going out tonight, darling? Andrew's going to call round at seven to take me to this dinner of his. You'll be OK with Sam?'

Alice felt a bit weird. It was a strange feeling, having a dirty face, even if no one else could see it. 'Guess so,' she said. 'Won't be a regular thing, will it – with Mr Watkins?'

'Doubt it, darling,' Megs said, with a sigh. 'But it will be nice to go out for an evening.'

When Alice got to the playground, Alex had a large lump of green plasticine in his pocket. 'We may need some more time,' he said. 'I tested this last night on the garden hose. It held for three seconds after I turned on the tap. Even that was two seconds better than the blutac. We need something more powerful.'

'What about a cork?' said Suzie. 'If we hammer it in just right that should give us some time. My dad bought a bottle of champagne at the weekend. Those corks have wires round them.'

'Genius,' said Alex. 'We trim it down and hammer it in at lunchtime, hold it in place with one of those wires, then whip the wire off just before the lesson. I'll measure the hose today and make it over the weekend. You with us, Alice?'

Alice nodded, rubbing her cheek and wondering if anyone could see the brown streak. Her hesitations about the plan grew stronger in assembly. There were severe and ominous warnings from the Deputy Heads about pranks in the last few days of term and especially damage to school property: 'Anyone caught will be severely punished, etc. etc.'

But then came double biology after lunch. The class was on its best behaviour. Rumours had gone round about Alex's plan and everybody approved. Some people were even expecting it today. The whole idea was to lull the Newtron into a false sense of security.

But Miss Newton was in the foulest of black moods and looking for trouble. Her right eye was fixed on the book in front of her as she droned through the dullest of lessons. Her left eye moved independently across the classroom looking for the slightest misdemeanour.

'Take down this definition and learn it by heart – sit up straight, Carter. Hormones are chemicals released directly into the blood. Julie Bates, stop picking your nails and pay attention. They are chemical messengers which travel – Williams, put that ruler down – which travel in the blood to activate target cells. They are vital for the functioning of the pancreas – put your hand down, Thompson, not now – and the reproductive system.'

Several of the boys at the front of the class giggled whenever the Newtron mentioned the reproductive system. It was enough to light the blue touchpaper.

'Anthony Papodopolos, come out to the front NOW!'

Anthony was a quiet, shy boy who never said boo to a budgie let alone a goose. No other teacher had ever singled him out for attention. The whole class went silent.

Anthony stood up, cheeks burning and lip quivering and made his way out to the front of the class. Every eye was on him. They knew what was coming.

'Anthony Papodopolos, what exactly is it you find amusing?'

Anthony's lips moved but no sound came out.

'Speak up, boy!' It seemed to Alice that the windows shook at the sound.

'Please miss, nothing miss,' he squeaked. The first tear rolled down his cheeks.

Alex and Suzie desperately tried to create a diversion to draw the fire. Suzie had a coughing fit. Alex stuck up his hand: 'Please miss, I need the toilet and I need it now.'

'Shut up. Detention, both of you. Now you, boy. There is nothing funny about the human reproductive system.'

Despite the seriousness of the situation a soft titter ran round the room.

'Over the weekend you will draw me a labelled diagram of the human reproductive system and bring it to me on Monday morning signed by your parents. Is that clear?'

Anthony looked at the floor, tears rolling down his face. ''Ss, Miss.'

Alice, Suzie and Alex exchanged looks. This time the Newtron had gone too far. Fire Hose Plan G had just moved to execution stage.

Sam and Tizzy went for a quiet drink after work, away from the usual crowd. It had been another tense day at the office. This time someone else was Richard's victim.

'It's just horrible,' said Tizzy for the ninth time as she set the drinks down. 'Why do people put up with bullies?'

'Happens everywhere,' said Sam. 'School, work, even families sometimes. Alice's dad, Nick, bullied my sister for years.'

'You've never said. Did he hit her?'

'I don't think it ever came to that. I didn't think that much about it while they were together. He's just so forceful all the time. Undermined her confidence. He rang up yesterday and wanted to take Alice abroad for Christmas.'

'Will she go?'

'Doubt it – Megs looked pretty determined. Her confidence is coming back a bit now but every time that toerag rings up she kind of wobbles. How's things with that boyfriend of yours, anyway? You haven't mentioned him for ages.'

Tizzy went quiet. 'Not great, actually. Wants things his own way all the time. Never listens.'

'He is a man, Tizzy.'

'More than just the usual.' She blew her nose and wiped her eyes. 'We had that bust-up last week after the weekend with my parents. I think he might be seeing someone else. He's away on his own this weekend.'

'Tough cookie,' Sam said, surprising himself. Normally he didn't do sympathy at all.

'Thanks,' said Tizzy, knocking back her drink. 'Sam – you don't fancy – you know – going out somewhere, do you? Just for a laugh. Make a night of it.'

Sam was about to say yes without thinking when his phone rang. It was Alice.

'Sam? Just checking you're on your way. It's Mum's big night. You were going to be home early, remember?'

'Jumping jellyfish, I forgot. I can just make it by seven if I dash. Just having a drink with a friend.'

'Idiot. Any text messages?'

'Nothing.' He hung up. 'Look, sorry, Tiz. Got to go. Megs has this date and I promised to be there for Alice. Nothing personal. Family. You know.'

'No big deal,' said Tizzy, standing up and giving him a hug. 'See you at the party on Monday.'

Sam legged it to the station and just made the train after his normal time. Even so, Megs was pacing up and down when he arrived home, all ready for Andrew.

'You look gorgeous, sis. Doesn't she, Alice?'

'I've already told her that umpteen times. I just don't see why she has to go out with a teacher from my school.'

'What's that on my face?' said Sam, looking over Megs' shoulder into the new mirror. He rubbed his forehead.

'Don't let Alice stay up past ten,' said Megs. 'And Sam, Mum rang. Dad's not been too good this week. Really run down. I told them to call a doctor.'

Sam was still staring at his reflection and scratching his chin.

Megs turned round. 'Looks fine to me,' she said. 'You're just trying to take my mind off things.'

The doorbell rang. Andrew Watkins swept in, said 'Hi' to Sam and Alice, looked stunned by Megs and swept out again in a matter of seconds. Alice waved goodbye from the window. Sam stood in front of the mirror rubbing his face.

'You too?' said Alice, coming to stand next to him and pointing at her cheek.

'You look fine to me,' said Sam, looking at her reflection.

'So do you,' said Alice. 'And I look fine in the bathroom mirror and the mirrors at school. But when I look in this mirror, there is a great brown streak all down my cheek and right down onto my shoulder. Nothing I can do gets it off.'

'Message' sang Sam's phone.

'Sam!' said Alice. 'You've got a new ring tone! Don't say you're growing up at last? Is it the code?'

'Three, eight, colon, one, four,' Sam read aloud.

'Perfect timing,' said Alice as she punched in the numbers. The new door was the same colour as the calendar itself and hard to see at first.

'What happens now?' wondered Sam after they had waited a few seconds. Alice peered out of the window to see if JB had arrived with another parcel. She turned back into the room.

'Sam! Look! The mirror!'

Sam spun round. The face of the mirror was once again cloudy and soft. Alice put out her hand and pressed her fingertips through the surface. They disappeared. It was like pressing them through a very thick layer of oil. She pressed one arm through next, then the other, feeling the empty space on the far side. Only then, like a swimmer putting her face through water, did she press her head through the mirror's soft surface and out the other side. She saw enough to be aware that she was entering a warm dark room, lit by lines of sparkling lights at floor level. Quickly Alice steadied herself on the frame of the mirror and stepped through, first one leg, then the other. Sam followed her and both of them took in the scene.

They had emerged in the middle of a vast indoor chamber, but they could see neither walls nor ceiling. The sense of a vast space was created by patterns of tiny lights running across the smooth black floor in random patterns like the cracks in very large crazy paving. The chamber was very still. The other sources of light were what looked like large fireflies, thousands of them, dancing, as it seemed, from point to point in the great space.

There was no sign of JB. Alice and Sam looked around to make sure they could find the mirror again and then began to move in the same direction into the chamber. Almost at once, Alice became aware of a low whispering sound coming from many different directions.

As her eyes became more used to the dim light, she began to see the other distinctive feature of the cavernous chamber. Suspended from the ceiling, still out of sight, were thousands and thousands and thousands of tiny black threads. At the end of each thread, at different heights above the floor, was either a speaker or a headphone. Each was at least a metre from any of the others.

The speakers themselves were all different. Some, like the headphones, were different sizes. Some looked as though they had been taken from a car stereo system. Others were larger, like the ones in televisions or hi-fi systems, Sam thought. Some were much smaller: the tiniest earpiece you can imagine. Others were shaped like shells or rusty cans at the end of a string.

The low, rustling sound was coming from these innumerable speakers or headphones which stretched away into the distance in every direction. As Sam and Alice wandered around the chamber and as their ears tuned to the silence, they began to hear snatches of what was being said. From each speaker came a different voice.

Alice stood next to one of the strings she could reach and put the earpiece close to her left ear. The words were in a language she could not understand but she instantly caught the notes of pain and distress in the woman's voice. Carefully, she let the headphone hang still again and went to another and then another. Each time the voice spoke a different language. It was like turning the dial on a radio tuner and listening to snatches of different programmes except each one was punctuated by sobs and cries.

A little way away, Alice saw Sam doing exactly the same. Then she found a voice speaking English. A woman in a broad Scottish accent, crying and pleading for the life of her child. As Alice listened, she learned that the young girl had cancer and was not expected to live beyond her fifth birthday. The next voice she could understand was that of an old man, crying out with loneliness. The next was a woman with a Yorkshire accent anxious and worried about her son, serving with the army far away in a foreign country. The next a young man in prison on the point of suicide. The next a young child's prayer for protection for his mother when her boyfriend came home drunk. The next the cry of someone close to death from a hospital ward.

'These are prayers,' she thought. 'I'm listening to real people, saying their prayers.'

As she listened to each whispered cry and let go of the headphones, Alice found she shed a tear. She and Sam came together and held hands. They looked across the great chamber and heard in the gentle rustle the cries and prayers of thousands and thousands of people in different languages from every point on earth.

Suddenly Sam pointed. One of the creatures Alice had thought was a firefly had come close to them and landed on a tiny speaker nearby.

The creature was surrounded by a bright light. As it came to rest, Alice and Sam were able to see its shape for the first time. They gasped. At the centre of the ring of light, the size, it seemed, of a butterfly, was a tiny angel. Its six wings beat faster than they could see as the creature hovered in the air near the earpiece, listening to the prayer. Sam recognised that the language was Spanish and the voice was that of a young boy but neither he nor Alice could make out the words. The tiny angel listened to the grief and pain until the voice came to an end. It seemed to Alice that its light burned just a little less brightly as it attended to the prayer. Then, in a moment, the angel was gone leaving a trail of light behind it. This particular speaker was silent for a time. Then a different voice began in yet another language. This one sounded Indian, Sam thought. Another angel came and listened in the same way and then flew upwards like a spark and was gone.

Sam and Alice let go of each other's hand again and walked forward, listening and watching the endless sequence of prayers from all over the earth, cries of the heart, spoken and yet heard. Gradually they began to notice that the pattern of lights on the floor radiated out from a central space like spokes on a wheel, so they let the pattern lead them and eventually it took them to the very centre of the chamber.

There, in the midst of the rough circle of light set into the floor were three wooden stools around a dark oak table. JB stood up to welcome them and invited them to sit with him. He offered them draughts of cold water served in simple wooden cups. There was fresh bread and a wooden bowl filled with wild honey.

Sam and Alice felt strangely weary after walking only a little way through the chamber. The simple meal revived them. For some moments each of them ate in silence.

After he had swallowed the last of the bread and washed it down with the cold, refreshing water, Sam turned to face JB. 'Tell us about this place,' he asked, speaking softly. 'Of all the places we have been, I think this may be the most strange and beautiful of all.'

JB acknowledged the truth of what he said with a sad smile. He spread his arms wide. 'Behold the Chamber of Laments,' he said. His deep voice seemed at one with the resonances in the great space, echoing softly off the distant walls and ceiling. 'This is the place where the cries and tears of all the earth are heard. Each minute and hour, each day and night, each long and weary year every prayer that is offered in hunger or sadness or despair comes to this chamber and is heard.'

'Can every prayer be answered?' asked Alice, her eyes wide.

'Every prayer is heard, child,' JB said. 'Each prayer which is the cry of a heart makes a difference. Each tear is counted. Many more are answered than you or I can know. But prayers are not like the wishes in your stories. Not all can be answered yet. There is too much that is still bitter and twisted and evil in the world. Too much is still to be set to rights. But the day will come. The day will come when the King returns and even this great chamber will fall silent for eternity. Then every sorrow and every sigh will flee the earth for ever.'

'Who is this King?' asked Sam. 'When will he come?'

'You do not know?' asked JB, standing and looking at each of them. He smiled sadly and indicated they should walk together back towards the mirror. First Alice then Sam shook their heads.

'You do not know? Yet your whole world is, supposedly, preparing to celebrate his birth. The very meaning of that birth is now forgotten. The story is retold as a fairy tale to children but they are no longer allowed to see its meaning.'

They drew near to the misty surface of the mirror suspended in the chamber. JB stood and faced them but continued speaking.

'Two thousand years ago, the King was born. He lived and served and loved and died. But death itself could not hold him. He lives still and reigns in heaven and wherever on earth men and women welcome him as Lord. He has a people scattered through the earth who give their lives in the service of this kingdom. And the time is nearer now – nearer than it has ever been – the time is near when the King will return to set everything to rights. And even this great chamber will fall silent.'

As JB motioned again with his arm, both Alice and Sam took a final look around the great, sad and weary space. Countless thousands of prayers and cries expressing such profound sadness: the weariness of the earth laid bare. JB helped first Sam and then Alice through the mirror's surface.

The front room felt very small and cold and empty after a place which was so sad yet so alive. Alice drew the curtains as Sam lit the gas fire. Then together they faced the calendar and looked.

The fourteenth door was open now. Just as Alice hoped, there in the doorway in a circle of light, hovering above the ground, was a tiny angel with six wings. If you looked very closely, you could see that its expression was (in a way that Alice could not understand) at the same time full of sadness yet full of hope.

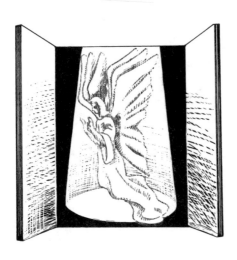

15 December

On Saturday, Alice slept late and was woken by the sound of the doorbell ringing persistently. She ran down the stairs. No one else was around.

'Hi, Josie. Come on in.'

'Is Sam up?' Josie didn't look too well.

'Not yet. Shall I try and wake him?'

'Please. Mind if I put the kettle on?'

Alice was already halfway up the stairs. She knocked at Sam's door. 'Sam. Wake up. It's Josie downstairs.'

'OK. Down in a minute.'

Megs stuck her head round the bedroom door. 'Is that the time? Slept in. Alice, get dressed, pet. I think your father's coming round this morning.'

By the time Alice came back downstairs, the house, it seemed, was full of people. Round the kitchen table sat Megs and Josie. Megs was dressed but her hair was all over the place. Opposite them, in T-shirts and boxer shorts, were Sam and Andrew Watkins, who had emerged from the front room. Everyone seemed to be getting on famously.

Alice's nice Saturday mood evaporated instantly. She slammed the kitchen door as loudly as she could, stormed into the front room and went to switch on the TV. As she turned, Alice caught a glimpse of her reflection again in the mirror. To her horror, the dark stain on her left cheek and shoulder had now spread to the right side of her face and covered both her hands. Her clothes were also stained. She looked as though she hadn't changed or washed in weeks.

Megs came quietly into the room with her cup of tea. 'Alice?' she said, quietly.

Alice grabbed two cushions, put them over her ears and stared straight ahead, eyes filled with tears.

'Alice, I should have warned you Andrew was here,' Megs began. 'I would have done but I'd no idea he was going to stay over. He stayed in here.'

Alice bit her bottom lip hard, determined not to cry. 'Alice, please.'

Alice turned her face into the sofa and her back to Megs, who touched her softly on the shoulder. 'We'll talk later, my love,' she said. 'Your father is coming at twelve. Andrew will be gone in half an hour. I thought we might get a tree later and put some decorations up.'

As soon as the coast was clear, Alice crept out of the front room and into the hall. She pulled on her boots and coat and scarf and charged out of the house without any idea where she was going. It was raining heavily. There was a stream of traffic heading into town and a bus just pulling up. Alice had some change in her pocket. She joined the queue and leapt aboard, paying for a single fare into town.

Back at the house, Sam was the first one to notice that Alice was gone. Megs came back into the kitchen and announced Alice was sulking. Sam was pleased for his sister but felt for Alice having to meet one of her teachers over breakfast. He knew, as well, how badly Alice felt about Nick leaving and how his visits always upset her. As soon as he could, he made an excuse and went to find her.

The front room was empty. Sam, too, gasped as he caught sight of his reflection in the mirror. His reflected clothes were ragged and patched. Through the holes, Sam could see his knees and arms were caked in dirt. His hair looked as if it had not been washed in ages. There was a bruise on his left cheek. As he touched it, the place felt sore.

He turned away to look at the calendar, out of habit more than anything. He looked first at the angel from yesterday and then saw, to his surprise, that a new door had appeared already. The frame was made of thin metal and the door itself looked and felt like darkened glass. His phone was upstairs. The message must have arrived when he was having breakfast.

'Sam,' said Josie, coming in behind him, 'can we talk? I came round this morning because I've got something important to say.'

'Sure, yeah,' said Sam. 'Sit down.'

Josie closed the door. 'It's not very easy,' she said. 'I've not wanted to tell you. I'm really pleased we got back together. I'm really happy about the way everything's worked out and that we're going make a go of it and keep the baby.' Josie rubbed her tummy as she said this and then took Sam's hand.

'I'd never have told you this before,' Josie said. 'But you've changed. You're so much — just so different really. It's just that while we were — you know — after we'd split up — I didn't mean to — but I went one evening with my old friends and got together with someone else. It was just for a night. It didn't mean anything. I was on a rebound. I'd had too much to drink. You know how it is. I just didn't want there to be anything between us now, you know, we're going to be parents ... '

Sam sat quietly, head bowed, cheeks burning. Something inside him felt very hard and cold and angry and hurt. Another part was telling him that all of that was unreasonable and that he should be gentle and understanding. Just for the moment, the cold, hard part was winning. He could feel the harsh words bubbling and boiling their way to the surface.

Megs stuck her head round the door after she had said goodbye to Andrew. 'Sam,' she said, 'have you seen Alice? She's not in her room and her boots and coat are gone. I thought she might be in here with you. Sorry to interrupt, Josie.'

Sam checked what he was going to say but withdrew his hand from Josie's. 'I heard the door bang earlier,' he said, 'while we were all in the kitchen. I came in here to look.'

'I'm really worried,' said Megs. 'She's never just gone off before.'

'She can't have got very far,' said Sam. 'You stay at the house. Nasty Nick's going to be here anytime. I'll go out and look for her. Josie, we'll need to finish this later.'

The last few words came out more sharply than he intended. Josie looked hurt. Megs winced.

Sam charged upstairs for his jacket and phone. There was a text message and a code: eleven, colon, thirteen. No time for that now. On the way downstairs he stopped to check in any case. No buttons had been pressed on the calendar. The surface of the mirror was hard and unyielding. There was no way Alice could have gone through without him.

'I'm going. Give me a call if she comes back.'

Megs was pacing up and down in the kitchen, really worried now. Josie put the kettle on, anxious about Alice but also about Sam. Neither of them wanted to use the phone in case Alice tried to ring. The rain ran down the kitchen windows.

Sam looked up and down the street, stepping back every now and then to avoid the water thrown up by the cars. There was no sign of his niece. 'Where would she go?' he thought. 'Alice hates being cold. None of her friends live nearby. She must have headed into town.' There was no queue at the bus stop. Sam took his place in the shelter and hoped the next bus would not be long.

Alice pressed her face to the bus window and let her tears flow. It wasn't fair. All the adults in her life just lived their lives with no reference to her. Her stupid father got a new girlfriend so she and Megs had to move miles away. She was just getting used to that when Sam split up with Josie and she had to get used to living with him. Her dad only made contact when he felt like it – which wasn't very often. Now Megs was clearly getting together with one of her teachers – the one half the school was in love with. Alice could imagine the taunts if it got out.

The bus arrived in the town centre and Alice got off. She mooched around for a while, not really thinking where she was going. The cold and the rain led her, with the rest of the crowd, to the indoor shopping mall. Everywhere was brightly lit. Everyone, it seemed, was shopping in twos and threes. No one else was on their own. Everyone was in a tearing hurry, rushing about, heads down.

There was a strange new shop, Alice noticed, on one side of the mall. The sign above the door read in small neat letters: 'The Christmas Preparation Shop'. There was nothing at all in the window. Completely empty. Inside there was nothing on the shelves.

'Strange,' thought Alice. 'Have they sold out already? Or is it so new that they haven't got any stock yet?'

She pressed her nose up against the window. Around the sides of the shop were little cubicles. Each was equipped with a telephone, pens, envelopes and paper but nothing else. There were no customers – unlike every other shop in the mall which was packed out. No one else seemed to take the slightest notice. There was a kind of reception desk just inside the door covered in green fabric. Standing behind the desk, perfectly still, was a small dapper-looking man in a smart suit and a bowler hat. He caught Alice's eye, smiled and raised his hat to her. Instantly, Alice looked away.

There was a coffee shop next door and Alice was now cold and hungry. She had dashed out of the house before breakfast. She had just enough money for a large hot chocolate, as well as the fare home. She paid for her drink, collected it from the end of the counter and looked around for somewhere to sit.

The only vacant seat in the place was at a table near the window. The tall scruffy man in a hooded coat who sat there had his back to her and was reading his newspaper.

'Excuse me,' said Alice. 'Do you mind if I sit here? There's nowhere else.'

'Be my guest,' said a deep, familiar voice. 'Delighted to see you.'

'JB!' said Alice, genuinely pleased. 'What are you doing here?'

'Drinking my coffee, reading my newspaper and waiting for you.'

'How did you know I would be here?' Alice asked.

JB just smiled and tapped the side of his nose gently.

'What about Sam?' she asked.

'He'll be along,' said JB. 'That's why we're in the window. Tell me about your morning. You've been crying.'

Alice told him all about it: Andrew Watkins, her dad, Megs, Josie, even Sam. 'They all treat me like an object. They all expect me to fit in with them, whatever. So I ran away. Not for ever. Just to teach them a lesson.'

JB said nothing. He was, thought Alice later, a very patient listener. A moment after she had finished, she jumped as JB tapped on the window. There was Sam, just outside the coffee shop, his eyes scanning the mall. Alice suddenly felt extremely guilty.

As he heard the tap on the glass, Sam turned round and took in the sight. He was cross and relieved at the same time and marched into the shop.

'Where have you been, young lady? Your mother's worried sick. Running off like that without a word. I didn't know where to find you. And haven't we told you not to talk with strangers? No offence, sir.'

'None taken,' said JB, with a smile, throwing back the hood of his great coat. 'But nor am I exactly a stranger!'

Sam gaped. 'This is a very strange morning,' he said. 'The code arrived earlier. We can punch it in when we get back.'

'No need,' said JB. 'What I want to show you today is right here.' He held out some money to Alice. 'Alice, would you mind getting Sam a cup of coffee while he sits down and takes all this in?'

'No problem,' said Alice.

'Tall Gingerbread Latte,' said Sam, looking a bit dazed, 'with cream – and some ginger biscuits – if they have any.'

As Alice turned away, JB addressed himself to Sam. 'So tell me what's been happening with you today.'

'Nothing really – just a normal Saturday. Megs has a new boyfriend. Josie came round. All fine – except for Alice running away. Hadn't I better ring home?'

'In a moment,' said JB. 'And that wasn't what I meant.'

'Oh!' said Sam. 'That. Not easy that one, JB. Josie told me she went with someone else. Hurts, you see.' He tapped his chest.

'I do,' said JB. Alice came back with the coffee and biscuits.

'It's time you two learned the most important lesson about getting ready for Christmas.'

'Presents?' said Alice but without conviction.

'Cards?' said Sam, with even less.

JB shook his head. Both of them looked outside at the shoppers for inspiration.

'Turkey?'

'Tinsel?'

'Tree?'

JB shook his head again and lifted his eyes to the ceiling. 'Clueless.' He took out a mobile and picked up a ginger biscuit, biting the end off. 'Phone home, Alice. Let your mum know you're safe and with Sam. We'll be home soon. You finish your coffee,' he smiled at Sam, dunking the biscuit.

The phone call to Megs was short and to the point. Alice still didn't feel very warm towards her mum. Nick had just arrived apparently. Josie was still there.

Sam finished the last of his drink. Alice passed him a napkin and pointed to her top lip. 'Cream moustache,' she said, smiling for the first time that day. JB led them both out of the coffee house and into the doorway of the new shop Alice had seen on the way in.

'I was looking at this before,' she said. 'It doesn't seem to sell anything.'

'Absolutely right,' said JB, opening the door and leading them in. 'It doesn't sell anything at all. Everything in here is given away.'

'So why is no one coming in here?' asked Sam.

'They can't see it,' said JB, sadly. He waved to the man behind the counter. 'Mr Gabriel,' he said, 'this is Alice. I think you've met Sam.'

'Miss Carroll,' said Mr Gabriel politely, raising his hat. 'Delighted. Heard so much about you. Mr Brown. Pleased to see you again, sir. Congratulations on the journey so far. We are most impressed, sir, madam.'

'Suffering sea snakes, we've met before,' said Sam. 'Hamleys. The Calendar Department.'

'Correct, sir. Delighted to be of service.' He turned to JB. 'What is it to be today?'

'We need to sit down a moment and then we'll need the screen.' He led them to a corner of the shop where there was a small table and three chairs and a large plasma screen.

'The most important lesson to learn about getting ready for

Christmas,' said JB, 'is the one about forgiveness. All over the world, all year long, people hurt those they love in terrible ways.' He picked up a remote control and pointed it at the screen. It divided into four sections. 'The pictures are live,' he said. 'Fortunately there is no sound.'

Alice and Sam looked. They saw a husband and wife quarrelling; two elderly people walking sadly apart from each other; a grown man nursing a grudge against his father; two sisters who never spoke. Every few seconds, one of the images changed. Sam and Alice saw a succession of lonely, broken people in a world that was fragmenting.

'Scratch the surface of any family,' said JB, 'and you will find deep fractures. Parents estranged from their children and children from their parents. Husbands and wives who live together still but whose hearts are full of bitterness. Brothers torn apart by jealousies which began in childhood. Sisters who never speak because of wrongs done to them years ago. Divorces which began with imagined neglect. Children separated from grandparents by pride which cannot make the first move. Lonely, estranged people carrying their own hurts, searching desperately for love.

'Why do you think it is,' he went on, 'that people spend so much on Christmas? What is it they are looking for in the bright lights and decorations, food and drink? Each one is lonely. Each one is chasing friendship and community.'

He flicked off the television screen. 'And that is why the most important lesson in preparing for Christmas is this: use these weeks before the Holy Day to practise forgiveness, to be reconciled, to let go of old hurts and wounds, to bring hearts and lives together again. There is no better way to get ready for the King.'

'How can you forgive,' said Alice, 'if you have been so badly hurt?'

'You have to want to do it,' JB said, 'really want to do it. Sometimes it helps to talk it through with someone else. But the best way is just to decide you will forgive and, if you can, let the person know. That's why this little centre is equipped with phones and pens and paper.'

'Shouldn't you wait, sometimes, for the other person to make the first move?'

JB shook his head: 'If each is waiting for the other, the waiting will last for all eternity. Make the first move. Make up. Be reconciled. Forgive and you will be forgiven.'

He stood up as he spoke and put one of his massive arms around each of them. 'Come!' he said. 'This is one lesson which is learned in the doing not the hearing.'

He waved to Mr Gabriel who lifted his hat a final time and JB led them through a curtain into what looked on the outside like a fitting room.

In the corner of the fitting room was a mirror with a soft and misty surface. 'You first, Sam. Put things right.' Sam squeezed his hand, stepped through carefully and found himself back in the front room. Alice followed. Both of them looked back, expecting JB to be with them but the surface of the mirror simply reflected back to both of them their shabby, dirty image.

Alice quickly turned away, not liking the sight but determined to do as JB had said. She somehow had in her mind a picture of Megs and herself drifting further and further apart all down the years ahead.

'Mum, I'm back,' she called. 'I'm sorry I ran off.' Megs came out of the kitchen, into the hall and caught Alice up in her arms.

'You absolute tinker,' she said. 'I'm so sorry. It was all too much too soon, I know.'

Alice set her feet back on the floor, held her mum's hands and looked into her eyes. 'Mum, I forgive you. I forgive you for everything. I love you very much.' Megs hugged her again and held her close. 'I forgive you, too, darling. We can get through this together.'

Sam went upstairs looking for Josie. He knew she wouldn't be in the kitchen with Nick and Megs. Sure enough, she was in his small bedroom, eyes red and swollen. He knelt next to her on the bedroom floor and took her hand.

'Josie – look – what you said earlier – it really hurt. I know that's daft and I had no right to take offence. I just can't stand the idea of you being with anyone else. Not now. I love you so much it hurts. But even though it hurts very much, I still think you were right to tell me. Nothing should come between us, not now.

And I want you to know that if there's anything to forgive – then I forgive you. It's over.'

Josie was in tears again and he embraced her.

Alice thought hard about her dad for the rest of the day. He took her out for lunch, just the two of them. It didn't feel right, somehow, to come right out and say she forgave him. Running off with someone else was on a different scale, somehow, to what Megs had done. But there was a sort of shift on the inside. And as they were saying goodbye, she managed to stammer out that Nick was still her dad and she loved him.

Later on, Alice and Sam sat together by themselves in the front room while Josie and Megs washed up after tea. Sam and Josie had been out to buy a Christmas tree and Alice was sorting through the decorations whilst Sam checked all the lights.

'JB was right, wasn't he?' said Alice. 'It's very, very hard. But it is the most important part of getting ready … to forgive.'

Sam couldn't speak. He just nodded and his eyes were drawn once more to the open door of the calendar. In the doorway two tiny figures were locked together in an embrace: reconciliation.

16 December

Megs kept her promise and took Alice to church on Sunday morning. Sam had offered to cook lunch to make up for last Sunday but Megs thought it wiser to put on a casserole before she left.

Alice took the red invitation with her again, just in case, and Megs put on her best coat. As they got ready, Megs admired herself in the mirror in the front room. 'I've wanted a mirror like this for ages, Alice. It's like a really nice early Christmas present. Come and look at yourself.'

Alice stood in front of Megs and looked carefully. She knew all Megs could see was a nicely turned-out daughter who was growing up fast. What Alice saw was someone who was stained and dirty from head to toe, whose clothing was ripped and torn, whose hair was streaked with dirt.

This week, of course, they were on time and Alice said hello politely as she was given a book and waved to the nice man who spoke to them last week. Brenda came over to say hello.

'Hello Alice. Good to see you again. Is this your mum?'

'Megs Carroll,' said Megs, holding out her hand.

'Brenda Fisher. Is this your first time here?'

Megs nodded. 'We've not lived here long.'

'You're very welcome,' said Brenda. 'Just make yourself at home.'

'That's nice,' whispered Megs as Alice led her to a seat.

To Alice's great surprise, Megs knew her way around the service book and guided her through. 'You know what to do!' Alice whispered. 'I never knew you used to go to church. Why have you never taken me before?'

'Tell you later,' said Megs. 'Shhh.'

Alice let the words of the service wash over her and just enjoyed the great space and the time to think. So much was happening to her and the people she loved. She found herself thinking about Abraham and Sarah and Col and JB and wondering what they would make of church. She said a prayer for Megs and Sam and Josie and Grandad, who was still poorly. Her favourite part was where the vicar lit another candle in the Advent crown at the front of church. There were three burning now. Only one more Sunday and it would be Christmas.

Megs led Alice forward when the time came to receive communion. Again, to Alice's surprise, Megs held out her hands and took a small piece of bread and drank some wine.

'What's that all about?' Alice whispered as she got back to the pew.

'Tell you later,' said Megs, squeezing her hand.

Josie was there for lunch again and Megs had invited Andrew, with Alice's permission. He said very nice things about the casserole. Megs said it was nothing special really but she had got up early to make it and her cheeks went a bit pink.

'So tell me, Mum,' said Alice after the first course, 'how come you know all about church and stuff and even took the bread and wine, and Sam knows nothing about it?'

'Charming,' said Sam. 'I wouldn't say I knew nothing.'

'I went to church until I was about your age,' said Megs, 'in Lincolnshire where we grew up. Grandma was very involved though your grandfather only ever went at Christmas and Easter. I was confirmed and everything – that's what happens before you can take bread and wine. I had lots of friends there.'

'But what about Sam?'

'I was too young,' Sam said. 'I was only five when we moved to Luton.'

'We just never started going again when we moved house,'

Megs went on. 'I found new friends, life kind of filled up. I've thought about going back to church from time to time – especially over the last few months – but never quite made it. Your father would get cross every time I mentioned it. He doesn't believe in anything. I never really wanted to go on my own.'

'I used to have to go when I was a kid,' said Josie. 'My mum and dad go all the time. All I remember is having to keep really quiet. Didn't you find it really boring?'

'I don't understand a lot of it,' said Alice. 'But that's not the same as boring, is it?'

'What about you, Andrew?' asked Sam.

'Choirboy and server,' Andrew said, blushing a bit. 'That's someone who helps at the front, Alice. But my mum died when I was sixteen. She had cancer. I stopped going after that. Blamed God, I suppose.'

Megs squeezed his hand. 'I'll get the pudding,' she said. 'I – er – made a trifle.'

The phone rang. Alice ran and answered it. 'It's Grandma for you, Mum,' she said. 'She sounds worried.'

Megs took the phone into the front room and Alice dished out the trifle proudly. Andrew and Sam asked for big helpings and teased her that the bowls were too small.

Everyone was laughing and giggling when Megs came back into the room. They fell quiet when they saw her face.

'It's Dad,' she said. 'He's been taken into hospital. He had some kind of seizure at lunchtime. Mum's just got back. She's really upset. I think one of us needs to go and see her.'

'Can't we all go?' said Alice.

'Not really, my love,' Megs said. 'We'll need to go and see Grandad in hospital and they probably wouldn't let you in. You'll need to stay here with someone.'

'Best if you go, old girl,' Sam said quietly. 'Not the best time for me to appear, is it?'

Megs and Alice both knew that Sam hadn't seen his mum and dad for about six months – and the last time they had seen each other Sam and his dad had quarrelled badly. Something about Sam's job and some money he owed them.

162

'Do you want me to take you?' said Andrew. 'No trouble. I could find something to do in Luton for a couple of hours.'

'Are you sure?' said Megs. 'You don't mind?'

'Least I can do after a lunch like that.'

'That's settled then,' said Josie. 'Leave the washing up to us. No excuses, Sam!'

Megs packed an overnight bag, just in case, and she and Andrew were gone ten minutes later. After the clearing up, Josie popped into town to do some Christmas shopping. Sam and Alice settled down in the front room to catch up on homework and the Sunday papers.

Alice had a French test the next day, so she spent twenty minutes trying to master irregular verbs. Feeling tired she went over, as she often did, to look at the calendar.

'Sam, you toad, there's another door!'

Sam was snoring quietly in the corner. Alice shook him awake. 'Wake up! Sam! There's a door. Where's your phone?'

Sam rubbed his eyes and stared. The new door was the grandest yet, made of some kind of crystal. He stumbled outside to his coat and fished the mobile out of the left-hand pocket.

As he came back into the room he shielded his eyes from his own reflection. His skin was caked in mud and his clothing was torn to shreds. They went through the familiar routine.

'Five.' Click. 'Four.' Click. 'Colon.' Click. 'One.' Click. 'Two.'

Cautiously, both Alice and Sam turned towards the mirror. To their amazement and great relief, the surface had turned cloudy. Sam went first this time. He pressed one hand through, then the other and waved his arms around. Nothing. Taking a deep breath he pressed his face through the viscous surface.

As he opened his eyes on the other side he heard JB chuckling. 'There is no need to hold your breath, Sam. Just come on through. The show is about to start.'

With some difficulty Sam drew his legs and body through the narrow space. As Alice followed him, he looked around. They were indoors – you could tell that from the temperature: warm and a bit stuffy. There was some kind of soft black carpet on the floor.

The room was dark apart from a small light burning in what seemed to be the centre of the space, near to where they stood. Right in the middle were three elaborate-looking chairs – like the ones in the dentist's or in the first-class compartment of an aeroplane.

Sam inspected the chairs, which were like nothing he'd ever seen, with all kinds of attachments. Alice looked above and around her. 'Stars,' she gasped. 'Thousands of them. And they are underneath us as well as above. Like we are in space but we can breathe.'

Sam saw more clearly now, as his eyes adjusted to the darkness, that the floor was a small circular platform surrounded by a guard rail at waist height. The platform was about the size of a large living room and seemed to be suspended in a huge sphere.

'Come and sit down,' said JB. 'Enjoy the show!' He took the seat in the centre with Sam on his right and Alice on his left and showed them how to get ready. There were special suits to wear made from very thin silver-coloured material, a headset with an earpiece and a safety harness securing them to the seat.

Alice got it first. 'Is it like an IMAX?' she said. 'It feels like the one I went to with Dad, near Waterloo station – only with seats.'

'Right first time,' said JB, securing Alice's straps. 'Only we've built a few refinements into this one.'

'It looks like the dome is 360 degrees,' said Sam, eyes widening as he took in the scene. Both Sam and Alice loved fairground rides and rollercoasters of every kind. 'Rollicking roosters!'

'Absolutely,' said JB. 'Only the best. The sound is pretty impressive. These earpieces are just so that we can talk to each other. The seats tip and move during the flight so strap in tightly. We've also added atmospherics: wind and temperature changes and some smells.'

'Amazing,' said Alice. 'When do we start?'

JB was strapping himself in. Sam saw he was still wearing his enormous coat and that his chair had some kind of keyboard strapped to it so he could start the performance.

'Can you hear me, Alice?' JB's voice was clear through the headset.

'Loud and clear,' she said and gave the thumbs up.

'Sam?'

'All clear, JB.'

'Then let's go!'

The journey began slowly in terms of perception – although Alice realised afterwards that in reality what seemed to be the slowest part of the experience – at the beginning – was actually when they were travelling the fastest. The seats moved into an upright position. The front of the platform fell away so it felt as though they were suspended in space. As she looked at the dome above and below her, stretching away as far as she could see, Alice noticed that the stars were no longer stationary but had begun to move towards her and past her. There was no sound or wind, of course, simply a sense of forward movement in the vastness of outer space. One particular star dead ahead of them burned larger and more brightly than all the others. They were entering the solar system.

The journey continued in silence for what seemed like half an hour. The sun grew larger on the horizon. 'Lower your visors now,' said JB. 'The sun will soon be too bright to look at directly. Look right.'

Sam turned his head. The coloured rings of Saturn flashed below them. The chairs banked left, as they spiralled into the solar system. In a matter of minutes the bulk of Jupiter appeared and passed beneath Alice's left shoe. A few seconds later, the chair shook and dived, navigating its way past the asteroids, and moments after that they passed the red planet, Mars, skipping round its atmosphere, ever bending inwards and conscious of the growing brightness of the sun.

A few minutes later, as it seemed, Alice caught her first glance of earth suspended in space, rushing towards them. They skimmed low over the moon's surface and were able to pick out craters, hills and plains and from there headed straight towards the earth, turning slowly on its axis. Alice gasped at the beauty of her own planet and picked out the familiar shapes of oceans and continents.

Sam jumped as somehow a great glass bubble was projected

around them and the chairs moved back into a flat position. As the craft entered earth's atmosphere the chairs lay flat and vibrated as they met resistance. The temperature increased and the bubble itself was coated in a sheath of flame.

The next moment the seats came upright again and they were flying through blue skies, through layers of cloud, descending all the time towards the earth's surface. 'Visors up!' came JB's command. As they descended, Alice could make out the coastline and the rivers, the vast desert spaces, the lakes and forests.

'Where are the towns and cities?' she asked.

'Wait a moment,' said JB. 'Remember this is not quite the normal view.'

As they came nearer to the earth's surface, the glass bubble around them retracted. They could feel the warm wind on their cheeks now and hear the gentle soundtrack of the earth without people. Alice noticed the way in which you had to listen carefully. The call of the gulls, the splash of waves on the beach, the cry of a deer.

Their journey paused over a series of low hills. Coming in, Alice had seen how their destination was a place where three great continents met: a crossroads of the world. They hovered at a height of about a hundred feet. JB pointed ahead and below. Alice saw the only signs so far of human life and habitation. A small wooden shack: a place for animals not people and, on a low hillside nearby, a wooden cross. There was nothing else.

JB pointed to the ground. 'Watch very carefully.' As they looked, something new began. A glistening, thin, deep-blue line appeared in the earth, then another, then another. They spread like a giant cobweb from the place where the cross stood and out for miles around covering the hillsides.

'Foundations,' called JB.

As the deep-blue lines spread outwards, Alice gradually began to see the shape of what looked like a great city: streets and squares, parks and gardens etched in sapphire. Sam looked back towards the centre. Clear crystals were appearing now in between the web of blue foundations, sparkling in the morning sun. Walls and houses, domes and turrets grew outwards from the centre.

Ribbons of gold formed streets in between the buildings. Towers grew and sparkled the deepest red. As they watched, the great outer walls of the city were growing now and glistened with every kind of jewel. They rose above and around the city, protecting it from harm. Within them were set twelve pairs of gates made of pearl, four on each side, facing north, south, east and west. The gates were not closed but wide open waiting to receive all who would come. There was a light over and within the whole city which was brighter and more glorious even than the rays of the sun.

The crystal city grew upwards and outwards before them through the course of a whole day. They moved around to different vantage points, now zooming in, now pulling back. Sam and Alice witnessed every part with cries of wonder and delight. JB let them take the controls and they were able to swing the joystick to the right and then to the left. Sam and Alice grew practised at swooping and diving over the city.

They saw a great river winding its way from the centre with mature trees lining its banks. They saw beautiful gardens and parks unfolding with towers and waterfalls, pleasant walks and every kind of flower and shrub. They saw spacious homes of every kind made ready and furnished: flats, mansions, terraces and squares. They saw what looked like fully stocked libraries and workshops, concert halls and galleries all prepared but standing empty. Within the city itself were vineyards and olive groves, allotments laid out and magnificent public squares. The city had grown vast in size: 'To walk across it now would be three days' journey,' said JB. 'To explore its wonders is the work of many, many lifetimes.'

There were no artificial lights in the city, no streetlamps or lights within the buildings. As evening came, Alice saw that none were needed. The city itself was lit from within in some way she could not understand. There were no shadows or dark places, no corners for wicked things to hide.

This growing of the city went on throughout the night. Once the basic features were laid out, Sam saw, more and more attention was paid to the detail: the crystal walls and towers were etched with beautiful carvings showing scenes from great battles and stories of the past. The pearl gates were inlaid with writing in many different languages. JB explained that they were words of welcome and of truth and the names of ancient tribes. Fruit ripened on the trees and in the allotments the vegetables matured to be ready for harvest. In the middle watch of the night, they flew low over the city from east to west and looked at the twelve foundation stones of its walls, which were inscribed with a different twelve names, again in many languages: 'Those who are honoured for all time,' said their guide.

And then, as the sun rose again in the east, they climbed a little higher above the earth and their ears caught the sound of singing. Alice pointed as angels in vast numbers flew from the east, out of the rising sun, and took up their positions at each of the gates and around the walls.

With the dawn, from north and south and east and west – from the whole earth JB told them later – came lines of pilgrims walking in orderly procession and singing as they came. Children and old people, helped along by those who were stronger. Husbands, wives and friends arm in arm. Groups of young people. Black and white, yellow and brown. To judge by their clothes and dress they were from every age and nation and tribe. The lines stretched back as far as the eye could see: a countless, countless host.

JB's eyes were full of tears. 'The pearl gates stand open to receive the pilgrims as they come singing to their eternal home,' he said, slowly and with great passion. He intoned words which seemed as ancient as the hills:

'No more shall there be in it an infant that lives but a few days or an old person who does not live out a lifetime. Death itself cannot come to this city. There is no war here, no hunger, pestilence or plague. Mourning and crying and pain will be no more.'

Above the sounds of the sea and the cries of the birds there rose now the song of the pilgrims as they entered the eternal city and were welcomed to their new homes. As each person passed the angels on the gates there came a moment, Alice saw, of looking and seeing: as the angel's eyes met the eyes of a child, or woman or man, all was laid bare and they were welcomed through the gates. But from time to time, she saw, one person or another was not able to enter the city. They gathered in small groups on either side of the gate, their loved ones clinging to them and begging them to come in.

'What's happening there?' Alice asked. 'Can we go down and see?'

JB adjusted the controls and they swooped low over one of the gates in the Western Wall. Alice saw now that each of those who were asked to wait outside was carrying something: a suitcase or rucksack or carrier bag.

'The people themselves are welcome,' JB said to them. 'But nothing unclean can enter the city. All falsehood and greed, uncleanness of every kind, must be left outside.'

Sam watched as a man urged and pleaded with his wife to leave a great suitcase in the small pile by the gateway and come inside with him. After some time she reluctantly set down what she was carrying, took her husband's hand and walked through the gate. They disappeared down one of the golden streets. An elderly couple were seeking to reason with a young man about Sam's age who could not be parted from a small black briefcase. In the end his mother tried to wrestle it from him and the young man ran away. Sadly, the couple let go and turned away into the city, joining their voices to the song of praise around them. Sam's eyes followed the man as he crept away beyond the city wall.

'What will happen to him and those like him?' he asked.

'There is a rubbish dump, a tip, a waste ground on the far side of the city,' JB answered. 'It is a place of filth and squalor. But it is the only place that such a man can live. There is no way back to the earth that was. And now come. Our journey is almost ended.'

Once more they ascended and flew around the walls, admiring again its majesty and greatness and the new life teeming within it. Then their view changed, so they were looking down and, as if they were flying upwards to a great height, the city itself grew smaller and smaller. Alice saw the very contours of the earth had altered so that this land was now in the centre and all roads, lined with pilgrims, led to the city.

And then their chairs tilted back into the start position, the harnesses were released, their view was, as it seemed, simply a blue sky on a summer's day, with streaks of cirrus cloud hanging low on the horizon. There, just behind them, was the shape of the mirror's misty surface.

'Thank you,' said Alice to JB. Sam squeezed the great man's hand.

JB helped them once more back through the mirror. The front room seemed small and cramped now after the vast expanses of space and the decorations seemed so dull after the beauty of the jewelled city. Only the calendar itself glowed with a new brightness. In the doorway for the sixteenth day, framed by crystal, Alice saw a gateway made of pearl, open and carved with words of truth and welcome.

17 December

After the vision of the dazzling city full of light and life and colour, Alice felt that somehow ordinary life was dull and grey and full of shadow. She could see more clearly the shabbiness of the wallpaper in her bedroom and the worn edges of the carpet. Somehow the mess and untidiness were much clearer as well. Even the breakfast cereal tasted grey.

The weather matched her mood exactly. The town was embraced by a damp fog which clung to everything. Only the calendar itself and the mirror stood out. The calendar seemed to light up the room now, to glow with life. The deep-brown frame of the mirror was vivid too against the dull patterned wallpaper in the front room.

Before she went to school, Alice made herself take another look at her reflection. She winced at what she saw, closed her eyes and then made herself open them again, peering through her fingers. According to the mirror, she was covered in filth from head to foot. The dirt was caked around her feet and ankles, up her legs and down her arms. Her clothes were nothing but filthy rags held together by a single piece of rope tied around her waist. Her hair was matted and full of dirt. Her shoes had fallen to pieces and rotted away. Her feet, she saw, were calloused and bruised.

Alice was so upset by the reflection that she went to find Sam only to remember he had left for work early that day. It was the office Christmas party. He'd not be home until very late that night

171

and they had made arrangements for Sam to phone home the code that evening if it arrived.

'Ready for school, darling?' Alice couldn't help noticing, even in the greyness of that morning, how much better her mum looked. She'd got back yesterday evening. Grandad was much better apparently and due home in the next couple of days. Andrew had been a real gentleman and Alice found herself warming to him. Megs had decided to invite the grandparents for Christmas Day instead of everyone going there and was now making grand plans for the dinner.

Suzie and Alex were full of the plans to disrupt biology. It was their very last chance before Christmas: school was due to finish the next day. Alice had forgotten all about the plot over the weekend: so much had happened at home. Alex proudly showed her the two corks he had made and the wire frames to hold them in place. 'They exactly fit the fire hose,' he said. 'Took me ages to carve them. This one's a spare.'

'I can't wait to see her face,' said Suzie. 'This is the moment.'

Alice had always had her doubts about the scheme and today they seemed bigger than ever. But the whole class was now in on the secret. For the first time that term, she and Suzie and Alex were accepted and part of the whole group. And she did absolutely hate the Newtron and so did the rest of the class. Maybe it would teach her a lesson.

English, French and Maths went very slowly but the class were on their best behaviour. After lunch, Alice and Suzie kept watch in the corridor as Alex crept into the biology lab and to the fire hose at the front of the room. He unhooked the hose, carefully pressed the cork into the end and fixed it securely in place with the wire frame. There was no sign of any teacher. Alice had discovered that there was some kind of drinks party in the staff room. The biggest challenge was keeping members of their own class out of the way.

Alex came out to report progress. 'So far, so good,' he said. 'Now comes the really tricky part. I'm going to turn on the hose. Stand by to scarper.'

Alice started to say something but he was gone. She went back to her post and scanned the corridor. Alex positioned the end of the hose very carefully so that it was pointing at Miss Newton's desk. Very gingerly he turned the wheel to release the water. He felt the pressure hose fill up and held his breath but the cork stayed in place.

'Yes!' he whispered, punching the air, and walked back out into the corridor, keeping his eyes on the hose the whole time.

'All set,' he said. 'All I need to do now is release the wire at the start of the lesson.'

'How are you going to do that?' Alice asked, hoping the whole plan would fail.

'I'll hide in the store cupboard when she comes in,' Alex said. 'I can just reach it from there if I creep out behind the blackboard. You'll have to distract her at the right moment until I'm back at my desk.'

Alice and Suzie chose desks in the back corner of the room. Suzie had smuggled in her mobile phone and was hoping to get some pictures or even a video. Alex saved a desk right at the front, nearest to the stock cupboard. For once, the whole class was there early, silent and attentive when Miss Newton came in.

Alice saw at once that she was not her normal self. 'Open your books please at the section on photosynthesis. We need to go back over some of the material we looked at in the last lesson but two. I've now marked the assignments and it is clear that some of you haven't grasped the basic principles.'

Suzie had put up her hand. 'Please, miss, Alice Carroll just kicked me under the desk.'

Over the Newtron's shoulder, Alice saw Alex creeping out, stretching his hand towards the wired cork.

'Please, miss, she kicked me first,' Alice protested.

'Quiet, please,' said Miss Newton, her eyes flashing with something like her customary fire. Suzie and Alice saw that Alex was now safely back in his seat. Then the teacher kind of deflated once again. 'The Head will be joining us in a few moments' time. He has a special announcement. Until then, please sit and read quietly.'

The knot in Alice's stomach tightened further and she and

Suzie exchanged glances and tried to catch Alex's eye. It was too late. The trap was set. A minute went by. The tension mounted. The whole class were watching, waiting, half of them silently hoping that nothing would happen and half of them hoping it would.

And happen it did. All at once. The pressure was building in the pipe. The Head came through the door at exactly the wrong moment. With a loud 'pop' like a champagne bottle opening, the cork shot from the pipe followed by a jet of cold water. Alice watched the cork fly through the air and land squarely on the stunned head teacher's forehead. The jet of water narrowly missed Miss Newton but soaked the first two rows before the end of the hose broke loose and pointed itself at the ceiling, spraying the entire lab in a fine drizzle. The whole class screamed and laughed and shouted to each other. Suzie calmly filmed the whole thing for her video diary. Some of the bolder members of the class danced on the desks in the drizzle coming from the hosepipe. Someone else switched on a ghetto blaster. Others ran out into the corridor.

A moment later, the automatic censor set the school fire alarms off and the whole school had to be evacuated. Teachers and pupils filled the corridors. Three fire engines arrived and the fire crews poured into the building. It didn't take the fire officers long to discover the cork and the wire and realise what had happened. The whole class knew who the culprits were and it was only a matter of time before Alex, Suzie and Alice were identified.

And so Alice found herself at the end of the afternoon with Alex and Suzie sitting in silence in an empty classroom, guarded by Miss Newton, the Head (who had a small lump on his fore-head) and a very large fireman, waiting for their parents. Suzie's dad and Alex's mum were already there when Megs arrived. Alice felt very small indeed.

The head teacher, normally a calm and rational man, had turned a bright shade of purple. The anger and embarrassment were swelling up within him, Alice thought, rather like – well, rather like a fire hose blocked with a champagne cork.

'In over twenty years of teaching,' he began, 'in over twenty years of teaching I have never, ever seen a school descend into chaos as rapidly as this. The behaviour of these students today has been absolutely disgraceful.'

To everyone's great surprise, Miss Newton had been looking extremely uncomfortable as if there was a struggle going on inside and now she interrupted.

'Head teacher, Mr Clarkson, before we say anything to the young people, I would like to make a short statement in their defence.'

Suzie, Alex and Alice looked at each other in amazement.

Miss Newton's face was as sour as ever but her tone of voice was less strident. 'I think it is only fair to say,' she said, 'that I have not been the best of teachers over this last term and that the class may have been provoked. As I've now explained to the head teacher (and he was about to explain to the class) I have been under severe stress looking after my elderly parents. I recognise that this has made me very short tempered, much more so than I should have been. Whilst there can be no final excuse for the kind of prank we saw today' (her eyes flashed with their normal fire at this point), 'there is, I think, a mitigating circumstance. I therefore ask, head teacher, that these pupils be given a second chance.'

The Head looked as surprised as the three pupils but her confession had taken the force from his temper and he was back in control. He thanked Miss Newton and spoke to the three culprits. 'Normally, I would have no choice but to exclude you from school for this kind of offence,' he said. 'However, I do accept what Miss Newton has said. I also believe that all three of you are fundamentally decent young people. Provided you apologise to Mr Clarkson and Miss Newton, your punishment will be six detentions to be served on Monday evenings next term. Let it never happen again!'

Alice, Suzie and Alex mumbled their apologies and thanked Miss Newton. Megs, Alice saw, was wiping her eyes and biting her bottom lip.

'I suggest you go home for the rest of the day now and return for the last day of term tomorrow.'

Megs and Alice walked to the car without speaking. Megs had parked a little way away from the school. As soon as they were inside the car, Alice burst into tears. 'Mum, I'm so sorry. I should never have got involved. It's been a kind of game all term planning something like this. Suddenly they were serious about it and I couldn't get out of it. I am so sorry.'

Megs gave her a big hug. 'It's OK, Alice. It's OK. You've learned your lesson, I think, haven't you?'

Alice nodded through her tears.

'Let's go home. I need to drop this old linen tablecloth into the dry-cleaner's on the way home for Christmas Day. Someone popped a card through the door for a new while-you-wait cleaning service just this morning. It's ever so reasonable.'

They parked near the shopping mall, busy as ever. To Alice's surprise, the new dry-cleaner's was exactly where the Christmas Preparation Shop had been two days before. There was a new sign above the door. 'Mum,' she started to say, 'this isn't … '

'This is the one,' Megs said and stepped inside.

The shop looked very different. There was a low counter now running along the front, just like any dry-cleaner's really, and a curtain leading to the back of the shop.

A smartly dressed man in a bowler hat came from behind the curtain as the door closed behind them.

'Mr Gabriel,' he said, lifting his cap and winking at Alice, ever so briefly. 'How can I help, ma'am?'

'It's this tablecloth,' Megs said. 'It's very old and I haven't used it in years. I wondered if you could get it clean for Christmas?'

'Let me see,' said Mr Gabriel. He took the cloth out of the bag and spread it out on the table top.

'I know it's very stained,' said Megs.

Alice saw that the cloth was made of very fine linen but it was rather discoloured with age. As Megs spread it out for Mr Gabriel to see she saw different coloured stains all over it. There was a particularly large red wine stain in one corner.

'New Year's Eve five years ago,' said Megs, pointing at the stain. 'My husband wanted to throw it away after that but it's been in the family for a long time. Can you do anything?'

'I think so, madam,' said Mr Gabriel. 'Come this way.' He lifted up the counter and held it open for Megs who went through. Alice was about to protest but he held his finger to his lips and winked again. The room at the back of the shop was a laundry containing an enormous chrome washing machine.

'My assistant, ma'am,' said Mr Gabriel. Alice smiled as the large, familiar figure turned towards them. He took the tablecloth, examined it carefully and placed it inside the large silver machine.

'Have a seat, ma'am,' said Mr Gabriel. 'This will only take a few minutes. A cup of tea?'

'No, thank you,' said Megs. 'This is a new kind of laundry.'

'Unique, ma'am, I think you will find. A very special service, is it not, JB?'

Alice watched as the old cloth spun round inside the machine and went through the wash and spin routine. The cycle seemed very rapid. In a matter of ten minutes, it seemed, JB was removing it from the drum almost dry. Without speaking, he took it into the corner and pressed it with an enormous steam iron.

'Is that to madam's satisfaction?' said Mr Gabriel proudly, as JB held up the cloth.

'Amazing,' said Megs, feeling the edge of the linen. 'It's like new. Better than new!'

'Thank you, madam,' said Mr Gabriel, tipping his hat and showing them back through the curtain. 'And of course it's free of charge. Introductory offer.' JB followed with the linen cloth carefully wrapped in brown paper and tied with string. 'Do call again if you need us.'

'Amazing,' said Megs as they drove home. 'Never seen anything like it.'

The phone was ringing when they came through the front door. Alice picked it up. 'Code's arrived,' said Sam. 'Got a pen?'

'But Sam ... ' said Alice.

'Can't talk now,' said Sam. 'Party.' Alice could hear the music and voices in the background. Sam sounded a bit the worse for wear already. 'Write this down and repeat it. One. Colon. One. Eight.'

'One. Colon. One. Eight,' said Alice. 'But Sam ... '

'Can't stop. Shee you later.' He hung up. Alice shrugged her shoulders and went into the front room. The new door in the calendar was strange and round and made of glass. 'If I didn't know better,' Alice thought, 'I would say it was the door of a washing machine.' As she looked closely, she almost thought she saw water swooshing round inside as if it was halfway through a programme. Nothing else happened. There was no sign of the door opening. The mirror's surface was sharp and solid, her reflection still the same awful picture she saw each morning.

'Teatime,' Megs called.

Sam was having an excellent time at the office party. The firm had been very stingy this year and, instead of going out, they were just having a few drinks in the building after work. But Tizzy had done a brilliant job with the food and decorations on a limited budget and different people had brought in extra booze. Some of the desks had been cleared away to make a space for dancing and one of the receptionists was acting as DJ with her portable music player wired up to a huge set of speakers. Wild dancing alternated with karaoke but now the music was slowing down. Even Richard seemed to be enjoying himself and relaxing just a bit. Sam had already entertained the entire company with his impersonations of Elvis, Meatloaf and his annual rendition of Slade.

He and Tizzy had been together most of the evening and Tizzy had made a particularly brave if drunken job of Gloria Gaynor's 'I Will Survive'. She looked absolutely stunning in what she was wearing.

As the party moved out of its most raucous phase someone turned out more of the lights and the music slowed down to George Michael's 'Careless Whisper'. 'Dance with me, Sam,' Tizzy called, pulling him close. Other couples were pairing up across the floor and some people were beginning to slip away. Sam waved to Germaine who had his coat on and was leaving. 'Happy Christmas!' he mouthed. Germaine mouthed something back and wagged his finger in warning, pointing to his wedding ring. Sam thought it might have been 'Josie' but he couldn't be sure.

Tizzy's arms were tight around his waist now and Sam noticed she was steering him gradually away from the dance floor and towards the stockroom. She reached up and whispered in his ear as they came closer. 'Let's go and count the envelopes. Like last year.'

No one was watching. They opened the stockroom door and slipped inside. The lights were on and they both closed their eyes against the sudden brightness. Sam felt Tizzy's head against his chest and was reaching out his hand to flick off the lights when, from the back of the room, there was a deep cough.

'Ahem.'

Sam and Tizzy sprang apart. Sitting on a pile of boxes against the back wall and watching them, was a large figure with a bushy beard in a massive coat.

'Aren't you going to introduce me, Sam?' asked JB, sadly, looking down.

Sam went very red and was sober in an instant.

'Tizzy, this is a friend of mine, JB. JB, this is my – er – colleague. Elizabeth Green.'

JB stepped forward and took Tizzy's hand. 'Good to meet you, child,' he said. 'Happy Christmas.'

'Happy Christmas,' said Tizzy, her cheeks burning. 'Sam, I'll – er – just go and check on the party. See you later.'

Sam nodded. He and JB stood facing each other in the empty stockroom. Sam could not meet the great man's eyes at first, dreading what he would find there. JB said nothing. When Sam finally met his gaze he found a strange blend of compassion and questioning.

'I'm sorry, JB,' said Sam, in the end.

'Then you must change,' said JB. 'Life is not a game. Some of the choices we make last for ever. Sam, your commitment to Josie and to your child is for life now. That means turning your back on certain things. Tizzy has to find her own way.'

'I know. But she needs a friend right now.'

'She does indeed,' said JB with a hint of anger. 'I think she needs a friend who will care for her not exploit her weakness.'

Sam was silent for a moment.

'You're right, of course,' said Sam. 'What can I say?'

'Like everyone else, Sam, you have turned Christmas into nothing but a season of eating and drinking and carousing into the night. Have you not seen yet it is also the time of new beginnings?'

He put his arm round Sam's shoulder as they moved to the door. 'Go home, Sam. Go home to Josie and to Alice. Start again.'

JB's final words echoed in Sam's mind as he said goodbye to Tizzy and the others. As he and Tizzy hugged he whispered, 'Sorry. Still friends.'

'I know,' she said. 'Still mates.'

JB's words echoed in his mind as he travelled home on the train, as he walked through the empty streets still wrapped in fog, as he opened the front door. Josie, Megs and Alice were having cocoa in the front room. Josie got up and gave him a big hug.

'Home early,' she said. 'Missed you.'

Sam wiped a tear away and blew his nose. Megs went to make more cocoa. Alice took him by the hand and led him to the calendar.

The strange door that looked like a porthole stood open now. 'Start again' came the echo in his mind. Inside the door stood a table spread with the whitest linen cloth Sam had ever seen. No marks, no spots, no blemishes. Start again.

18 December

Sam slept badly and woke early. His mind was in turmoil now about all that had been happening. He took a long look at himself in the bathroom mirror and realised that he did not really like what he saw. He put on his work clothes, came downstairs and for the first time took a very long look at himself in the new mirror in the front room.

He could hardly bear the sight reflected back to him and screwed up his eyes. He made himself remember Josie and JB and what had almost happened last night and forced first one eye open and then another.

He hardly recognised the creature staring back. His skin was caked in mud and slime. His hair was matted, dank, twisted into knots. His clothes were filthy, shredded rags hanging from his limbs. His shoes were split and the soles worn through. He was a much thinner version of Sam with sunken eyes and cheeks. His flesh was covered in wounds and sores. The creature cowered inside the mirror. The eyes which stared back into Sam's were burdened and afraid.

Sam sunk down and perched on the edge of the armchair, eyes still fixed on his reflection. 'Is this what I've become?' Sam whispered to himself. 'Shallow, pointless, scared? "Start again" was what he said to me. But how?'

Just then, Sam thought he heard someone call his name, from faraway. It sounded like JB's voice but he couldn't be sure. He reached out to touch the mirror, then pulled his fingers back. His hands had met those of his reflection. They were worn and calloused and cold.

Head bowed, Sam turned away. Time for work. At least it was a half day.

When Sam arrived at the office, it was half empty as he expected. Those who were there were simply going through the motions. He was relieved to see that Tizzy had stayed at home. There was a faint smell of alcohol and crisps in the normally sterile corridor.

Richard came by and made a sarcastic comment about not expecting to see Sam at work that day but otherwise he was left undisturbed. All that morning, his mind tangled with the problem caused by JB's advice: 'Start again.' But how? He was the person he had become through years of choices or not making choices. Again he caught the echo of a voice calling his name from very faraway: 'Sam!'

He was meeting Josie for lunch and Christmas shopping. At least here he could make a beginning. Although he and Josie got on well, he knew there were so many things he wasn't saying. They ordered soup and a sandwich.

'Josie, can I say something?'

'Sure. What is it?' Sam thought he saw a shadow of fear flash across her face. He took her hand.

'I just want to say that I'm not very proud of the way I've been and the way I am. That's a bit of an understatement really.' Sam's mind was full of his reflection in the mirror. 'I'm not sure I can, but I want to do better. For you. For the baby. For me.'

'Sam!' came the voice calling from faraway. Sam turned his head towards the door.

'What is it?' asked Josie.

'Nothing,' said Sam, turning back. 'I just wanted to say that. I want to be a better person. If I can.'

'So do I,' said Josie, taking his other hand. 'I really want this to work, Sam. You and me.'

'You and me,' said Sam, his mind still full of his reflection.

Unlike Sam, Alice slept in that morning, clattered down the stairs at the last minute and was whisked away to school. The whole morning was acutely embarrassing. Alex had managed to bunk off for the day so she and Suzie had to face the music on their own.

The Head came to see the whole class in the first lesson with Miss Newton. He explained to them the stress the biology teacher had been under for the whole of the term and that she would be taking compassionate leave for the next few months. They were to have a supply teacher in the new year. Suzie's and Alice's cheeks burned red. He then talked at great length about health and safety and responsible behaviour and wasting the time of the fire services who could have been needed in a real emergency. Alice and Suzie felt extremely small. He then singled them out, talked about when pranks go too far and about how they deserved to be excluded from school but Miss Newton had intervened, and gave strict instructions that the class were not to emulate their behaviour. Alice and Suzie wished the classroom floor would open up and swallow them in green smoke. 'Where is Col when you need him?' Alice thought grimly.

Whatever the Head said to their own class, to the rest of the school they were some kind of heroes. People came up to them in the corridors and at break time and clapped them on the shoulders. Alice would have done a great deal not to be famous in that kind of way. From time to time during the morning she thought she heard someone calling her name from very faraway, across the other side of the playground but whenever she looked there was no one there.

School ended just after lunch with an assembly in the big hall. Once again, the Head told the story of yesterday, emphasised what a serious, stupid prank it had been and read out the names of those responsible. All but the worst behaved kids in the school now knew that they had gone too far and Alice knew that they knew. The incident would live on and grow in the school's memory and her name would be linked with it for ever.

Normally breaking up for Christmas was one of the best days of the entire year but Alice left the yard with Suzie in silence, shoulders drooping. They hugged as they said goodbye for the holidays. The only good thing to come out of the whole incident was cementing their friendship. Each knew she would have an ally in getting through the next term.

Again, as she left school, Alice thought she heard her name being called: 'Alice!' It was the kind of voice that makes you want to see the person, but whenever she turned round, there was no one there.

Alice arrived home to an empty house. She ran straight upstairs to change out of her uniform and came back downstairs to the front room. The calendar lifted her spirits as it always did and she spent a few moments tracing the different images and adventures of the last week. Today was the sixth day, she realised. Today they should face some kind of test and say goodbye to JB. The way she was feeling, this just might be the last time they entered the world of the calendar.

Reluctantly, Alice turned and looked into the mirror. She saw what Sam had seen before her, though she was not aware of it. A sad, frightened creature stared back at her from the mirror's surface, clothed in rags, caked in dirt and covered in the most horrible sores. 'No more than the truth,' she thought and even as she thought it, she heard her name called again, from somewhere deep within the mirror: 'Alice!'

She heard keys turning in the front door. 'In here, Mum,' she called, biting her lip. But it was Sam.

'Home early,' he said. 'Half day. How was school?'

Alice just looked at him.

'They might have forgotten, you know, after Christmas.'

Alice looked at the floor and sighed. 'Message!' said Sam's phone.

Both of them brightened up at the thought of whatever awaited them in the calendar. Sam dashed upstairs to change into jeans and trainers. Alice inspected the new door. It was framed in tiny coloured and glazed tiles. The door itself was blue and made of wood.

'Alice!' came the call again. Sam came back into the room and read the code. 'Five. Three. Colon. Five.'

They turned round. 'The mirror,' Sam said. 'The surface has changed. Ready?'

'Let's go,' said Alice. 'Remember it's a test. Don't mess up. I want to make it through till Christmas Eve.'

Sam climbed through first, Alice followed.

They found themselves standing on a simple pathway, leading away from the mirror, flanked on each side by a grove of the most ancient olive trees. From the branches on the ground, they recognised the wood of the mirror's frame and of the calendar itself. It felt like evening or perhaps early morning: just enough light to see by but not very clearly.

Alice turned to look at Sam and flinched. Sam looked at Alice and did the same. Then they both looked down and realised what had happened.

Each had become the creature in the mirror, their own reflection: covered in layers of dirt, clothed in filthy rags, with broken, worn shoes, covered in sores, weak and thin and frightened.

'Is this what you looked like in the mirror?' said Sam.

Alice nodded, still looking down.

'Me too,' said Sam, ashamed.

'I want to go back,' said Alice, turning back towards the mirror.

'Alice!' 'Sam!' came the voice from faraway, back down the pathway.

'Sam, I can't stand being like this. I want to go back.'

They both turned back towards the mirror. To Alice's surprise, it had become solid again: there was no way through. She peered into the frame, expecting to see only her own reflection.

Instead she saw the front room and the person she had left behind looking back and walking away from the mirror. She saw the room change and this same person growing older and, she thought, harder. The pictures in the mirror flashed before her: fierce quarrels with Megs and her father, even with Sam; her dress becoming weirder; smoking and drugs; becoming sloppy with her homework; sneering at her friends; left alone.

The mirror once again turned misty.

'Alice!' 'Sam!' called the voice.

She turned back to Sam and flinched as she saw the creature in front of her and knew she looked the same.

'What did you see?'

'I saw myself turning my back on the mirror. I saw snapshots of the coming years. Josie and I got married but it didn't work out. We had a son. I couldn't cope with what was happening. I played around, lost my job, everything fell to pieces. You?'

'Same kind of thing. What do we do?'

Sam was quiet for a moment, reaching within.

'I think this is the test,' said Sam. 'The test this time is not to turn back. We need to go forwards.'

'I'm not sure I can,' said Alice. 'I'm not sure I can be like this.'

'I have to go on, Alice,' said Sam. 'I can't stop this now.'

Alice reached out her fingers and touched the surface of the mirror. It would be so easy to turn around, to step back through, for the adventure to stop, to go back to the way she was. She couldn't stand the rawness of the way she looked on this side of the mirror. For a moment her whole story was poised, balanced on a knife edge.

'Alice,' came the call again.

Alice closed her eyes, took a deep breath and made her choice.

'OK,' she said to Sam. 'This is the hardest thing I've ever done. And I couldn't do it on my own. But it's the right decision. Let's go.'

Alice and Sam turned and walked down the path, through the olive grove and away from the mirror. Progress was slow. It was painful to walk on bruised and blistered feet. They were cold and hungry in the twilight of early morning though it was growing just a little lighter. The voice called them forward. From time to time it would call out 'Alice!' or 'Sam!' as if it was longing for them to come.

'Is it JB?' said Alice.

'I thought it was at first,' said Sam. 'I've been hearing it all day. But now I don't think so.'

The trees on either side of the path thinned out as it led up towards a low hill. In the distance was a town. The path wound around the side of the hill. The call seemed to come from the far side.

They came slowly and painfully round a sharp bend and stopped in their tracks. Both Alice and Sam had seen pictures, of course, but nothing had prepared them for this.

A man of Sam's age, perhaps a little older though it was hard to tell, was stretched out on a cross on the hillside above them.

Like them, he was covered in dirt. Like them, he was clothed in rags. Like them, his body was covered with bruises, sores and wounds. He was suffering and close to death.

They knew now that he was the source of the voice which called them. As they watched, he lifted himself up on the cross, at great cost, and called again, this time in relief that they had come: 'Alice!' 'Sam!'

They stood in silence for a little while, taking in the awful sight. Then both of them knelt in silence.

'Why?' said Alice, aloud. 'No one has ever told me. Why?'

'So there could be a new beginning,' said a woman's voice behind her. 'So that we can start again.'

Sam and Alice turned to see a woman wearing a blue cloak standing behind them, gazing at the figure on the cross. Her shawl was drawn across her face.

'Who are you?' asked Alice.

'That is for another day,' said the woman, with immense gentleness. 'There is more to this story yet. Now that you have seen and understood, follow the path to the river. It is not far.'

They looked once more at the figure suffering on the cross and then turned, slowly and painfully, away from the scene. The path led downwards now, bending through the trees. Alice ached all over from the sores. She felt cold and hungry, sorry and ashamed. Only the voice calling her name sustained her on this final part of the journey.

A little way on and the trees began to clear again. An enormous crowd of people lined the near bank of a wide river. All were turned towards them. As they appeared, a loud cry and cheer went up. Sam and Alice looked into the faces of the crowd. They were strangers yet they seemed familiar. Everyone seemed to know them. Each one called out in encouragement.

As they drew nearer to the river the crowd parted and created a pathway to the bank. Sam saw that the river itself was deep and wide with a strong current.

Five metres out from the bank, bracing himself against the flow, stood the familiar figure of JB holding out his arms in welcome. His massive coat, for once, was lying on the bank. Both Alice and Sam shrank back, conscious of how they must appear to this huge crowd but the applause and encouragement drew them on.

Down they went to the water's edge. JB waded towards them and gave them each a mighty hand to hold. 'Are you ready?' he said. 'A new start?'

Alice and Sam nodded and JB led them out into deeper water.

'You must be washed,' he said. 'The old life must die.'

Again they nodded.

There was nothing dignified in what happened next. JB seized both of them by the rags which were around their shoulders and plunged them down into the river's flow. Alice and Sam had time only to take a deep breath and hold it. The water was icy cold. The current flowed past them and through them. For Alice there was a sense of everything being stripped away, of simply trusting the hand which held her. For Sam, it seemed the waters flowed inside as well as around him, into every place, washing and cleansing and carrying away the dirt and grime of years. For both, there was an incredible sense of strength flowing into them and through them.

When it seemed to Alice she could hold her breath no longer and would burst, JB pulled them up. There was a mighty roar from the crowd on the bank as they began to walk to the shore. Alice looked at Sam first and then herself. The old, filthy and wounded creature was gone. Instead, Sam was shining from head to foot – but still his old self. She looked down at her body, still clothed in the old rags. Each wound, each bruise, each sore on her flesh was gone. She was made new.

JB waded back to the shore with them.

Women greeted Alice and pulled her out of the water. Men met Sam in the same way. They took them each to one side, gave them warm towels to dry their bodies and stripped off the remains of the rags which had been their only clothing. There were combs for their hair and sweetly smelling oils. In place of the old rags, they were given fine, new, white robes, sandals for their feet and a ring for their finger. Each white robe had a bright red sash. Best of all (Alice thought), there was a mirror. She rubbed her eyes as she saw her likeness restored, sparkling and new on the inside as well as the outside.

When they had changed, they were led away again to a great tent where a feast had been prepared. Sam and Alice were seated at the very highest table, on either side of JB. The table was spread with the most delicious food. The feasting went on through the whole day. As they ate together, first one then another in the crowd would come and welcome Alice or Sam silently: they did not often speak (other than their names). They simply smiled, touched their hands or shoulders in welcome and turned away.

As the meal ended, JB turned to them both. 'This feast has been in your honour but now we must go. Walk this way.'

He pointed back along the clearing. They followed him, the journey much easier now. Both Alice and Sam held back as they came to the hill, but the cross stood empty now, alone and defeated on the skyline. Even so, the three companions stood for a moment in silence, heads bowed. They came in due course to the olive grove and to the mirror suspended a little way above the darkened pathway between the trees.

'A new beginning,' said JB. 'Use it well, my children. It was marked by the water but won at incredible cost. And go well. From tomorrow, you will have a new guide, the greatest of all.'

'Thank you, JB,' said Sam. 'Thank you for everything.'

Alice hugged him for a final time. Together they stepped through the misty surface of the mirror and into the front room. As they did so, the white robes disappeared to be replaced by their ordinary clothes.

Sam and Alice stood side by side, facing away from the mirror and afraid to turn around. Without speaking, together, they once more faced their reflections. The old, emaciated creatures were gone. Instead, each saw their reflection as they had been a few minutes ago, face and hair shining, dressed in new white robes.

Alice smiled and led Sam over to the calendar. The blue door was gone now. In the middle of the doorway stood an ancient stone bowl. In the bowl water sparkled and glistened with life. Lying next to the bowl, side by side, each with a red sash, were two white robes, shining and new.

19 December

Alice slept in, of course, the next day – the first of the holidays. She was woken by the phone around ten and stumbled downstairs in her night things, not quite awake.

'Hello.'

'Alice, it's Josie. I'm trying to contact Sam. He's not answering his mobile.'

'You OK?' Josie sounded frightened.

'Not feeling too good. I just need to get hold of Sam.' There was a retching sound at the end of the line.

'Hold on,' said Alice, and bounded back upstairs. She checked Sam's room. Devastation everywhere. No sign of him but the mobile was on the bedside table. Alice picked her way between the dirty socks and worse to retrieve it. A whole line of missed calls showed on the screen. She ran back down to the hall.

'He's left his mobile at home, Josie. I think he must have slept in. Try his work number.'

'I've lost it. I just have his mobile and your number there in my phone. Can you see if you can get hold of him, Alice? I need to get to the doctor's. Ask him to ring me.'

Josie sounded worried and in pain now. Alice took Sam's mobile through into the living room and flicked through the address book. There was no work number listed but there was a mobile number for Tizzy. Alice knew Sam worked with her. She pressed 'dial'.

191

'Hi, Sam. What's up?' The person at the other end sounded as if she had just woken up.

'Tizzy. It's Alice, Sam's niece. He's left his mobile at home and we need to get hold of him. Can you give me his work number?'

Alice held her pen ready as Tizzy told her the number. She rang Josie straight back but it was engaged, so she rang Sam herself from the home phone.

'Sam? It's Alice. Listen, this is important. Josie has been trying to reach you but you left your mobile at home.'

'Shivering sea lions!'

'It's serious. I don't think she's very well, Sam. She sounded as though she was throwing up.'

Sam's mobile ring tone sounded again in her left hand. It was Josie.

'Alice, did you get through to Sam?'

'He's on the other line.'

'What's happening, Alice?' called Sam in her left ear.

'Shut up, Sam, I'm trying to listen to Josie. What's the matter?'

Josie was breathless on the phone. Her voice was pitched higher than normal.

'There's something wrong. Stomach cramps and I've been throwing up all morning. I've rung the doctor and they want me to go straight to the hospital. Tell Sam – ooooohh, that's a bad one – tell Sam to meet me there in the maternity wing at Chase Farm. I'm going to take a taxi. Tell him to be quick.'

Alice repeated the message into the other phone. Sam sounded unusually serious.

'Tell her I'm on my way, Alice. I'll go straight to the hospital. And Alice ... '

'Yes?'

'Tell Josie I love her very much.'

Alice raised her eyes to heaven and blushed. She repeated the whole of Sam's message but there was no reply. She pressed redial but the number was engaged. Josie must be calling for the taxi. She picked up the home phone again but Sam had hung up as well.

'Charming,' said Alice, standing in the hall in her pyjamas. 'Absolutely charming.'

⧖

Sam had his scarf and jacket on and was in the lift before you could say 'Josephine'. In fact, that's all he did say to Germaine as he charged past. There were only a handful of people at work in any case on the morning after the morning after the party. People were taking sickies or holiday in preparation for Christmas. Even Richard hadn't surfaced. He sprinted to the tube, jumped onto the train as the doors closed and arrived at Liverpool Street just in time for the 10.36. Through the whole journey he sat on the edge of his seat and thought of nothing except Josie and what was happening, fearing the worst.

As the train drew into Gordon Hill, he leapt from the carriage as the doors opened and covered the journey to the hospital (mainly uphill) in ten minutes. Red faced, breathless and with a stitch in his left side, he burst through the double doors into the maternity unit.

'Josie Liddell?' he gasped at the nearest receptionist.

'And who are you, sir?' asked the woman, as if there was all the time in the world.

'Boyfriend. Fiancé. Father of the – you know ... '

The receptionist looked at her screen. 'She's in radiography now. You should just make it. Down the corridor turn left, second door on the right.' Sam raced off. 'No running,' shouted the receptionist as he burst through the double doors and sent trolleys scattering right and left.

'Turn left, second door on right.'

Sam crossed the corridor and opened the second door only to find himself confronted by a woman he had never seen before in labour, screaming at the top of her voice surrounded by midwives and birthing partners. One of them had a digital video camera and was filming the entire event. She turned the lens round to face Sam.

'Who are you?' she yelled above the noise.

'Radiography?' asked Sam, looking desperate.

The midwife looked as though she was about to hit him with a bedpan. 'Back down the corridor. You turned right instead of left.'

'AAAAAAAHHHHHRG ... ' screamed the woman in labour looking straight at Sam.

'Push, darling,' urged the birthing partners.

Sam turned white. He fled back to the crossroads, took time to read the signs and fell into the radiography suite.

'Sam Brown,' he gasped. 'Josie Liddell?'

'Sam, in here,' came Josie's voice. 'You're just in time.'

Sam went into the radiography room and took in the scene. Josie was lying on her side, facing towards him. Her face lit up as Sam came into the room and she put out her hand. Sam took it. A woman in a white coat was squeezing something from a tube over Josie's stomach. A stern-faced middle-aged woman was standing in the corner of the room in her coat and hat.

'Great! You made it!' said Josie. 'You remember my mum?'

Sam shook hands. 'Great to see you again,' he panted, still badly out of breath. The woman nodded, opened her mouth as if to say something and then shut it again. Her eyes flashed rather dangerously. Sam vaguely remembered Josie saying she was a Presbyterian or something and hardly ever smiled.

He took Josie's hand again and collapsed onto a stool.

'What's happening?'

'I woke up this morning throwing up.' Josie wiped her eyes with the back of her hand. 'I had these really awful stomach cramps. I just felt so frightened, Sam.'

'I'll wait outside,' said Mrs Liddell, disapprovingly.

The radiographer took control. 'The midwife doesn't think there is anything the matter but thought it best to have a scan, even though your wife is at an early stage.'

'Oh! I'm not ...' Josie began.

'Not yet anyway,' said Sam, squeezing her hand.

'Let's see what's happening,' said the woman, who introduced herself as Mim, short for Miriam. She smiled and pressed the sensor to Josie's stomach.

Neither Sam nor Josie had a clue what to look for but watched the screen for something that looked like a baby. Mim said nothing for a while, moving the picture around, scanning the whole area very carefully.

'Is everything OK?' asked Sam, anxiously.

'I think so,' said Mim. 'Both of the babies seem absolutely fine.'

Josie and Sam looked at each other and then at the screen, lost for words.

'Both of the babies?' they said together.

Mim nodded. 'You're having twins. Congratulations!'

It was after lunch by the time Sam left the hospital with Josie. They dropped her mum off on the way home.

Josie explained to Sam that she hadn't actually told her mum she was pregnant yet. She'd been waiting for the right moment. Also, they had only just decided they were going to stay together. The visit to the maternity hospital had come as a bit of a shock. That would explain, Sam thought, what happened when Josie announced that she was expecting twins. Mrs Liddell clutched her handbag tighter and opened and closed her mouth without actually saying anything. She looked rather like a goldfish (except for the hat and winter coat).

Alice spent the first half of the day worrying until Sam phoned through on Josie's mobile to say everything was all right. She spent the afternoon half-heartedly looking for her Christmas presents (normally a favourite pastime in the holidays) but with no success.

Megs arrived home at three and had just made a pot of tea when Josie and Sam arrived. She hugged them both and brought them into the kitchen. Josie sat quietly. She looked, Alice thought, remarkable pale but very happy.

Sam had brought cream cakes: two huge éclairs, a French horn and a vanilla slice. Alice chose an éclair.

'Celebration,' Sam explained. 'Big announcement. Josie is expecting twins. Ta-da!'

'Twins!' said Megs. 'Fantastic. No wonder you've been so rough.' Everyone stood up and hugged. 'Boys or girls?'

Josie blew her nose but she was still smiling. 'It's too early,' she said. 'We can go back in four or five weeks and have another scan. They gave us the pictures.'

Alice peered at the fuzzy black and white pictures from the scan. Josie and Sam pointed out the two tiny shapes that were living, growing human beings. 'Wow!' was all she could say. 'Amazing.'

Megs asked Josie to stay to tea but she thought she ought to get home. 'Mum's still in shock,' she said. 'I want to be there to tell Dad myself when he gets home.'

Megs announced that she was going out to dinner with Andrew. 'Do you two mind if Sam stays here tonight with Alice? He's booked a table and everything.'

Josie and Sam didn't mind a bit. Alice thought Sam looked quite relieved.

'Sam can come round and meet Mum and Dad properly later in the week – when they've – erm – got used to things,' she giggled.

Sam took Josie home around six. Andrew called for Megs at seven. It was half past seven before Alice realised that she hadn't even thought about the calendar once that day.

'I'll see if there's a text,' said Sam. He picked up the phone from the table in the hall where Alice had left it and came back into the front room. 'Here it is. Arrived about twenty minutes ago.'

'Perfect timing as ever,' said Alice going over to the calendar. 'There's a new door here, Sam. A wooden house-door with a stone lintel. Numbers?'

'Nine, colon, six,' said Sam slowly. Alice pressed in the buttons. Both of them looked over towards the mirror, expecting to see the misty surface once again.

Alice touched it with her fingers. The surface was hard and cold. All she saw now was her normal reflection.

Sam looked carefully at the calendar. 'The door's started to open just a little. But nothing else is happening.'

Out in the street there was the distant roar of motorbikes heading towards them. 'What on earth?' said Sam.

Alice went to the window. 'Come and look,' she said. Three

massive motorcycles were heading down the dark street, head-lamps like searchlights. The one in front was a bright yellow three-wheeler. The two behind were silver and gold. The riders were dressed from head to foot in black leathers. As Sam and Alice watched, the bikes stopped right outside their house. The riders revved their engines, daring the neighbours to challenge them. There was no one else to be seen in the whole street but one or two curtains were twitching. The lead rider dismounted, took something out of the panniers and walked towards the front door. Alice saw he was carrying a bundle under each arm.

'It's the calendar,' she said, pushing past Sam and opening the door. 'Are you our new guides?'

The man took off his helmet and shook his head. He had long dark hair and an oriental face. 'Mel,' he called over the revving engines. 'Pleased to meet you. We've come to take you to your guide.' He handed both of them a helmet and leather jacket.

Alice checked she had her keys and locked the front door. 'You ride with Caspar,' he said, pointing to the gold bike. The rider waved a gloved hand. He had a Russian look to him, Alice thought: dark eyes and beard. 'Sam – you ride with Bal.' Bal was black and smiled back when Alice waved.

In no time, they were mounted on the back of the bikes, on proper pillion seats, each holding onto the waist of the rider in front. Mel's engine roared into life and the yellow three-wheeler set off. Alice saw curtains twitching again all down the street.

The riders headed back the way they had come down the street away from the town centre but turned left suddenly down a lane Alice had never noticed before which seemed to lead straight out into the countryside. The trees and hedgerows whizzed past. Alice felt perfectly safe as she leaned into the bends with Caspar. She caught flashes of yellow and silver in front as they sped into the night. The bikes seemed to be accelerating faster and faster now. All around was a blur except for the back of the rider in front of her. It seemed, just for a moment, as if their wheels left the ground and they passed through some kind of invisible barrier. Then they were slowing down again, cutting their engines, gliding to a stop just outside a large single-storey stone house with a flat roof. Alice thought she recognised the door of the house from the calendar.

Bal, Mel and Caspar dismounted and took off their helmets and leather jackets and stretched. They pointed not towards the house but up into the sky. It was early evening. The brightest star Alice had ever seen was shining right above the place they had come to visit. Caspar indicated they should walk up to the door and knock. 'No need to be afraid,' he said.

Sam led Alice to the threshold and tapped lightly on the wooden door with the back of his hand. It was opened almost straight away by a girl just a little older than Alice herself. Both of them took her for a servant. She kept her shawl over her head and her gaze to the floor as she beckoned them with a smile inside the warm stone building. There was a fire burning in the grate and the smell of a delicious soup filled the air. Tiny oil lamps lit the space in the centre of the room leaving long shadows. The starlight came in through each of the three high windows.

The girl seated them at a wooden table in one corner and then brought them the broth with newly baked bread, butter and cold fresh water. She indicated with smiles that they should help themselves. Sam supposed that her master would join them after the meal. The soup itself was delicious. Layer upon layer of flavour as if it had been cooking for a very long time.

After they had eaten, the girl cleared away the dishes to a corner of the room and gestured for Sam and Alice to come and sit on two comfortable wooden chairs, one on each side of the fire. There was now a sharp sense of expectancy in the air.

The girl stepped away from them and for the first time stood in the pool of light at the centre of the room. She stretched to her full height, threw back her shawl and shook out her long dark hair. Her eyes flashed with the reflected starlight.

Alice gasped. She was so beautiful. So brimming with life. So full of joy and sadness finely woven together. Young yet full of years. Her voice was rich and full of pleasure and her smile lit up everything around her. Alice was sure she had seen her before.

'Welcome, Sam Brown. Welcome, Alice Carroll. You are my guests. My name is Mary. You have tasted the food prepared for you. Now you must listen to my song.'

Without waiting for any reply or answer, Mary began to sing. Her song filled the home and spilled over to the waiting world. Alice had never heard anything more beautiful in her whole life and knew she never would.

The first part of the song was lament. There were notes of longing and of waiting. As she sang, Sam had visions of darkness over the face of the earth; of cruelty and wrongdoing; of war and hatred; of a world weary for change. Alice felt herself caught up in hope and expectation, longing for something somewhere to be different, waiting for something but not knowing what it was.

The note of lamentation died away and for some moments there was silence broken only by the rhythm of Mary's foot tapping faster and faster. And then Mary sang once more, a sharp cry of joy and wonder, a joy which celebrated life and hope and wisdom and love taking human form. As she sang, Sam's mind was filled with the flash of angels' wings and blinding light, of moments of fear and danger, of long journeys to far places, of escape in the night. Alice saw visions and felt the wonder of a child conceived in Mary's womb, of hope and joy after years of waiting, of fear conquered, of the proud and powerful put down, of poor and humble people lifted up, of all that was wrong now beginning to be put right, of promises which had been kept. She caught the wonder and the mystery of life taking shape, wrapped in human flesh, formed within a young girl's body, light itself caught, distilled, made visible, at rest.

The song spoke of all that was familiar in the story: of shepherds and wise kings; of stables and the donkey. Yet she saw it now through different eyes: eyes which had been watching and waiting for generations, longing for this moment, eyes which understood, a little, the great cost and promise locked inside a tale which is often told yet seldom understood. And she saw, or thought she saw, a child: growing, playing, learning, laughing, crying, settled at his mother's breast, pulling at his mother's arms, hiding from his mother's eyes, resting in his mother's love.

For Sam, the final part of the song spoke to him so deeply of the wonder of conception and the precious gift of life: the essence of two natures, the spark of gift and grace, the slow formation of a child, the solemn charge to love and give and share.

As Mary's song ebbed now to gentle lullaby, both Sam and Alice closed their eyes and rested.

Alice was the first to wake, at home again, the room lit only by the fire. She shook Sam gently. 'Wake up. We're home.' The song had left an echo of wonder and stillness in the room.

Together they stood and turned back towards the calendar. The new door was fully open now, swung back on its hinges. Inside, hanging in the vastness of a dark sky, as Alice knew it would be, was the brightest of all stars. Glimpsing its light, Alice caught echoes of Mary's distant song.

20 December

Megs had the day off work on Thursday. She and Alice had planned to finish the Christmas shopping. To Alice's great relief, there was no sign of Andrew Watkins *and* Megs seemed to be in a very chirpy mood. They buttoned up well against the December weather and caught the bus into town. The shopping mall was a sea of people.

'Strange,' said Megs. 'That new laundry has disappeared. I thought they were very good.'

Alice smiled, half expecting to see Mr Gabriel somewhere in the new Fair Trade gift shop which had opened just in time for Christmas. There weren't that many people inside – not compared to Boots or Smiths. There was no sign of a bowler hat – but one of the women waved at Alice and Megs and beckoned them to come in.

'It's Brenda,' said Alice. 'Brenda Fisher from the church.'

She dragged Megs inside by the hand. Brenda was standing behind one of the tills. 'What are you doing here?'

'The vicar had a telephone call last week,' said Brenda. 'The company which had rented the shop before Christmas pulled out with only a few days to go. They suggested we might like to run it for charity. We already have a Fairly Traded Shop at church once a month and we managed to get hold of some more stock. What do you think?'

'It's brilliant,' said Alice. 'But what's Fair Trade?'

'It's where the farmers and producers in poorer countries get a fair price for their goods,' said Brenda, showing them her stock. 'The food is over there. Clothes are against that wall and the craft things are in the middle.'

'There aren't many people here,' said Megs.

'It got busier yesterday,' said Brenda, defensively. She busied herself rearranging some of the chocolate bars and didn't meet Megs' eyes. 'Especially around lunchtime. People are looking for something a bit different these days. The only trouble is, we're really short of help. I don't suppose either of you could lend a hand?'

'Well, I'm not … ' Megs began to make her excuses.

'I will,' said Alice. 'I'd rather do something useful than trail round the shops.'

'What about your own Christmas shopping?' said Megs. 'Last chance?'

'I can buy what I need here.'

Megs looked less than enthusiastic. Alice was unsure whether it was the thought of her daughter helping out in the shop or the prospect of an African wood carving as a Christmas present.

'Won't you be in the way?'

'Not at all,' said Brenda. 'There's plenty she can do. Just leave her here for a couple of hours while you whiz round the shops, then we can see how it's going.'

'OK then. If you're sure that's OK. Call me if you get bored or anything and I'll come back to get you. Bye.'

'Mum!' said Alice.

'What?'

'Aren't you going to buy anything? These tea towels would be just right for Grandma.'

Megs grimaced and got out her purse. 'How lovely, darling. I'll take two.'

'Four pounds, please,' said Alice, holding out her hand.

After Megs had gone, Brenda introduced Alice to the other two volunteers in the shop: Wendy and Carla. Alice's job was to look after the food area. The morning was extremely quiet and Alice had plenty of time to look at the stock and read the posters on the wall. It all seemed so obvious really: giving people a fair price for the goods they produced. The only trouble was, people streamed past the shop without seeming to notice it was there. She even saw Alex and waved desperately but he never looked inside.

The shop doorbell rang at a quarter to twelve and a familiar figure in a bowler hat came in.

'Mr Gabriel,' said Alice. 'What are you doing here?'

'How do you do, Miss Carroll,' said Mr Gabriel, lifting his hat. 'Delighted to see you again. Who are your companions?'

'This is Brenda from the church,' said Alice. 'These ladies are Wendy and Carla.'

'Delighted,' said Mr Gabriel again. 'Is business good?'

'Not brilliant,' admitted Brenda. 'We could do with a few more people.'

'I'll see what I can do,' said Mr Gabriel, mysteriously, and winked at Alice. 'In the meantime, Miss Carroll, I simply called to deliver this.'

He took a large, crisp white envelope from inside his coat and placed it in Alice's outstretched hand. 'Good morning!'

Wendy held the door open for him as Mr Gabriel walked out into the shopping mall.

'What is it, Alice?' said Brenda. Alice examined the outside for a moment. The envelope was embossed with gold with a very fancy crest on the back. She opened it carefully and took out a white card, again edged in gold.

'To Alice and Sam,' she read aloud. 'He's my uncle. "You are invited to a wedding. On Thursday 20 December. The car will collect you at 4.00 p.m. Wear your smartest clothes.'

'That seems short notice,' said Brenda, looking over her shoulder. 'Is he alright, that Mr Gabriel?'

'Yes, very much so,' said Alice. 'I think you might find he was the person who phoned the vicar about the shop. But strange things happen when he's around. Is there a phone I can use?'

Wendy pointed to the payphone at the back of the shop. A few more customers were drifting in now so the three women were needed at the counter. Alice went and rang Sam to tell him the news.

'Fascinating. No problem,' he said. 'I'll come home after lunch. It's dead here anyway. I can tell Richard I need to do some work at home.'

When Alice returned to the shop floor she had to rub her eyes in disbelief. The store was now packed to bursting point with more people coming in every moment. More than that, they were not just looking but buying. For the next hour, Alice worked flat out on the food section. Wendy was on clothes and Carla sold the ornaments. Brenda brought out the boxes of stock from the back room. Everything was selling as fast as they could put it on the shelves.

By half past one, they had sold their entire stock and Carla turned the sign on the door to 'Closed'. Even so, they saw a stream of people coming up to peer in the window only to turn away disappointed. The two old tills were full to bursting with cash, cheques and credit card slips. The three women and Alice sipped cups of tea and drew breath.

'Whew!' said Brenda. 'Our best day so far. Fantastic.'

'We'll have to get some more stock for tomorrow,' said Wendy.

'What's the money for anyway?' said Alice. 'Does it go to the people who made the stuff?'

'They've already had a fair price,' said Brenda. 'We're going to divide the profits between the shelter for the homeless and the church roof appeal. Looks like both will get a special Christmas present. I'd better ring the Vicar.'

There was a tap on the glass and Carla went to let Megs in, burdened with plastic carriers. 'Had a good morning, darling?'

'We sold everything,' said Alice pointing to the empty counters.

'Strange,' said Megs. 'Everywhere else was really quiet after about eleven. I got all the shopping done. Ready to go?'

Alice nodded, hoping that no one would mention the invitation. Brenda was on the phone but waved. 'Thanks, Alice,' she said. 'See you at the Carol Service?'

Megs had no time for questions all afternoon. She had to wrap the presents she had bought. Alice hoped there were some good ones. Andrew was taking her up to see the grandparents in Luton again. He came round at three and Sam was home about the same time. Alice was in the bathroom when they left so there were no awkward questions.

'You look very smart,' she said to Sam, dressed in his best suit, white button-down shirt and tie.

'Thank you,' said Sam. 'You're still wearing jeans.'

'What's wrong with jeans?' said Alice, defiantly.

'No one wears jeans to a wedding,' said Sam.

'Well I do,' said Alice.

'Message' sang the mobile phone. 'Here's the code,' Sam said. There was a new arched door on the right-hand side of the calendar. 'Five, five, colon, one.' Alice pressed the buttons and looked out of the window. An enormous stretch limousine was making its way down the road.

'Look at this, Sam!'

They watched as the car pulled up outside and their three escorts got out of the front seats dressed in sharp suits and sunglasses. Mel was driving and he stayed by the car. Caspar and Bal came to the front door.

'Wedding party ready for collection?' asked Caspar walking through into the hall.

'Ready and waiting,' said Alice, holding out the white card.

Bal took off his glasses and inspected them both. 'Very smart, Sam,' he said. Then all three of them looked at Alice.

'No one wears jeans to a wedding,' they said, simultaneously.

'I do,' said Alice, weakly.

'Not this time, young lady,' said Bal. 'Change. Quick or we'll be late.'

Alice sensed it was not the time to argue and sprinted up the stairs. With great reluctance she put on her one smart dress and smart black shoes and tied up her hair in matching ribbons.

The three men were waiting at the bottom of the stairs, looking at their watches.

'Spectacular,' said Caspar as she came down the stairs. 'Worth waiting for, young lady.'

They escorted Alice out of the house, standing on each side like bodyguards. Mel opened the rear doors of the limousine and Alice climbed inside. It was the height of luxury. Sam and Alice sank into the soft leather seats. There was room to extend your legs right out, a television, even a minibar with soft drinks.

'Fasten your seat belts,' said Mel through the intercom. Both of them complied as the car slid smoothly away from the pavement and out onto the main roads. The glass was tinted so Alice and Sam could see out but no one could see them. Alice sipped a fruit punch cocktail and looked out of the window. It was great to see heads turning as they passed, everyone wondering who was inside.

It was growing dark outside now and the streetlamps were on as well as the Christmas lights. The car sped out of town and onto the motorway which (for once) was almost clear of traffic. The television news came on and Sam and Alice watched the headlines: another famine loomed in Africa; record crowds in the shops pre-Christmas ... When Alice peered through the smoked glass again they were on smaller country lanes but still moving at a worryingly high speed.

'Here we are,' said Mel from the front. Sam could see a great stately home ahead, at the end of a long driveway, full of light and colour. It looked like a castle. 'The party's in full swing.'

The limousine came to a stop on the gravel drive in front of the house entrance. Caspar opened the door, Bal held an umbrella over Alice and Mel held one over Sam. They parted at the door. 'Enjoy yourselves,' they called.

Sam and Alice joined the party. The ladies were all in dinner gowns. The gentlemen wore suits. Alice was glad, for once, that she had followed instructions. It was like something from one of Megs' celebrity magazines.

A waiter came up balancing a tray of elegant glasses. 'What's the choice?' asked Sam.

The waiter coughed and looked embarrassed. He spoke with a thick French accent. 'Tonic water or orange juz?' Alice took an orange juice.

'Nothing stronger?' asked Sam (now in a party mood).

'I'm very sorry, m'sieur,' said the waiter. 'Zer 'as been some sort of mix up.' He beckoned to Sam who bent his ear close to the waiter's mouth. 'Ze wine 'as run out. Zis 'as never 'appened before, you understand.'

'At a wedding?' said Sam, stupefied.

The waiter nodded and raised his eyebrows. "Eads will roll,' he mouthed and shimmied to the other side of the room.

'What's the big panic?' said Alice, sipping her orange juice. 'Look at this yummy food.' There were more people serving now, bringing in platters of food for the guests. Alice helped herself to a mini Yorkshire pudding with a sausage inside. Sam had a tiny prawn in batter with a couple of chips. They made their way slowly through the great hallway and into what looked like the main ballroom. Over on the far side, Alice could see the bride and groom making their way through the crowd. There was a string quartet on the stage. Every so often they caught a snatch of conversation from one side or another:

'Have you heard? The wine's run out.'

'Did you ever hear of anything like it, my dear?'

'I'm not one to complain but, honestly. What about the toast?'

'The best man looks distracted, darling.'

'The bride's mother has had to go and lie down, poor thing. They say she has a heart condition.'

Alice was beginning to feel more and more sorry for the bride and groom, whoever they were. Nobody had spoken to Sam or herself since they came in. They gradually moved back to the side of the room.

'There you are,' came a familiar voice, in a soft whisper. 'How do you like the wedding?'

'Very nice, thanks,' said Sam, his mouth half full of mini-pizzas, which he managed to spray over Mary.

She looked older than the last time Alice and Sam had seen her but unmistakably the same: the life shone within her eyes. She was dressed as one of the waitresses and carried a tray of orange juice. Even so, if you looked into her eyes, she was the most beautiful person in the room.

'How do you like it, Alice? Have another orange juice.'

Alice took a glass. 'It's a lovely party,' she said. 'Thank you for inviting us. It's a shame about the wine running out though.'

'Wait and see,' said Mary, laughing. 'Here's the head waiter now. I've just suggested how he might sort it out.'

A very anxious head waiter came over to where they were standing. He spoke to Mary, ignoring Sam and Alice.

'Did you do as I asked?' Mary said. 'Did you speak to him?'

'I did,' he said. 'I know you zaid 'e was special – but the advice is –'ow you say – very strernge.'

'Will you do as he asks?' Mary asked.

'I werll,' said the head waiter. 'We 'ave nothing to lose. It will be an 'our before the supplies arrive from the ware'ouse. If it is not solved by then, I will lose my job.'

'These are friends of mine,' said Mary, 'Alice and Sam. Can they come downstairs and watch?'

'Only if they change first,' said the head waiter. 'No guests are allowed downstairs.'

'Do you want to watch?' said Mary. Alice and Sam nodded. They looked behind them as the waiter led them away and Mary continued offering the tray of orange juice.

'Do you think they … ?' said Alice.

'Come on, come on. I 'ave not got all day,' said the waiter.

He took them straight to the changing rooms and sorted out a small black dress, apron and cap for Alice and a dinner jacket and bow tie for Sam. They were changed in no time.

'Now, follow me,' he said. 'Anton, Georges, you come too.'

'What are you going to do?' asked Alice.

' "Do whatever he tells you," Mary said. "Do whatever he tells you." It seems mad to me but zis is what 'e zed. "Go downstairs to ze kitchens. You will find zix enormous stone jarz."'

At that moment they burst through the double doors into the cauldron of activity that was the kitchen. Fifteen chefs busied themselves with the preparation of the main course, due to be served in twenty minutes. An under waiter ran in behind them: 'The receiving line 'as begun. Stations everyone.'

Alice thought the effect was like stirring an anthill with a stick. Everyone scurried round even faster carrying vast silver tureens of steaming food.

'Can you see the jars?' said Sam.

Alice and Claude, the head waiter, scanned the room. 'Over there, by the old fireplace,' called Alice.

Each jar was as tall as Sam. 'We 'ave to take zem to ze old castle well and fill zem,' shouted Claude above the racket. "Urry, zere iz not much time.'

They managed four on the first trip, with Alice holding the doors open. The stairs down to the old well from the kitchens were steep. The well was out of doors in a tiny round courtyard right in the centre of the old keep. Sam dragged the heavy lid from the mouth of the well. Anton and Georges went back for the other two jars. Alice released the bucket on its chain and sent it plummeting down into the water below.

Claude took off his jacket and turned the handle which pulled the chain and raised the bucket. As it reached the top, Sam poured the contents into the first jar and sent it straight back down again.

'Wait,' called Claude as the bucket reached the top for the second time. "Old zis.' Sam took the winch handle and Claude drew out a cup of the water and tasted it. 'Sweet and fresh,' he said, handing it to Alice. 'At least we will not be poisoning ze guests.'

It took six enormous buckets of water to fill one of the jars to the brim. By the time Anton and Georges returned with the final jars, two were filled with water. The four men took it in turns to haul up the bucket. All were now out of breath and red in the face.

Claude asked Alice for a progress report on the wedding banquet. Alice sprinted back up the stairs, through the chaos of the castle kitchens and up another broad, carpeted staircase to the ballroom. The last of the guests were moving through the receiving line to be greeted by the bride and groom and their immediate families. Any moment now, the bride and groom would enter the hall. The best man looked increasingly desperate and the bride's father was full of fury and pacing up and down, mobile phone pressed to his ear.

Mary caught her eye and came over. 'It's almost time,' she said. 'Is Claude ready?'

'Almost,' said Alice.

'As soon as the final jar is full, not a moment before, tell Claude to draw off the water into a decanter and, without tasting it, take it to the best man.' Mary handed Alice a silver jug. Alice took it in both hands and sprinted back down three flights of stairs, dodging waiters carrying hot tureens of food on the way up.

The last bucket was filling the final great jar as she ran into the small courtyard. Sam, Anton and Georges had collapsed on the floor with their backs to the wall.

'As soon as the last jar is full to the brim, draw some of it out into this decanter,' said Alice. 'Without tasting it, take it to the best man.'

Claude raised his eyes to heaven. He was too out of breath to speak but took the decanter from Alice, held it by the handle and pressed it down slowly into the first jar they had filled, carefully so that nothing was spilled.

'Let's go,' he said to Sam and Alice. 'You two stay 'ere. Don't let anyone in.' Anton and Georges simply moaned in response and remained slumped on the floor.

As they passed through the kitchen, Claude found a tray of glasses for Sam and gave Alice the decanter. He led them, then, in stately procession up the two flights of stairs (taking care to avoid the waiters on the way down with empty platters), through into the main hall and to the table on the dais at the far end. Alice noticed that Mary slipped in behind them as they passed the door of the hall. The conversation stopped as they moved down behind the rows of guests. People nudged and pointed towards Alice and the decanter she carried. As they came to the top table, the whole room fell silent, set down their knives and forks, fingered their empty glasses and looked towards the best man.

Claude coughed discreetly, rather from habit Sam thought because everyone was already staring at him. 'M'sieur. Ze wine for your approval.'

The best man smiled with relief. 'Someone found an off-licence. Well done, Claude,' he whispered. 'Let's see what it's like. Not expecting anything much but any port in a storm.'

Claude coughed discreetly again and took a glass from the tray Sam was carrying. Alice could see that his hand was trembling and there were beads of perspiration on his forehead. She offered him the decanter. He took it by the handle and poured.

Out came the richest, deepest red wine. Its bouquet filled the room. All of the guests inhaled at the same time. The best man's eyes lit up. He took the glass from Claude and Alice took the decanter back. The best man raised the glass to his lips, sipped, swilled it round his tonsils, arched his eyebrows, swallowed, sipped again and beamed from ear to ear.

He stood and addressed the guests. 'Ladies and gentlemen: simply the best I have ever tasted. Let the festivities begin!'

There was a great roar from the hall, a round of applause and the feasting and conversation began again. The best man turned back again to Claude.

'How much of this stuff do we have?'

Claude was stretched out on the floor at his feet in a dead faint. Alice replied on his behalf: 'About 180 gallons, I think.'

'This will be some wedding!' said the best man.

Sam was bending over Claude, slapping his cheeks to bring him round. He came to and instantly sent every waiter down to the water jars bearing jugs and decanters, even vases, so that the wine began to flow. Anton and Georges did not appear and word came back that they too had tasted the wine (rather a lot of it) and were in no fit state to carry it through the hallway.

Claude and Mary walked out again to the vestibule with Sam and Alice. 'Dear madame, 'ow can I zank you?'

'Not at all, Claude,' said Mary, bowing slightly. 'Excuse me, I must say goodbye to my guests.'

Mary walked them to the door where Bal, Caspar and Mel were waiting with the limousine. 'Remember what you have seen,' she said. 'Store it in your heart. Think of it as a sign of something greater.'

She kissed Alice on the forehead and shook Sam warmly by the hand. Their three escorts bowed very low to Mary and helped them back into the car. The journey home seemed to take no time at all. Neither Sam nor Alice spoke, turning over in their minds all that they had seen.

Megs and Andrew were not yet back from Luton. Alice and Sam said goodnight to Mel and ran through into the front room. There in the open door of the great castle, on a floor littered with confetti, stood six stone jars filled to the very brim with the richest and best wine there has ever been.

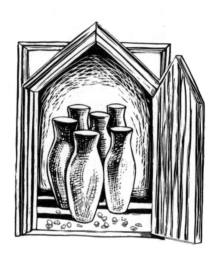

21 December

The next morning, Alice slept until half past eight. She skipped downstairs in her pyjamas, her mind full of the ride in the limousine and the banquet. There were voices coming from the kitchen but Alice turned right into the front room and scanned the calendar.

There wasn't that much space now: just room for three more ordinary doors and the one in the centre which had been visible from the beginning. She gasped: the new door had appeared already in the bottom left-hand section. It was completely black, surrounded by a thin wooden frame. There was no sign of an opening.

'Sam!' she called, running into the kitchen. Megs and Sam sat at the kitchen table with mugs of tea. Both of them looked very serious. Megs had been crying. They were holding hands.

'What's the matter?' asked Alice. 'How come you're not at work?'

'It's Grandad, love,' said Megs, softly. 'He was taken ill again in the night. Grandma rang. This time it could be very serious.'

Sam squeezed her hand.

'We need to go and see him,' said Sam. 'All of us. Gran has asked us to go.'

'I want to see him,' said Alice.

'Run and get dressed then,' said Megs. 'I need to finish getting ready as well. We'll leave in about half an hour. We've decided to take a taxi and train. Can you sort that, Sam?'

Sam's two-seater was too small and not good in any case on long distances. Andrew had gone away for the day.

Alice sprinted upstairs and pulled on some nice clothes. She was back in the front room in five minutes, with Sam. He pulled out his phone to call a cab.

'There's a message – a code.'

'I was coming in to tell you,' said Alice. 'The new door is there.'

Sam opened the message. 'Two, five, colon, seven. Then it says "For immediate use. Taxi".'

'Whoever sends the messages must know what's happening,' said Alice. 'It's always been OK before. Shall I punch in the code?'

Sam thought for a moment. Just for a second, he imagined he was back on the forest trail with Abraham and Sarah, trying to work out which way to go. 'Punch in the code,' he said. 'We'll take a chance.'

Alice pressed the buttons: 'Two, five, colon, seven.' One day soon she must ask someone what they meant. There was a soft click and the new door began to slide open.

Megs came down the stairs calling: 'Sam – did you call the cab? The normal number is by the phone.' Alice thought she was in shock.

The doorbell rang. They got up to go but heard Megs answer it. A very familiar voice said: 'Taxi, madam? To the hospital?'

'That's right,' said Megs. 'But just to the station. You were very quick.'

'Just waiting for your call, madam,' said Caspar, raising his chauffeur's cap. He was wearing the complete uniform and dark glasses.

Bal and Mel were outside, dressed the same way as Caspar and standing on either side of a black unmarked Range Rover with dark tinted windows. Megs looked up and down the street for the taxi.

'There must be some mistake,' she said. 'We only ordered a cab to the station. This will cost a fortune.'

She looked at Sam accusingly, as if it was his fault. Bal opened the passenger door: 'Complements of Mr Gabriel, madam. An upgraded service. No charge.'

'The man from the dry-cleaner's?' said Megs in a bit of a daze. 'Strange – but very kind of him. How did he know?'

Caspar gave Alice a poke in the ribs. 'I saw him yesterday,' she said, 'at the charity shop.'

'All aboard, madam,' said Mel, soothingly. Megs did as she was told and climbed into the back, followed by Alice and Sam. Bal motioned to them both to keep quiet.

'We are going to the hospital, aren't we?' Sam enquired just in case there were any strange journeys involved. Bal nodded and tapped his watch impatiently.

There was a flask of coffee in the back seat with cups, milk and sugar and a selection of pastries. Alice decided that this was a very good thing as she'd not had breakfast. The car pulled away from the kerb quietly and out onto the main road. It was a strange thing that whenever she was driven by her three new friends, there was very little traffic.

'So when did you find out about Grandad?' asked Alice. 'How was he last night?'

'Not great,' said Megs. 'We stayed as late as we could, then dropped Grandma off at home. You'd gone to bed when we got back. Sam and I stayed up late. Grandma phoned at eight o'clock this morning. She'd rung the hospital and apparently he's had another bad night. Chest infection on top of everything else.'

Megs looked tearful again. Sam passed his sister some coffee and helped himself to a pastry. He looked out of the window for a moment and noticed that they must be going at least a hundred miles an hour.

'Is Mum meeting us at the hospital?' he asked.

'She'll be on the intensive care ward now,' said Megs. 'Mobile phones aren't allowed so we can't ring ahead. At least there are no hold-ups.' Megs blew her nose. Alice and Sam exchanged looks.

The car pulled up at the main entrance to the hospital. Caspar and Mel leapt out and opened the doors for Megs and Sam. Bal stayed at the wheel and drove off to park the car. The others came into the hospital with them, one on either side and very much on the alert.

'There's really no need,' said Megs, coming round a bit now.

'All part of the service, madam,' said Caspar. 'Mr Gabriel would insist.'

Sam followed the signs for Intensive Care and found it first time thanks to a couple of coughs from Bal when he missed vital turnings. The escorts stayed outside the door of the ward. Alice, Sam and Megs were invited in, though only briefly.

Alice ran and hugged her grandma who looked very thin and frail next to all the machinery. Both of them burst into tears. She could hardly recognise her grandfather who was stretched out on the bed with pipes and tubes running in and out of him, fixed to great machines. Sam embraced his mum and squeezed his dad's hand. He, too, seemed very choked up. A nurse came over and asked them to step into the relatives' waiting room. The doctor would be with them in a minute or two.

The waiting room was not very big to start with but with the four of them and the three solemn escorts in dark glasses against the back wall it felt very crowded indeed. Gran was oblivious to everything and sat on the sofa clutching Alice's hand.

The doctor came in after a couple of minutes, shook hands with the family and acknowledged their three companions.

'I am afraid Mr Brown has been very sick,' he began. 'Fortunately, his condition has now stabilised and the antibiotics are beginning to work. We think he is out of danger.'

Megs, Sam, Alice and Grandma all heaved a huge sigh of relief together. The doctor went on, 'We will move him out of Intensive Care this afternoon if all goes well. Then, in two days' time, he should be well enough to leave hospital. The only thing is, he must have people around who can look after him. With respect, Mrs Brown, I don't think that you will have the strength by yourself.'

'Can Grandad come to our house?' suggested Alice, instantly.

'Would it matter if we're so far from the hospital?' asked Megs.

'Not at all,' said the doctor. 'We can give you a number to call for the hospital in your local area. That should be very satisfactory. It is much better to be with those you love at Christmas time, is it not?'

Gran nodded. 'If you're sure it's not too much trouble.'

'You and Grandad can have my room,' said Alice. 'I'll go in with Mum.'

'That's settled then,' said the doctor and stood up to leave.

It took a few moments to make the arrangements for the rest of the day. Megs would remain at the hospital with Grandma, then stay overnight with her. Sam and Alice would travel home with their escorts. Either Megs or Sam would hire a car on Christmas Eve to collect Grandma and Grandad from the hospital and bring them home for Christmas.

⧖

Half an hour later, Alice and Sam were walking down the main corridor of the hospital feeling somewhat conspicuous with Mel on one side and Caspar on the other. Bal had slipped away, they supposed to collect the car. Alice couldn't work out why they were being so protective. 'It's not as if we're in any danger,' she thought.

Just at that moment, she caught sight of a curious figure dressed completely in dark grey slowly coming up the corridor towards them. He wore a hooded cloak and carried a great scythe over his shoulder. Alice saw that he kept to the edge of the corridor and that no one else could see him. He turned left into one of the wards, leaving a cold, slimy trail behind him like a slug.

'What was that?' said Sam.

'There's another,' said Alice.

An identical figure had turned into the corridor from the main entrance and was moving away from them to another part of the hospital. He was followed by a third, then a fourth, coming straight for them. Their tracks glistened for a few moments, then faded away.

'The grim reapers some call them,' said Mel. 'They are no friends of ours or of any human. They are the messengers of death. They come to spoil, to rend, to draw life's sweetness to a bitter end.'

Alice and Sam shuddered and drew back into the protection of their escorts as the reaper approached them. There was no face inside the grey hood. The cloak covered its feet. Black gloves gripped the scythe which was a dull metallic grey but razor sharp. A putrid stench of decay surrounded the creature like a cloud.

When it drew close to them, the reaper stopped, sensing rather than seeing something wrong. Its voice was cracked and low, coming from deep within the shroud it wore, echoing around the corridor:

'You have no place here. This is our domain.'

'For a time only,' said Caspar. 'You will not prevail.'

The creature turned its hooded face to look directly at Alice and at Sam. They saw only the deepest blackness within. Alice gagged at the smell.

'All are ours,' it hissed. 'One day you will come to us. This scythe or one like it will cut the cord of life. The end of everything is death.'

The last word hung in the air as the reaper turned and continued its malodorous passage through the corridor and away to one of the wards. Alice and Sam felt a deep chill settle in their bones.

'Can't you stop it?' said Sam.

'There is only one answer,' said Caspar. 'Come, our Lady awaits.'

They moved more quickly now down towards the main exit. Alice saw two more reapers making their way down the corridor in the distance. They passed a group of three huddled together outside a single doorway. 'The Morgue,' Mel explained. Outside the main doors there were a group of three or four waiting, it seemed, for some signal before entering the building.

They crossed the courtyard to a wide open space beyond the car park. A sleek, white and silver helicopter was waiting on the launch pad. As he saw them approach, Bal started the engines and the rotors began to turn. Mel and Caspar guided Sam and Alice underneath the rotors and helped them climb on board, before strapping them into the passenger seats.

Bal's voice came through the headsets in their safety helmets. 'All aboard?' he asked. Sam and Alice put their thumbs up. The helicopter took off and began to move away towards the south.

'Look down and to the right,' said Bal. 'Use the binoculars. This is what we want you to see.'

Sam and Alice picked up the two large pairs of binoculars in lockers under their seats and scanned the horizon. It took Alice a few moments to see it clearly but once she saw it, the vision never left her. Stretching out across the towns and cities and villages – everywhere people lived – was something like a blanket of thick black tar which hadn't set. It lay across the roofs of the houses, it stretched across the roads, it covered the office blocks and factories, even the schools and the hospitals. It covered the whole of human existence. Through the binoculars it looked to Alice as if it were choking the very life out of every community.

'What is it?' called Sam.

'The shroud of death,' came Bal's chill voice through their ear-pieces. 'It covers the whole earth. However much you do not like to talk about it, it remains a terrible reality. Death steals our loved ones and casts its long shadow forward over every life. In the end, it takes us all and ruins all we love. It is heaven's enemy.'

Alice shuddered again and made herself look. 'Why are you showing us this? How can we bear it?'

'We are showing you what you already know,' said Bal. 'But we must show you clearly so that you can appreciate and understand what has been done. Hold tight.'

The helicopter banked sharply up to the right, forcing Alice and Sam back into their seats. As they climbed higher, both of them continued to stare through their binoculars, surveying the black, sticky blanket which embraced all of human living. Alice found as she focused the lenses that she caught sight of rapidly moving grey specks: the reapers going about their sad business. They passed at lightning speed over countries and whole continents. The whole world over it was the same.

Up ahead of them, suddenly, a mountain rose high above the plains. It stood out brightly against the skyline: a haze of greens, browns, yellows and blues reflected from the sky in numerous pools of water. Only over this mountain was there no grey shroud.

Bal brought the helicopter down in a clearing on the lower slopes and cut the engines. Caspar undid Alice's and Sam's seatbelts and helped them climb out of the helicopter. The air was sharp and fresh after the hospital and the flight. Sam took deep breaths. Mel pointed to a path which led up the hillside. 'Our Lady waits.'

Sam and Alice set off, once more leaving their escorts behind them, enjoying the bright sunshine, the flowers and the birdsong. They walked uphill for ten minutes, perhaps more, with the path before them clearly marked. The shadows which had settled within them in the hospital corridors began to fade away.

The path ended in a garden. To Alice's great delight, roaming freely in the garden were six stately peacocks with their mates, their plumage on full display with a thousand eyes dancing on their tails. They were tame and came to greet them, curious at the intrusion, then went about their business, lighting the space with colour and beauty.

In the centre of the garden was what looked like a small cave cut into the rock. A large stone had been rolled away from the entrance. There beside the empty cave, on a simple wooden bench, sat Mary: still brimming with hope and life but now, Alice thought, a little older and a little sadder than when they saw her last, yet still at peace. She stood to greet them. They bowed low before she took their hands.

'Come,' said Mary. 'Sit and eat. Refresh yourselves.'

She sat them on the bench and set before them a wicker basket filled with different fruits from the garden. Sam chose a pear; Alice selected some strawberries and a plum. The tastes were fresh and sweet like the air on the mountain and restored them a little more. One of the peacocks came and stood beside them. Alice offered him a strawberry and he took it in his beak.

Mary knelt beside them as they ate and waited quietly for them to finish.

'And now,' she said, with joy, rising up and shaking the grass from her skirts, 'now you must listen again to my song.'

She stepped away from them and stood in front of the stone which had been rolled away, lifted her arms to heaven and began to sing. As she sang, she moved in the most stately dance.

The first part of the song spoke once more of a mother's love and pride in her son. The verses told of a young man, strong and well loved, following his father's trade, a carpenter. They spoke of the call of God to fulfil all that he was meant to be, of travelling and friendships. Mary sang of water changed to wine, of lives mended and renewed, of new hope for the poor, of the hungry being fed. Alice saw the flashing wings of a dove, baskets of food in abundance, a great catch of fish. The music filled Sam's heart with hope. He felt the call to leave everything, to follow.

Then, gradually, the song's tone changed and the dance changed with it. Mary's voice picked out and followed the minor keys which had been present from the beginning. She sang of jealousy and conflict. She sang of challenge which turned to hate, of a call to suffering and death. With the notes now clashing, Alice felt the anguish of betrayal and capture, torture and trial, and Sam's mind was stirred to turmoil by images of agony and death. Through it all, the song spoke of suffering, yet of a mother's love sustained and sustaining through every time of trial.

The moment of death was followed by silence, then a soft, tender lament. They washed his body and covered it with spices, and laid him in a tomb, a cave.

The song spoke of three days of waiting, watching, hoping, the longest days, and then the music burst once more to life and as she sang, Mary danced for joy, weaving in and out of the trees, creating circles and patterns and always at the centre was the empty tomb. The great hymn spoke of death defeated once and for all, of new life given and available to all, of love and friendship which endures for ever, of an abundance of joy and laughter and plenty. And now both Sam and Alice saw the same picture in the song: they saw the great sticky shroud of death which lay over all the earth defeated, rolled back, cleansed and swallowed up in the new life of Mary's son and gone for ever.

The hymn of triumph turned into a song of praise. Sam and Alice could not help but stand and join in as best they could. They were no longer watching and listening only but drawn to share again in heaven's song:

> 'Death has been swallowed up in victory.
> Where, O death, is your victory?
> Where, O death, is your sting?'

As the song came to its end there was silence and rest. Then Mary embraced them both. 'It was necessary to see the terror of death so that you can understand the wonder of life.'

They nodded, breathless but at peace.

Mel carried a tired Alice back down the pathway to the helicopter. Both she and Sam slept on the journey back. Without knowing how or where, they transferred again to the Range Rover and woke again as they arrived home.

Sam unlocked the door and Alice pushed past him into the front room. Together they looked once more at the calendar. The twenty-first door was open now. In the background, Alice saw a beautiful sunlit garden. In the foreground, laid across the door frame, was a brightly coloured feather taken from a peacock's tail.

22 December

Alice woke late on Saturday, realised what day it was and grumpily turned over in the bed. Nick and Janie were taking her out today as a Christmas treat. She was not looking forward to it.

Alice knew that Nick's original suggestion had been to take her away for a holiday over Christmas. To her great relief, Megs had vetoed the idea. She'd found her weekly phone calls to her dad a bit easier over the last two weeks. At least he had rung. At least he was making the effort to take her out for the day. In spite of all that was happening with Grandad, Megs was a lot happier than she was in November.

'The trouble is,' Alice said to no one in particular, 'I think I can learn not to mind about the little things. But it's really hard to let go of what he did to Mum. Leaving us. Making us move house.'

'Alice! Rise and shine! They'll be here at eleven!'

'Coming, Mum.'

Despite herself, Alice found she took a little extra care with her appearance and picked out her best jeans and sweatshirt. Even so, Megs gave her a thorough inspection when she came downstairs. Megs herself was up to her armpits in advance cooking for Christmas. The kitchen was full of steam and wonderful smells. There were two dozen mince pies on wire cooling racks. Megs was stirring her famous pineapple stuffing for the turkey: a family tradition and an annual treat.

Sam was at the kitchen table, doing his best to distract Megs so he could steal a mince pie.

Alice poured out her muesli and sat down next to Sam. 'I wish I didn't have to go today,' she said, pulling a face. 'I'd much rather be at home getting ready.'

'I think it's starting to snow,' said Sam. As Megs looked out of the window he grabbed a mince pie and burnt his fingers as he hid it behind his folded arms. 'Where are you going anyway?'

The snow was just beginning. 'Coo!' said Megs. 'I hope you'll be OK going out in this.'

'We're going out for Christmas lunch in a restaurant,' said Alice. 'Just the three of us.' She turned up her nose. 'Then shopping so I can pick out some new clothes.'

'Spend lots!' said Megs. She noticed the mince pie was missing and took a string bag of sprouts from the vegetable basket and tossed it across to Sam.

'You need to earn your snacks, Sam. Peel!'

'Got to go in five minutes, sis. Lunch with Josie's mum and dad, remember?' He pulled a face.

'How many for Christmas lunch now, Mum?'

'The three of us,' said Megs. 'Mum and Dad, Josie and – erm – I've kind of invited Andrew. Is that OK? He was going to be on his own.'

'Cool,' said Alice. 'Seven. Will they all bring presents?'

The doorbell rang.

'That'll be your dad. You let him in.'

Despite herself, Megs straightened her hair and glanced in the kitchen mirror. 'You look fine, sis,' said Sam.

Alice brought Nick and Janie into the kitchen. They were smartly dressed today and Alice thought everyone was determined to be on their best behaviour. Nick was wearing a dark suit and an open-necked white shirt. Janie was wearing a short white leather skirt and bright red top. The grown-ups all shook hands. Sam and Janie hadn't met before.

'Time for a coffee?' said Megs in the kind of voice which hoped the answer would be no.

'We probably need to get going in a few minutes, if that's OK?' said Nick.

'These are for you, Alice,' said Janie, holding out a carrier bag full of brightly wrapped presents.

'Thanks,' said Alice. 'I'll put them under the tree. Come and look at the Advent Calendar.'

Everyone trooped into the front room. Alice moved back so Janie and Nick could see.

'Never seen anything like that,' said Janie. 'The pictures are really detailed. What are these buttons on the bottom?'

'It's ever so good,' said Megs. 'Every day a new code comes through to Sam's mobile. Alice's phone broke in half-term. Alice punches in the number and the door opens by itself.'

'Let's see it then,' said Nick.

'Can't just now,' said Sam a bit defensively. 'They come at a different time each day.'

'It doesn't seem to have much to do with Christmas,' said Nick. 'Where are the wise men and the shepherds? Load of mumbo-jumbo anyway, if you ask me. Let's go.'

Alice counted to ten to calm herself down as Megs wrapped her in a big hug. 'Love you,' she said.

'Be good,' said Megs in reply.

Nick had a new sports car. Megs tried not to think of how much it might have cost as he drove away. For Alice, it was nothing like as comfortable as the limo or the black Range Rover.

Lunch in the posh restaurant was really very nice and, despite herself, Alice enjoyed the first part of the day. Janie and Nick talked about their new house and their last holiday and their next holiday. They were flying to New York on Christmas Day because the fares were so reasonable. Alice listened quietly and didn't say too much. Janie was trying too hard to be nice and Nick was showing off but the food was excellent.

'So what are you doing over Christmas, Alice?' said Janie. 'Lots of presents?'

'We'll go to church tomorrow,' said Alice. 'There's a carol service at the one round the corner. I've never been to church at Christmas before.'

'Me neither,' said Janie. 'I wonder what it's like.'

'Boring claptrap, if you ask me,' said Nick. 'I don't want any daughter of mine getting mixed up in that nonsense.'

'What's happening on Christmas Day?' asked Janie, sensing the chill in the air.

'There are seven of us for Christmas dinner,' said Alice, without thinking. 'Grandad's been really poorly so he and Grandma are coming to stay. Josie is coming – that's Sam's girlfriend. She's expecting twins.'

'Bloody hell,' said Nick. 'That's only six, Alice.'

'Andrew's coming as well. He's the PE teacher at my school. He and Mum have been out on a couple of dates.'

Alice looked straight at Nick as she said this and, as she hoped, she saw him flinch. 'Ha!' she thought. 'Stick that in your combat trousers.'

'All finished?' said Janie, filling the awkward silence. 'Let's hit the shops.'

Sam was looking forward to meeting Josie's parents even less than Alice was looking forward to seeing Nick and Janie. He'd hardly met them before and now he was about to become part of the family.

He stood on the doorstep hopping from foot to foot. In one hand he clutched a bunch of flowers from the filling station and in the other a bottle of wine. Josie had told him there had been an almighty bust-up on Friday night.

She answered the door. 'Come in,' she said, giving him a kiss. 'Mum and Dad are in the kitchen.'

'Mrs Liddell, Mr Liddell, good to see you!' Sam smiled his most charming smile.

Mrs Liddell was attending to the gravy and nodded to the pan in acknowledgement. At least she doesn't wear her coat at home, Sam thought to himself.

'Roger and Dorothy,' said Josie's dad, holding out a big hand. He was a retired police sergeant and looked the part. 'Come on through, er, Sam. Lunch isn't quite ready. Fruit juice?'

'Please,' said Sam.

The four of them settled on the sofas in the front room. There was a bit of a pause as Roger supplied everyone with a soft drink. Then even more of a pause as they took a first sip.

'It has all been a bit of a shock,' said Dorothy to the fire.

'Now, Dorothy,' said Roger. 'We agreed I would handle this. What we want to say, Sam and Josie, is that we're delighted that Josie has found someone she really loves and that she wants to settle down.'

'I just wish it hadn't been so sudden!' said Dorothy, speaking to the mantelpiece.

'So we want to welcome you as part of the family, Sam, very warmly.'

'Thanks,' said Sam, meaning it.

'It's all a bit back to front though,' said Dorothy, looking at the television.

'We're also pleased,' said Roger, looking hard at his wife, 'we're also very pleased that we're going to be grandparents at long last.'

Josie's eyebrows shot up a little at this point but she kept her lips tightly shut.

'Twins!' said Dorothy to the lampstand, a first hint of enthusiasm in her voice.

'Things have happened a bit in the wrong order, we have to admit that,' said Roger. 'Josie did seem upset earlier in the year when you – you know.'

'Dad!' said Josie.

'But she does seem very fond of you and well, we're delighted. Aren't we, Dorothy?'

Dorothy smiled weakly and nodded towards the back garden. 'Twins,' she said.

'The thing is,' said Roger, looking slightly awkward now, 'the thing is, Dorothy and I are very committed to our church, especially Dorothy. We've lots of friends there. We've tried hard to bring up Josie to follow our faith.'

'She was never interested,' said Dorothy. 'Not since she was young.'

'Now, Dorothy!' said Roger. 'This isn't the time.' He turned back to Sam.

'The thing is, we very much hope that, when the time comes to, you know, get married, do the honourable thing, we very much want it to be a church wedding.'

'But it needs to be soon,' said Dorothy, 'before things show. I need to be able to hold my head up in church.'

'Mum!' said Josie. 'We've not had time to talk it through, have we, Sam?' Her voice cracked a little.

'Can I say something?' said Sam, coughing.

'Yes, of course, lad. Go ahead,' said Roger, slightly surprised that he had a contribution to make.

Sam cleared his throat, feeling very young all of a sudden. 'First, I want to say thankyou for your welcome, in the circumstances. Perhaps I've not been the most responsible person in the past, but I want to put that behind me.'

'Bit late for that,' said Dorothy to her handbag.

'Let him finish,' said Roger.

'I love Josie very much,' said Sam, getting into his stride and taking Josie's hand. 'And I intend to stand by her and by our – er – the twins. We've talked about getting married and we want to do that. We think it's the right thing to do.'

'So we can talk dates, then?' said Dorothy, brightening and looking at him.

'Not just yet,' said Sam, trying to sound firm. 'Josie and I will need to make our own decisions about where we get married and when. Josie is clear that she doesn't want the wedding to be in your church.'

'But you don't know anywhere else,' said Roger.

'Well, there's a church round the corner from where I live,' said Sam. 'I took my niece along two weeks ago. We're going back tomorrow for the Carol Service. That's what we're thinking at the moment. Something simple.'

Roger and Dorothy looked at each other for a moment and seemed to reach an understanding. Dorothy shrugged her shoulders.

'Well,' said Roger, smiling. 'I think the dinner's ready. Come on through and you can tell us a bit about what kind of work you do.'

Just after three, Sam took his leave of Roger and Dorothy. The meal was a bit of an ordeal: the vegetables were overcooked and the meat was chewy but he managed to ask for seconds of apple crumble and Dorothy had obviously made an effort. The conversation stuttered along but kept going, more or less. Sam had helped with the washing up. Even Dorothy had begun to thaw out a little by the end.

Josie walked him to the car. 'You were wonderful,' she said. 'I never imagined you could be like that.'

'Least I could do,' said Sam. 'Will you be OK?'

'Absolutely. You get back to Alice. I'd best stay here.'

Megs and Andrew were staying near Luton overnight to check on Grandad and bring him back first thing on Christmas Eve. Andrew wouldn't hear of Megs hiring a car and driving over on her own. Neither Sam nor Josie begrudged Megs a night away. Both of them liked Andrew very much and even Alice was coming to terms with what was happening.

'See you tomorrow. Love you.'

As Sam parked in his usual place at the back of the house, his phone announced there was a message. Sure enough: the code.

Alice was waiting for him inside. 'How did it go?'

'Grim at first but alright in the end. How about you?'

'Started well but ended badly. Nick teased me about going to church so I mentioned Mum's new boyfriend. That put him in a really bad mood. Then I spent lots of his money.'

'Well done. Code's arrived.'

'Perfect timing. Mum and Andrew left ten minutes ago.'

The new door looked like a metal hatch leading underground. Alice punched in the code as Sam read it aloud: 'Four, two, colon, three.' The instant she pressed the final number, the doorbell rang.

'I didn't hear a car,' said Sam as he went to answer it.

'We were parked outside already,' said Caspar. 'No time to lose.'

The black Range Rover was blocking the road. One of the neighbours honked his horn, trying to get past. Mel, wearing his dark suit and glasses, got out and just looked at him. He waved back in a friendly, ingratiating manner. 'Take your time,' he called. 'No hurry!'

Caspar took the wheel. 'Where are we going?' said Alice, strapping herself in.

'Heathrow,' said Mel, checking his watch. 'We'll just make it. Bal is meeting us there.'

Sam pressed his nose to the dark glass as they drove into the airport. To his surprise, the Range Rover was waved through the security gates and they drove out onto the tarmac in the section of the airfield for private jets. A blue and silver Lear jet was warming up on the runway.

Bal waved to them from the cockpit as they climbed aboard. Caspar made sure they were comfortable as the plane taxied down the runway and took off. Once they were airborne, Mel served snacks. Alice giggled when he offered her peanuts.

'Where are we going?'

'Rome,' said Caspar.

The flight took about an hour, Sam thought. This was some jet. The inside was sumptuous leather with a blue and silver trim. There was a second identical Range Rover waiting for them on the Rome runway. Caspar drove again. Bal and Mel had motorbikes and cleared a way through the traffic.

The city sped by. Alice pressed her nose to the car window catching all she could of the strange sights. For once when their escorts were with them, there was traffic everywhere. At every corner there were old and famous buildings. 'Sorry we haven't time for the full tour,' said Caspar. They headed into the very centre to a space beside a small church just outside the Vatican.

Sam and Alice climbed out of the car. There was a fresh smell of cut flowers on the cool night air. Bal was bending over a circle of metal in the earth, unfastening padlocks and chains.

'The door,' said Alice, 'on the calendar.'

'We've come to the catacombs,' said Bal. 'One of the oldest and most holy places in Rome.'

Mel went first down the iron ladder, Alice followed, watching her step, then Sam and Caspar. Bal stayed to watch the entrance. They passed along long corridors lit by oil lamps. Dark passages led off to the right and to the left. The walls were carved with strange markings and symbols. Sam sensed they were going deeper, though the slope on the pathway was very gentle, right under the centre of Rome.

At last they reached their destination. In a small hallway, carved out of the rock and lit by oil lamps, Mary was waiting for them. She stood as they entered, moving more slowly, Alice thought. Mary showed them a bowl of water where they could wash their hands and face, gave them each a soft linen towel and then flat honey cakes and clear water to refresh them after their journey.

Alice sat on the simple stone bench next to Sam and looked at the carvings around the walls. She tried to imagine who had made the markings, the community which had gathered here. The space they had come to was larger than it seemed. You could fit sixty people in here, maybe more.

In front of them, there was a single small spluttering lamp on the low stone table. At Mary's feet, bulrushes and lilies grew in a pot of earth. Once again, Mary looked a little older than when they had last seen her. Her hair now was grey and her face lined, yet the same life and passion burned within. At times as Alice watched her, she was no different from the young girl they had met only four days ago. At others, she could sense the ageing more than see it.

As the silence of the holy place settled into them, Mary began her story in a whisper.

'There were not many of us in the beginning. Six score followed the call and remained in the city. The early days were wonderful, despite the sadness. The strangest mix of sorrow and of joy. I had lost my own son and then discovered him again, for ever. God's own breath came upon us. There were signs and healings. Thousands joined us and became followers of the Way.'

The lamp spluttered on the table in front of them. Alice caught the sense of wonder and excitement as the small community grew stronger. Mary's voice dropped further as the story unfolded.

'But bitter persecution followed. Suffering, forced exile, death for some. We were arrested and put in prison. Nothing could silence the good news. Some fell away or were corrupted. But the faith of those who were left grew stronger. The message spread from place to place carried by merchants and travellers, by those fleeing for their lives, by those called and sent out.

'Within a single generation, there were followers in many different places and even here in Rome. This is where we gathered on the first day of the week. You can still see the marks we made as we assembled here in these caves, often in secret. Codes and passwords were part of our life. You can still see the tombs of those who died for their faith.'

Sam looked around at the walls of the cave and, in his mind's eye, saw the room filled with people who were lit with an inner joy – a joy strong enough to withstand fear and danger, even death itself. He felt the same joy and life rising inside him.

'We did not know it at the time,' said Mary softly, her eyes shining, 'but by our witness the world was changed.'

There was a deep silence for some minutes in the cave.

'What are these?' said Sam, pointing to the lamp and to the bulrushes.

'We had many lessons to learn, dear ones,' said Mary, smiling sadly. 'Even in the midst of trial and difficulty. They are lessons which have often been forgotten. These are symbols of those lessons. There was a prophecy, a code, almost a riddle, one of many about my son.'

'Can you tell us what it said?' asked Sam.

Mary sang the words as a lullaby. Alice wondered if, long ago, she had sung them to her baby boy:

> 'A bruised reed he will not break,
> A dimly burning wick he will not quench.'

Mary knelt by the bulrushes and the spluttering lamp. 'The lesson is needed today more than ever,' she said. 'God's ways are paths of gentleness and hope. Find the life that is there,' she said. 'Nurture it. Even if the reed is bruised and broken, do not give up. It can mend, given time. Even though the lamp burns low, do not put it out. Tend it and protect it until it burns strong again. We are not simply those who bear a message. We are those who live the Way in the strength that is given to us. The way of my son is the way of gentleness and hope.'

They sat quietly for a while, both of them taking in the symbols which were set before them. For Sam especially, there was a challenge, a shaping, an inner strength born in that moment.

Then Mary's gentle voice brought the moment to a close: 'Our time is at an end. You must go, children.'

She embraced them both. Caspar led them again out of the catacombs, up the ladder to the waiting car. They sped through the busy evening streets of the city to the waiting jet. The jet carried them swiftly through the night skies. From Heathrow, their escorts brought them safely back again to the familiar street and home.

Neither Sam nor Alice slept this time on the journey but neither did they speak. Each carried in their minds the wonder and the challenge they had heard. Mary's story and her final words burned within them.

They said goodnight to Caspar, Bal and Mel. Sam turned on the light in the hall but they left the lights off in the front room as they went to inspect the calendar.

In the centre of the door was an oil lamp burning dimly, flickering and almost going out. By its light, Sam and Alice saw clearly, trampled underfoot yet never to be broken, a bruised reed. The symbols of the gentle way.

23 December

On Sunday morning, Alice woke early. She felt lighter and cleaner than she had for a long time. 'Only two days to Christmas!'

Megs had left a long list of chores for Sam and herself. Josie was coming round to help and arrived when Alice was halfway through breakfast. 'Sam's still asleep,' Alice said as she let her in. 'Cup of tea?'

'Please,' said Josie. 'Sam!' she called up the stairs. 'Action stations. Megs will be back at lunchtime.'

A low mumble came from the direction of Sam's room.

'What's on the list, Alice?'

'Mainly cleaning,' said Alice. 'Front room. Grandma and Grandad are sleeping in Sam's room. There's more room. Mum threatened to get a skip. The food she ordered from the supermarket should arrive around ten.'

Sam staggered into the kitchen in his dressing gown and hugged Josie. 'C'fee,' he pleaded. Alice raised her eyes to the ceiling.

Josie and Alice sorted out dusters and buckets of soapy water while Sam had his shower. They started on the front room. Josie hoovered and Alice dusted round. She polished the mirror carefully. The surface was still solid, the reflection still normal. By the time she had finished rubbing, the glass sparkled.

Alice came to the calendar itself and ran the duster first over the four edges and then, very carefully, across the buttons and, last of all, in between the doors. There was just one empty space left, in the bottom right-hand corner, where today's picture would appear.

'You've got lots of presents, Alice,' said Josie. 'You must be excited.'

'I am,' said Alice, quietly, looking at the calendar, focusing this time on the picture of the tiny angel from the Chamber of Laments. She realised she hadn't actually thought very much about the adventure of the calendar coming to an end – but there were just two doors left.

The doorbell rang. Sam answered it on his way down. 'Shopping,' he said. Josie and Alice went to help carry what seemed like a hundred plastic bags through into the kitchen. A cold wind blew through the house as the delivery man brought everything into the hallway.

'Food,' said Sam, peering into the bags.

Alice slapped his hand and gave him three bin-liners. 'Two for rubbish,' she said, speaking as much to Josie as to Sam. 'One for laundry. It's got to be finished by twelve. I'll put the shopping away.'

'It's got to be finished by eleven,' said Sam, running up the stairs. 'I need to do some Christmas shopping.'

Josie helped Alice put the shopping away. 'What time is Megs arriving?'

'Around lunchtime was all she said.'

Sam arrived back with three full bin-liners and collected the hoover. 'Impressive,' said Josie. 'You might have time to go to the shops after all.'

In the end, they all went into town together. Megs rang to say they wouldn't make it home until two o'clock at the earliest. The shops were heaving with men. 'We only come out two days before Christmas,' said Sam. He made his excuses and slipped off to do his shopping.

Alice and Josie nosed around the shopping mall more window shopping than anything else. Alice was more interested in the people. She watched the expressions on their faces. Why was everyone in such a hurry? In the corner of the market square, a brass band was playing Christmas carols but no one stayed to listen. It was the only peaceful area in the whole town centre, it seemed. The music seemed stronger, somehow, at least when you'd been listening to the tinny jingles in the shops. There were long queues at all the cash point machines and at all the tills. She caught snatches of conversation as people charged past her.

'Hurry up, why can't you? I'm sick of shopping.'

'Can't we go home now?'

'You always spend too much on your parents – every year it's the same.'

'I hate Christmas. I'm exhausted already.'

Sam came back to meet them, looking pleased with himself and carrying a number of parcels. Alice and Josie tried to peer into them but without success.

They got soaked waiting for the bus on the way home and arrived back later than intended. Megs was already there with the grandparents. Grandma was stooped and thin and grey but very happy to be there. Grandad looked older than she remembered and weaker but a hundred times better than in the hospital bed. Alice hugged them both.

'Come on in,' said Grandma. 'You're all soaking wet. You must be Josie. Lovely to meet you. Congratulations.'

'You never said how pretty she was, Sam,' said Grandad from the chair, smiling. Josie blushed.

'Where's Andrew?' asked Alice.

'He had to go,' said Megs. 'Said something about last-minute Christmas shopping.' She winked at Josie.

'How are you, Dad?' asked Sam.

'Glad to be out of that hospital ward, Son,' said his father. 'And glad to be all together for Christmas. Especially now the family is expanding.'

'I'll put the kettle on,' said Grandma. 'Why don't you give me a hand, Josie, and tell me all about yourself?'

'And you, young lady,' said Grandad. 'You tell me all about this calendar. I've never seen anything like it.'

'We had a card through the post,' said Alice. 'Sam collected it from Hamleys on 30 November. Every day we get a text message. It's like a code. We punch it in and a new door appears.'

'It's not like any advent calendar I've ever seen,' said Grandad. 'What are all these pictures? I can't see them so well without my glasses.'

'This one's a dove,' said Alice. 'This is a golden thread in a forest. This one is a new road dug through the mountains.'

'Is it indeed?' said Grandad. 'Do you know what they mean? It's not as though any of them come from the Christmas story, is it? What's that one in the corner there?'

'A new shoot,' said Alice, 'growing from an old stump.'

'Is it now?' said Grandad, smiling. 'I think I begin to see.'

'See what?' said Alice.

'When I was little,' said her grandfather, 'my mother made me go to Sunday School. I quite liked it really. Never kept it up, though your grandma went to church when we first got married. Say one for me, I always used to tell her when she went out on a Sunday.'

'What's that got to do with the pictures in the calendar?' asked Alice.

'When I was small, I was very good at remembering things,' said Grandad. 'They used to give a prize to the person who could learn Scripture verses by heart. Some of those verses have rattled around inside my head all these years, just odd words and phrases. Lately, I've been trying to bring them back into my mind with, you know, hospital and that.'

Alice squeezed his hand.

'The thing is,' said Grandad. 'I don't know what they have to do with Christmas – but some of those pictures remind me of those old Bible verses. I think there's more to this calendar than meets the eye.' He tapped his nose and winked. Alice smiled.

'Mark my words. The answer's in the Book.'

Before she could ask any more questions, Megs ordered Alice upstairs to get ready for church.

Sam and Josie were planning on going to the Carol Service with Megs and Alice.

'Are you sure you'll be alright, Mum?' said Megs for the sixth time since tea. 'I can stay at home with you and Dad, if you like.'

'You go, love,' said Grandma – also for the sixth time. 'It's been a busy day. We're not used to so many people around.'

Sam was putting his coat on when there was a familiar sound. 'Message!' sang the phone.

'I didn't know you'd changed your ring tone,' said Megs. 'Is that the code for the calendar?'

'How exciting,' said Grandma. 'Put it in before you go to church, Sam. Let's see one of these doors open. It's just like magic. Honestly, the things they can do these days.'

'Suffering swordfish, look at the time,' said Sam moving towards the door. 'We'll be late for church.'

'Brenda said they were expecting a lot of people,' said Alice, shifting from foot to foot. 'We want to make sure we get a seat.'

'Don't be daft,' said Grandad. 'It's a church not a cinema. There's always seats in a church.'

'Go on, Sam,' said Josie. 'I've never seen how this thing works either.'

'Nor have I,' said Megs. 'I've never been around when you punch in the code.'

'But...' Alice began.

'Just get on with it!' said Megs. 'Or we will be late.'

Sam nodded at Alice and opened the text. Alice could see the faint outline of the new door in the remaining space. A dark brown garden gate. You could hardly see it against the wood of the calendar.

Sam read out the numbers: 'Five, five ... '

'At least it's not Col,' Alice thought as she punched in the numbers. 'I can't imagine what the coloured smoke would do to Grandad.' Push. Click.

'Colon ... '

'On the other hand it would be fun to take the whole family on an adventure.' Click.

'One, one.'

'Perhaps Caspar will be at the door with a minibus.' Push. Click.

Sam and Alice tensed themselves for something strange to begin to happen. The others all peered at the calendar.

'I'm sure those numbers mean something,' said Grandad.

'There's nothing happening, love,' said Grandma, disappointed.

'It – er – sometimes it takes a while to open,' said Sam, relaxing just a little.

'Well, it really is time to go,' said Megs. 'We don't want to arrive halfway through the service.'

Alice ran to the front door and opened it slowly. No sign of any strange vehicles in the street.

'Mum, I think I might have tummy ache. Can I stay at home and Sam can look after me?'

'Don't be silly, Alice. You're the one who wanted to go to church. Out of the house. Now!'

Sam and Josie walked two steps behind. Alice kept looking round all the way to St Philip's. 'What's going on?' she mouthed to Sam.

Sam shrugged his shoulders – then grinned inanely at Josie.

'Alice is acting a bit strange,' she said. 'Wonder why?'

'Probably because she's expecting a cloud of blue smoke or a helicopter to appear any moment,' thought Sam to himself. 'Girls,' he said aloud. 'Honestly!'

Josie elbowed him in the ribs just as they turned into the church entrance. There were crowds of people all making their way inside at the last minute which meant there was a queue at the door. Brenda was giving out the hymn-books.

'Hi, Alice! Great to see you. Thanks for your help the other day.'

'Hi Brenda. You met Sam, my uncle. This is Josie. They'd like to get married here soon.'

'Not so fast, Alice,' said Sam. 'We were just wondering, you know.'

'Give the vicar a call after Christmas,' said Brenda. 'He's a bit tied up just now.'

'Sure – course,' said Sam, poking Alice hard as they squeezed into a pew near the front.

The church was full and lit only by candles in all the window spaces with very dim overhead lighting so people could read their carol sheets. People were mostly in family groups though some looked as though they were on their own. The organ music stopped for a moment and the vicar invited everyone to stand from the back of the church.

The first carol was one Alice knew: 'Once in Royal David's City'. She turned round during the first verse and gasped. Caspar was standing two rows behind her singing in a deep bass voice. He was dressed in a dinner jacket and bow tie with a warm winter overcoat and bowed towards her.

Alice nudged Sam. 'Look behind.' Sam turned, nodded to Caspar, then looked to the right and to the left. Sure enough Bal and Mel were there too, dressed to match. Two rows behind them was Mr Gabriel, for the first time without his bowler hat. He seemed to be enjoying the singing but winked in their direction.

'Stick out a bit, don't they?' Sam whispered in the lull after verse four.

There was a reading next, then another carol, then readings and carols alternating in a pattern. Alice enjoyed the whole thing. Church was even better when it was full. Just before the final verse, the vicar stood up to make an announcement.

'We are very fortunate to have three guests with us from an international choir visiting London: the Bethlehem singers. They have kindly offered to sing solo parts in our final hymn.'

Alice looked around. Sure enough, Caspar, Mel and Bal were moving out to the front of the church.

'That's why they're wearing dinner jackets,' whispered Sam.

'That means a change to our final carol from "Hark the Herald Angels Sing",' said the vicar. 'We don't normally sing Number 25 until just after Christmas, but I am sure we can make an exception for our guests. Would the congregation please stand and join in the chorus of "We Three Kings".'

The organ played the familiar tune. Caspar, Mel and Bal launched into the song in a harmony which soared and filled the church. The power of the words lifted the congregation and drew from them the best music of the evening.

> 'O Star of wonder, star of night,
> Star with royal beauty bright,
> Westward leading, still proceeding,
> Guide us to thy Perfect Light.'

Each of the soloists offered one verse with unusual passion. Each produced gifts as they sang and set them on the altar. Then all three came together in a new harmonic arrangement for the final cry of praise, filling the church and singing:

> 'Glorious now behold Him arise;
> King and God and Sacrifice;
> Alleluia, Alleluia,
> Earth to heav'n replies.'

'You were fantastic,' Alice said to Caspar over a mince pie after the service.

'Very well done,' said the vicar coming up to shake the three guests warmly by the hand. 'We've never had as many people in church for a Carol Service. You really lifted us at the end. What passion!'

'Any chance you can stay back and help sort things out for a bit, Alice?' asked Brenda. 'There's a lot to get ready for the Christmas Eve midnight service.'

'Allow us to help, ma'am,' said Mel.

'Are you sure?' said Brenda. 'There is a lot to do.'

'We need to get back,' said Megs, coming over with Josie, 'but you stay on with Sam if you like, Alice.'

'Thanks, Mum. We won't be too long.'

Mel and Bal started with the washing up. Sam and Alice collected the service sheets and stacked them at the back.

'Thanks,' said Brenda. 'The vicar's gone home to put his feet up. That's his tenth Carol Service this week but I could tell he enjoyed it the most. I just need to pop home and get some more wine. We don't like to keep too much in the vestry these days. Will you be alright here?'

'No problems,' said Sam.

'Bolt the door behind me and I'll knock three times,' said Brenda. 'Thanks.'

As soon as Brenda had gone Bal and Mel dried their hands and put their jackets and coats on. 'This way,' said Caspar, leading them down to the front of the church. Just to the right of the main altar was a side chapel. They stopped and bowed before a small bronze statue. Alice gasped. It was Mary as they had seen her on the first day, full of life, and with a child in her arms.

'This way,' said Mel. 'Bal will stay here in the church.'

He led them past the bronze statue to the very far corner of the building and pulled back an old tapestry. There was a strange old door set in the wall. Bal lifted the latch and pulled it open.

Alice blinked and screwed up her eyes. Bright sunlight streamed into the church.

'Come through,' said Caspar, leading the way.

Sam stepped through over the threshold and Alice followed. They looked around and breathed in the warm spring air of early morning. Alice felt uncomfortable already in her winter coat. She took it off and left it on the ground by the doorway.

The four of them were standing at one end of an enormous field. The earth had recently been ploughed and had deep furrows ready for sowing. The field's boundary was marked by a dry stone wall. Beyond it was another and then another as far as the eye could see.

'Welcome,' said Mary, who had been sitting on a low bench beside the door next to a gate into the field. Mel and Caspar bowed low. Sam and Alice followed their example now.

Mary was as they had first seen her: young and full of passion and yet at the same time old and full of wisdom.

'This is the last time we will speak together in this way,' Mary said. 'Tomorrow is the calendar's last day when we shall meet but there will be no time for conversation. Today you must walk with me. Take these.'

Mary handed them both a large, heavy canvas satchel on a strap. Alice and Sam put them over their shoulder and saw that Mary had one also.

'What is it?' said Sam.

'Seed,' said Mary. 'Good seed to sow in the earth. Watch and follow.'

They set off around the edge of the field. As they walked, Mary took great handfuls of seed and flung them out onto the earth. Sam and Alice followed, doing as she did. There was no breeze and the seed hung in the air before it settled onto the soil.

Together they worked their way across the ploughed field. It was hard work. Alice found the soil stuck to her shoes and, after a while, her arms ached from the throwing. Yet it was also a solemn and exciting experience, not knowing what would grow.

'What are we sowing?' called Sam, as they drew near to the end of the field and their bags grew lighter.

'All kinds of good things,' said Mary. 'But now you must see what happens to what is sown.'

She led them back across the centre of the field to begin their walk again from the place where they had started to sow.

Out across the field, Alice saw green shoots beginning to appear through the soil. 'What you will see takes many of your months,' said Mary, 'but watch and learn.'

Around the edges of the field and in the places where they had walked, nothing grew. Sam looked more closely. 'Birds,' he said. 'The seed has been eaten.'

Alice walked over to the left side of the meadow where the seed was growing quickly, shooting upwards. Then, as she watched, it began to wither and die.

'No root,' said Mary, bending down and picking up a large rock. 'The ground here is full of stones. There will be no harvest here.'

Sam ran ahead of them. There was boggy ground up ahead. The plants were shooting up here as well, but growing alongside and tangled in among them were weeds and thorns.

'Worries, cares, pleasures,' said Mary. 'They start well but the life is choked out of them. No harvest here either.'

As Sam looked at the thorns entangling the young plants, Alice had run ahead again to the middle of the field, where all kinds of good things were growing. There was corn and wheat, poppies and flowers of every kind, vegetables, fruit bushes which would yield berries, oats and barley, rice and millet all side by side.

'Look at how much is growing!' she exclaimed. 'Look how it grows from the tiny seed!'

'Look, indeed,' said Mary. 'And remember. And think. And see if you can understand.'

By now they had walked the full circuit of the field and come back to the door where Caspar and Bal were waiting. Mary embraced them both.

'You have travelled almost the whole journey through the calendar,' she said. 'The seed of life has been sown.' She turned back towards the field and pointed to the different places they had walked together.

'Make sure nothing snatches away the seed.' She tapped Sam on the forehead.

'Make sure that there is depth for the seed to take root and grow.' She tapped Alice on the chest.

'Make sure that the seed is not choked by worries, cares and pleasures.' She took them both by the hand and turned to face the centre of the field.

'Let there be good fruit. Go well.'

One by one, they stepped over the threshold and were back in the quiet chapel at the side of the church. The lights were on but even so the building felt cold and gloomy after the spring sunshine. Mel was sweeping the broad central aisle. There were three loud knocks on the door.

'Sorry to be so long, my dears,' said Brenda. 'Thanks so much for waiting. It looks so clean. I'll be fine now if you want to carry on.'

'Goodnight, Brenda,' said Alice, looking back down the church, ready now for the services on Christmas Eve.

The three companions walked them home.

'Will we see you tomorrow?' said Sam.

'You may see us, but there may not be time for conversation,' said Caspar with a smile. 'Travel well. Tomorrow is the last door but also the greatest. Be ready and stay in the house.'

Everyone was in the front room when they arrived – even Andrew.

'Hi!' said Sam.

'What happened to the calendar?' said Alice. 'Did anything appear?'

'I never thought to look,' said Grandma. 'Let me get my glasses. Well, I never did.'

'There's more to this than meets the eye,' said Grandad.

'How do they do it?' said Josie.

Alice and Sam looked and saw what they expected: an open door, a tiny snapshot of a field ploughed and ready for sowing. Tiny dots on the wind: seeds of life falling into good soil.

24 December

Alice was up early on Christmas Eve. The excitement of the last part of the journey twisted and danced inside her. As far as she was concerned, there was only one thing that mattered today. She never wanted the adventure of the calendar to end. Yet she also wanted, more than anything, to reach that final door, the one that had been visible all the way through, the very large one right in the centre.

At five minutes to eight, she crept into the front room. Sam was still asleep. Alice looked at him with new respect. The change in Sam over the last few weeks had been remarkable. Even Megs said so. But he still snored like a train. Alice didn't wake him just yet – though she would never have dreamt of not sharing this last adventure with him. She wanted a few moments by herself before it began. She felt sure the message would arrive in the early morning – the only time the house would be still and they would be alone with the calendar.

Alice squatted in the corner of the room, enjoying the darkness. The Christmas tree was in the corner. She could smell it and see its shape outlined against the light that spilled in at the window whenever a car came round the corner. It cast long pointed shadows on the chimney breast. At the base of the tree were the gifts: a pile that grew larger by the day. Last year on Christmas Eve, Alice got into the most terrible trouble for trying to peel off the wrapping paper. She half-grinned to herself as she remembered how preoccupied she had been in years gone by with the coloured paper and the strange boxes. It was true – this year she'd hardly given the presents a thought. At least three new large parcels had arrived since she went to bed last night.

Over on the opposite wall, of course, was the calendar. Doors one to twenty-three were open. The minute candle in the first door still shone as brightly as before giving enough light to see what was in each tiny space. Alice looked at them one more time, remembering the different conversations and adventures. The tiny dove. The wild animals sharing a common home. The burning coals, the six stone jars, the new road. The man, woman and child dancing after being brought back to life. The broken chains. The tiny, bubbling stream of water. The peacock' feather.

Alice looked at her watch one more time. It was almost eight o'clock. She shook Sam.

'Whassup?' Sam rubbed his eyes. 'What time is it?'

'It's eight o'clock. It's the final day. We need the code before anyone else is awake. There will be people here all day. Let's go.'

Sam reached for his phone. A text message had arrived. Alice stood by the calendar, finger poised. 'Call out the numbers.'

Sam brought up the message: 'You've won a holiday in Benidorm. Ring this number immediately for more details.'

'Sam, stop teasing. It's not the time.'

'No, seriously, that's what it says. Maybe it's not time yet. Yesterday it didn't come until just before six. Still, I may as well ring and find out what I've won.'

'Don't you dare!' yelled Alice. 'It has to be now. It's the only time today. Are you sure your phone's working?'

Sam checked, nodded and slipped off to the loo. Alice paced up and down. Sam came back. Still nothing. They had breakfast. Still nothing. Megs came down yawning, dreamily chattering about all they had to do. Still nothing. Grandma and Grandad emerged and they made Grandad comfortable in the front room – opposite the calendar. Even Sam was on edge by now.

'Anyone coming shopping?' Megs said to them both.

'Busy,' muttered Sam sheepishly. 'Presents to wrap.'

'Can't, Mum,' said Alice. 'Television.'

Megs looked at them both curiously. Something was going on. 'Tesco calls,' she sighed. 'Last-minute stuff. Wish me luck.'

Somehow Alice and Sam shuffled through the morning. Sam checked the mobile every ten minutes. Still no code. Alice tried punching in yesterday's, but all of the buttons were still in place. She played on her Game Boy. Sam made a serious attempt to wrap up a present for Josie. In the end Alice rescued him. Together they made a half-decent job of it. The minutes dragged by. As Alice put Josie's gift under the tree, she had a closer look at the three gifts which had arrived in the night. They were beautifully wrapped, with classy paper and trimmings, not like the ones they normally gave each other.

'Sam! Look at these,' said Alice. 'Look at the labels.'

Sam came over and they pulled out the three gifts. Each one had a similar label. The first was very heavy. 'To Alice and Sam with love from Mel.' The second was light and smelled fragrant. 'To Sam and Alice with love from Bal.' The third was wrapped in dark paper and was of medium weight. It gave off a powerful, sweet smell. It was from Caspar.

'Should we open them?' said Alice.

'It says "Wait for Christmas Day" on the back of the label,' said Sam.

Morning turned into lunchtime. Megs came back from Tesco's and Sam and Alice meekly helped put the food away. The cupboards and the fridge were full to exploding point. Alice opened the cupboard to put the plastic bags away and 5,000 fell out on top of her. Megs and Grandma spent the afternoon preparing yet more food. Alice tried to watch the television. Normally she liked the old films but not today. Christmas Eve always dragged but on this one every second seemed like a minute and every minute like an hour. When would it come? Bal had said to be ready and not to leave the house but he never said what time. Even waiting for Father Christmas when she was very young had never seemed this bad.

At four o'clock, while Grandad slept in his chair, Sam tried the emergency number given by Mr Gabriel. Perhaps something had gone wrong. There was just an annoying voicemail message in a very cultured Welsh accent. Alice tried the number 266 433 555 herself and listened to the message:

'Hello, Gabriel here. Thanks for calling. So sorry I can't take your call. It's Christmas Eve and I'm rather busy. Please leave a message or call back another time. In an emergency text 4447 7772 4442 44. Goodbye.'

'What use is that?' said Sam and popped out to the shops. He'd remembered he needed to buy his Mum and Dad's present. 'Won't be more than half an hour. Promise!'

Alice played around with Sam's mobile for a while. She resisted the temptation to read his text messages – except the different codes. All of this time she'd never really figured them out. They seemed like random numbers when they arrived.

Grandad woke up just after Sam had gone out. 'I meant to give you something earlier,' he said, getting up. 'We brought it yesterday. I didn't bother to wrap it up. Hope you don't mind. Those codes have been on my mind. I don't know but you might find it has something to do with this.'

He passed over an old book in a brown paper bag. Alice took it out. It had a plain black leather cover, gold leaf on the edge of the pages and was clearly very old and well read.

'Belonged to my grandfather,' said Grandad. 'He was a preacher, I think. Wanted you to have it. Kind of an heirloom.'

'Thanks, Grandad,' said Alice. 'I'll always keep it. But what's it got to do with the codes?'

Grandad yawned. 'That's the curious thing,' he said. 'If I remember rightly, there are sixty-six books inside that one cover. Every book has a different number of chapters. Every chapter has a different number of verses. So every verse has a reference, see?'

Grandad opened the book at the first page. 'This first book is called Genesis. This is chapter 1, verse 1. Only the way you write it would normally have a colon in: one, colon, one. Chapter 1, verse 1. Like your codes. Make sense?'

'It does,' said Alice, excitement stirring. 'I thought they must mean something. But how do I know which book?'

She went back through the codes in the phone and wrote them down in sequence: 9:2, 2:4, 11:6 and so on. Surely they must mean *something*. Everything about the calendar had a meaning to it. Her mind worried at problems sometimes like a dog with a bone. She tried a few mathematical formulae out but nothing seemed to stick. Then she tried applying the first code to the first book in the Bible and so on but that didn't make sense either. She dialled Gabriel's number again and got the same message. This time she wrote it down. What kind of number was the emergency text line? It wasn't like any phone number she'd ever seen. She wasn't really in an emergency but she was tired of waiting.

She went into text mode and typed in the sequence of numbers, just for interest: 4447 7772 4442 44. 'Giggsssaigai,' Alice read aloud. 'What kind of word is that?'

'Has it come?' said Sam, back from the shops. 'Sorry I was a bit sharp earlier. Tension.'

'Nothing so far,' said Alice. 'But Grandad had a really good idea about the codes. He thinks they are references to verses in here.' She held out the Bible. 'He gave it to me as a present.'

'Coo,' said Sam. 'Makes sense.'

'The only problem is, which books? I'm trying to make that number of Mr Gabriel's answerphone mean something. I typed it in to see if it was a code.'

'How about turning off the predictive text?' said Sam. 'That might be another kind of code.'

'How do I do that?' Alice asked. 'I didn't know you could turn it off.'

'Press star and hold it,' said Sam. 'Now type the number in again. Each sequence of numbers is a letter. Press 4 three times, 7 four times and so on.'

Alice followed his instructions. A word appeared. It was one she recognised from flicking through the old book. Her hands were shaking. 'What was the first code again – remember when we went to Choshek?'

Sam ran his finger up the list Alice had made. 'Nine, colon, two,' he said.

Alice found the place and read the first code, a tremble in her voice. There was an exact match with the adventure and with the picture in the calendar. The second was the same. And the third.

Now the time flew by. Megs came in first, then Josie, then Grandma. 'Reading the Christmas story, darling? That's nice,' she said.

'No, Grandma. Just checking something out. It was Grandad's idea,' said Alice.

Grandad woke up at that point and they took him through the sequence once again – although Sam wasn't sure in the end he understood text messaging.

Alice had to break off for tea on day thirteen. Every adventure and every picture meant more now. It was after eight when she got back to her place by the fire.

Andrew arrived for the evening and sat on the sofa with Megs and seemed kind of, well, at home. Josie sat cosily in an armchair. Sam looked proud and content. Grandad dozed off, then woke up and said something funny. There was a half-hearted family game going on around her. Alice joined in a bit, getting sleepier and sleepier.

And then, just as she got to the final code, it happened. Grandma and Grandad had gone up to bed, having had, they said, 'Enough excitement for one day.' Josie had gone home. Megs and Andrew had popped out to the pub for half an hour. For the first time since morning, Sam and Alice were alone in the room with the calendar. The phone broke wind. The code arrived.

'Didn't know you'd changed it back again,' said Alice.

'Some bits of me don't want to grow up just yet,' Sam smiled. 'Ready for the final adventure?'

'You bet. Read it out.'

'Seven, colon, one, four,' called Sam. They stood in front of the calendar for the last time. Alice resisted the temptation to look up the reference. That would come later. She solemnly pressed each button as soon as Sam read it from the phone. Each clicked as before. As the last one was pressed into place, at exactly the same instant for Sam and Alice, the house and the calendar and everything in it were taken away.

They were on a hillside on a clear spring night. There was enough moonlight to see by. There was a nip of frost in the air and light from a small town in the valley.

Together they took in the scene. All was still. Then they heard voices and turned to look back up the path. Coming towards them at great speed down the hill was a crowd of the roughest-looking men Alice or Sam had ever seen, calling to each other in a strange language. Just in time, Sam pulled Alice out of sight behind a big gorse bush. Alice stifled a cry as the thorns pressed into her legs through her jeans.

'What did you do that for?' she hissed as the men ran past.

'I don't think they're supposed to see us,' Sam hissed back. 'Did you see their faces? They looked scared out of their minds but at the same time you would have thought that they had won the lottery. We're meant to follow them.'

Alice didn't ask Sam how he could know that. She knew it as well, as clearly as if someone had told her out loud. They hurried down the path, keeping out of sight. The men were half walking, half running down the hillside towards the town. They were all ages: young lads and older men. The ones at the back kept looking behind them as if they expected to be followed. Sam and Alice kept diving behind rocks and bushes.

Alice supposed later that they covered about a mile. She had a stitch and was out of breath in no time and so was Sam, but they kept going. Nothing was going to make her miss this.

They came now to the walls of the small town. There were gates but no one was guarding them. There was hardly anyone around. They passed through the gate following where they guessed the men had gone and came to what looked like a large inn. The light from the lamps spilled out through the windows into the street. Alice caught a glimpse of the hustle and bustle and life inside. They were close behind the last of the men and she felt sure they would go straight inside. Sam was ready for a drink.

But no, they went straight past the door, then darted down an alleyway. There was a strong animal smell mixing with the town's drains and the beer from inside.

Both Alice and Sam saw them at the same time. They had looked at them often enough over the last few weeks. There round the back of the inn was a life-sized version of the doors in the centre of the calendar. One of the shepherds they had been following took hold of each door and pulled them backwards. Inside there was only the dimmest light from a dozen small lamps.

Alice and Sam crept nearer, behind the shepherds who were moving more slowly now, faces still full of joy and fear combined. Alice pushed her way through the cattle to the very back. Her feet brushed against the straw on the floor. The warm bodies of the animals made the small stable feel warm and comfortable but the smells were strong. All she and Sam saw next were the shepherds in a line, hats off, heads bowed and eyes down. Then someone said something and the line of shepherds parted.

And there was Mary, sitting in the centre of all those rough men, exhausted yet smiling. Her eyes met Alice's at once and there was understanding and joy and love and a challenge too – then the same for Sam.

And there he was, the tiny child, sleeping in his mother's arms, wrapped in rough blankets: the one she had learned to call by so many names, the one at the centre of the whole story.

There was no need for words. Time stood still. There was silence in the stable and great peace. Sam and Alice had reached their destination. With one mind with the shepherds, both of them knelt on the rough stable floor and gazed and wondered and wanted to stay there for ever.

If you asked Sam, in later years, what he remembered about that moment, he would stop and think for a while, savouring it again, returning to the scene captured so vividly in his mind's eye.

'The silence,' he would say. 'The silence was awesome. In that one moment, I swear, earth and heaven held their breath. In that one instant in all of time, everything changed.'

'I've been very blessed,' he loved to say. 'So much has gone right for me.' He would point you, then, to the pictures he carries of Josie and the twin boys and the two girls who followed on.

'But that moment is beyond words, beyond describing. To be there. To be so close. To be changed, completed almost.'

And Alice? Alice grew up to be beautiful and strong and wise, a source of life to all who knew her. In later years she had a smile to lighten any burden, a listening ear to unravel the most twisted pathway, love and strength in abundance for those who needed care.

And in those years, when she poured tea and offered strength to the many who came, you would sometimes catch her looking over the shoulder of her visitors, especially if the tale they told was particularly dark or sad. Her eyes would rest on a curious and ancient calendar made from olive wood in the shadows in the corner of the room. She would hardly ever show it to her guests. Some of our inner stories, you see, even the happiest ones, can never be fully told.

But she would say, if you asked her, that the best part of the adventure was not that she once lived in the story and visited for a while (although she never, ever forgot the events of that December). She would tell you, if you asked her, that the best part of the story was that for ever and for ever and for evermore, the story lived in you.

Help Alice and Sam crack more Advent codes, send Advent e-cards, solve new puzzles and lots more on our *Advent Calendar* website!

Visit www.dltbooks.com for more information.